SketchUp 7.1 for Architectural Visualization

Beginner's Guide

Create stunning photo-realistic and artistic visuals of your SketchUp models

Robin de Jongh

BIRMINGHAM - MUMBAI

SketchUp 7.1 for Architectural Visualization
Beginner's Guide

First published: April 2010

Production Reference: 1210410

Published by Packt Publishing Ltd.
32 Lincoln Road
Olton
Birmingham, B27 6PA, UK.

ISBN 978-1-847199-46-1

www.packtpub.com

Cover Image by Robin de Jongh

Credits

Author

Robin de Jongh

Reviewers

Thomas Bleicher

Colin Holgate

Acquisition Editor

David Barnes

Development Editor

Rakesh Shejwal

Technical Editor

Tariq Rakhange

Indexer

Hemangini Bari

Editorial Team Leader

Mithun Sehgal

Project Team Leader

Lata Basantani

Project Coordinator

Poorvi Nair

Proofreader

Aaron Nash

Graphics

Geetanjali Sawant

Production Coordinator

Adline Swetha Jesuthas

Cover Work

Adline Swetha Jesuthas

Foreword

Unwittingly about four years ago I woke up to be an Internet celebrity. I discovered that an idea I had previously left up for review on a SketchUp Gallery forum had grown to be the largest thread on the site. It was about a non-photo real visualization technique -people were actually calling it in my honor "the Dennis Method", and now I was receiving requests to give speeches and teach seminars. The technique lives on to be included in this book along with the other gems of visualization wisdom meticulously collected for your reading pleasure.

This is the first book ever on SketchUp that goes beyond the basic modeling exercises that you can typically find in the online video tutorials. It contains a kind of instant information that anyone using SketchUp needs to deliver a knock out visual punch.

As a registered architect I often rely on the power of SketchUp generated imagery to help a client to become comfortable with a solution that I am proposing. "Seeing is believing", says the proverb, well done visualization helps people to believe in the possibility of the design.

Personal proof of this for me came recently when I had to sell an idea of an underground shopping mall to provincial Chinese officials. The prospect of having to educate them for hours on patterns of pedestrian retail traffic; means of vertical circulation and the importance of natural light, especially if you consider my less than perfect Mandarin, was rather daunting. However, an effective visualization did all the work for me and secured the client.

This book shows you how to set up your work and dress it up for a kill in such a way that it jumps off your screen, grabs your audience by the guts and never lets them go.

The newest gems of SketchUp visualization wisdom are here for the taking. Read on, my friends, and see your models shine like they never did before.

Dennis Nikolaev, AIA

About the Author

Robin de Jongh is a consulting engineer and designer who has successfully used SketchUp for multi-million pound new developments, and a whole bunch of smaller projects, from steel staircases to new product prototypes. He previously ran an architectural and product visualization company. Robin holds a degree in Computer Aided Product Design and is a professional engineer registered with the Institution of Engineering Designers in the UK. He writes a blog about SketchUp for design professionals at www.provelo.co.uk.

I would like to thank my wife for her unfailing support during the writing of this book. As a divergent thinker I come up with scores of ideas daily, only a few of which will come to fruition. This book is one of them and I thank her and my commissioning editor for believing in the book proposal in the first place-and of course rejecting the bad ideas. My thanks go to all the SketchUp newbies whose faces light up when the software is demonstrated to them; I hope my enthusiasm for bringing the power and simplicity of SketchUp to you comes across in this book, and that it echoes your own.

Special thanks to all those whose images are included in this book; to my diligent technical reviewers and editor whose suggestions were invaluable; and to Poorvi for keeping me on schedule!

About the Reviewers

Thomas Bleicher graduated in Architecture at the TU Braunschweig in Germany. Since then he has been working as Architect, Lighting Designer and IT consultant. As a student he started using daylight simulation software and began to program computer software. He is working in London as a daylight designer and in his free time he writes plugins for SketchUp.

Colin Holgate has been programming for almost 30 years, with the last 22 years involving multimedia authoring tools, including HyperCard, Director, Flash, and Unity. He uses 3D models in his work, in both touch screen kiosk applications, and in online and offline simulations, and has been a SketchUp Pro user since 2004. Using SketchUp models, he has developed a virtual walkthrough of the future World Trade Center site.

For Debbie

Table of Contents

Preface

SketchUp 7.1 for Architectural Visualization: Beginner's Guide shows you how to master SketchUp's unique tools to create architectural visuals using professional rendering and image editing techniques in a clear and friendly way. You'll be able to get started immediately using SketchUp (free version) and open-source rendering and image processing software. The book also shows you how to create watercolor and pencil style sketchy visuals. In no time you'll be creating photo-realistic renders, animated fly-overs, and walkthroughs to show off your designs in their best light!. You will also create composites of real and rendered images, creating digital and paper presentations to wow clients. If you're impatient, you'll find a "Quickstart" tutorial is provided in the first chapter to get you rendering a photo-realistic scene immediately. The rest of the book builds on this knowledge by introducing you gradually to in-depth concepts, tricks, and insights in an easy-to-follow format through quick tutorials.

Using easy step-by-step explanations, this book opens the door to the world of architectural visualization. With no prior visualization experience you will quickly get to grips with materials, texturing, composition, photo-compositing, lighting setup, rendering, and post-processing. You'll also be able to take SketchUp's unique sketchy output and add the artistic touch to create pencil and watercolor scenes. With this book you'll be able to get started immediately using the free SketchUp download and open-source rendering software.

What this book covers

Chapter 1, *Quick Start Tutorial*: This chapter is an immediate fix if you're impatient to get photo-realistic rendered SketchUp scenes. Straight away you will learn how to model the gallery scene, fix up lighting, add materials, add a photo background, and finally render in Kerkythea.

Chapter 2, *How to Collect an Aresenal Rambo Would Be Proud of*: Did you know that by downloading a few free plugins and other software you can turn SketchUp into a free, fully functional 3D visualization and animation suite similar to high end commercial software? Follow this chapter to obtain all the goodies.

Chapter 3, *Composing the Scene*: In this chapter you will learn how to take the hard work out of modeling by setting up your scenes prior to starting modelling work. You will learn how to start from CAD plans, site images, or Google Earth, and build the scene optimized for quick rendering or animation later.

Chapter 4, *Modeling for Visualization*: SketchUp is so easy to use that we're tempted to jump right in and model everything. But this can lead to ineffective presentation later and large polygon counts, which slow the computer. This chapterwill lead you through some of the professional modeling methods you need to learn to save you time and hassle, and to make photo-real rendering a cinch.

Chapter 5, *Applying Textures and Materials for Photo-Real Rendering*: Most visualizers are crazy enough to use the materials bundled with rendering software. But this methodology was developed during the ice age! Now that we all have digital cameras and access to unlimited free online image resources, we have a far more effective way of "dressing" the model. The tutorials in this chapter show you how to use SketchUp's unique photo and material handling tools to create ultra-real textured models mega easily.

Chapter 6, *Entourage the SketchUp Way*: Now that you've created the scene, modeled the buildings, and applied materials, you can add life to the scene with Entourage. Learn how to find the best free people, foliage, vehicles, and furniture online, and better still learn how to easily create your own with the foolproof methods in this chapter. In no time you'll be able to build up a comprehensive library to use or give/sell to others.

Chapter 7, *Non Photo Real with SketchUp*: Exporting images from SketchUp is not the only way to produce sketchy visuals. Combining several image layers in GIMP, a powerful free photo editing suite, you will learn how to simulate sketchy pencil and watercolor styles. Fans of these methods will be pleased to know the famous Dennis Technique is presented in this chapter, along with Dennis's own creations.

Chapter 8, *Photo-Realistic Rendering*: Here, the amazing Kerkythea introduced in Chapters 1 and 2 is explored in more depth, giving you the skills and confidence to tackle any rendering project. A hassle-free method of working is introduced along with proven best settings for test renders and final outdoor and indoor scenes. This chapter covers everything you need to get professional photo-realistic renders from your SketchUp model that you'll be personally amazed with.

Chapter 9, *Important Compositing and After Effects in GIMP*: The rendering process isn't the end of the line, because there are lots of subtle but important after-effects you can apply to make the image even more effective. This chapter covers how to add reflections without rendering, creating depth of field effects from a depth render, adjusting levels for realistic daylight scenes, and compositing real and rendered images.

Chapter 10, *Walkthroughs and Flyovers*: The crowning glory of your visualization project is likely to be a rendered or artistic-style animation. The tutorials in this chapter will take you through this step-by-step, showing you how to create storyboards, set up cameras and paths in SketchUp with extra plugin functionality, export test animations and final renders. Photo-real animations are then composited to make a simple show reel.

Chapter 11: *Presenting Visuals in LayOut*: Layout is bundled as part of SketchUp Pro and is introduced in this final chapter for those who wish to explore the free trial before committing to Pro. You will learn how to bring together SketchUp models and artistic or rendered output into a screen presentation or printed portfolio, adding borders, text and dimensions.

What you need for this book

The basics are: Google SketchUp (Free) 7, Kerkythea 2008, GIMP 2.6, and VirtualDub. Also the book touches on Google Earth, MPEG Sreamclip, Microsoft MovieMaker, SketchUp Pro, and Layout (Installed with SketchUp Pro). An Internet connection is needed for some sections of the book.

Who this book is for

This book is suitable for all levels of Sketchup users, from amateurs right through to architectural technicians, professional architects, and designers who want to take their 3D designs to the next level of presentation. SketchUp for Architectural Visualization is also particularly suitable as a companion to any architectural design or multimedia course, and is accessible to anyone who has familiarized themselves with the basics of SketchUp through Google's online videos.

Conventions

In this book, you will find several headings appearing frequently.

To give clear instructions of how to complete a procedure or task, we use:

Time for action – heading

Action 1

Action 2

Action 3

Instructions often need some extra explanation so that they make sense, so they are followed with:

What just happened?

This heading explains the working of tasks or instructions that you have just completed.

You will also find some other learning aids in the book, including:

Pop quiz – heading

These are short multiple choice questions intended to help you test your own understanding.

Have a go hero – heading

These set practical challenges and give you ideas for experimenting with what you have learned.

You will also find a number of styles of text that distinguish between different kinds of information. Here are some examples of these styles, and an explanation of their meaning.

Code words in text are shown as follows: "Save it in the `My Documents` folder."

New terms and important words are shown in bold. Words that you see on the screen, in menus or dialog boxes for example, appear in the text like this: "Select the image you want to use and click **Open**".

 Warnings or important notes appear in a box like this.

 Tips and tricks appear like this.

Reader feedback

Feedback from our readers is always welcome. Let us know what you think about this book—what you liked or may have disliked. Reader feedback is important for us to develop titles that you really get the most out of.

To send us general feedback, simply send an email to feedback@packtpub.com, and mention the book title via the subject of your message.

If there is a book that you need and would like to see us publish, please send us a note in the **SUGGEST A TITLE** form on www.packtpub.com or email suggest@packtpub.com.

If there is a topic that you have expertise in and you are interested in either writing or contributing to a book on, see our author guide on www.packtpub.com/authors.

Customer support

Now that you are the proud owner of a Packt book, we have a number of things to help you to get the most from your purchase.

Errata

Although we have taken every care to ensure the accuracy of our content, mistakes do happen. If you find a mistake in one of our books—maybe a mistake in the text or the code— we would be grateful if you would report this to us. By doing so, you can save other readers from frustration, and help us to improve subsequent versions of this book. If you find any errata, please report them by visiting http://www.packtpub.com/support, selecting your book, clicking on the **let us know** link, and entering the details of your errata. Once your errata are verified, your submission will be accepted and the errata added to any list of existing errata. Any existing errata can be viewed by selecting your title from http://www.packtpub.com/support.

Piracy

Piracy of copyright material on the Internet is an ongoing problem across all media. At Packt, we take the protection of our copyright and licenses very seriously. If you come across any illegal copies of our works, in any form, on the Internet, please provide us with the location address or web site name immediately so that we can pursue a remedy.

Please contact us at copyright@packtpub.com with a link to the suspected pirated material.

We appreciate your help in protecting our authors, and our ability to bring you valuable content.

Questions

You can contact us at `questions@packtpub.com` if you are having a problem with any aspect of the book, and we will do our best to address it.

1

Quick Start Tutorial

So, you've decided to learn how to use SketchUp for architectural visualization? Maybe an architect or a visualizer told you how easy it is and you decided to give it a go yourself? Maybe you've read a book on basic SketchUp and want to take it further? You already know that SketchUp is the easiest, most powerful, effective, and fun-to-use application you could wish to use for 3D work. With this book you'll learn how to use SketchUp and other free software to achieve great architectural visuals in no time. You will need some basic knowledge of SketchUp, but can be a complete beginner in visualization.

With this Quick Start Tutorial you will get up and running immediately. It gives you a flavor of what is in the rest of the book. In this short tutorial you will learn how to:

- Produce a photo-realistic rendering of a scene modeled in SketchUp
- Produce real-world shadows and lighting using a physically accurate light simulator
- Create materials that reflect or absorb light
- Produce realistic windows
- Set up a camera at eye level
- Use photos for background and decoration

When you've followed the tutorial and seen how easy it is to produce great results with SketchUp, you'll be able to go on and refine your skills and technique in the subsequent chapters. The rendering software you'll be using is Kerkythea, which is a free, professional-level lighting simulator. To find out more about it and install it, jump to Chapter 2, *How to Collect an Arsenal Rambo Would Be Proud of*—but come back again!

For this tutorial you will need:

- A Windows PC or MAC
- SketchUp or SketchUp Pro
- Kerkythea (available free from `www.Kerkythea.net`)
- The SU2KT plugin (from the same website)
- A background photo (`.jpg` or `.png` format)
- Photos of some artwork

Can SketchUp really produce pro visuals?

What do you mean you're not sure about SketchUp visuals? You've heard it's just for simple stuff? And all the images you've seen are always cartoony? Ah, but those are just myths. Actually, top movie studios and world renowned architectural practices use SketchUp. Just because something's easy to use and free that doesn't mean it's not great, right? And just because beginners immediately want to post their results on the Internet, doesn't mean your results will be like theirs. It simply indicates that SketchUp is easier to learn and more accessible than other software. Take other free Google products like Google Search for example. There's nothing out there to rival it, period. And the same goes for SketchUp. Here's what you can expect from just 20 minutes modeling and rendering:

Reflection and absorption, even using simple SketchUp materials:

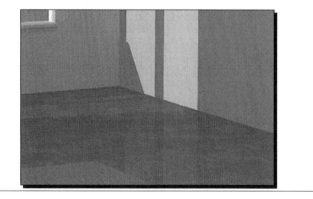

Accurate glass reflections:

Soft shadows from multiple light sources:

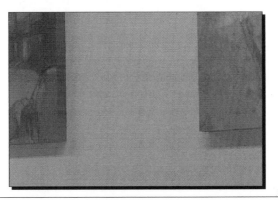

Physically accurate lighting, especially on indirectly lit surfaces:

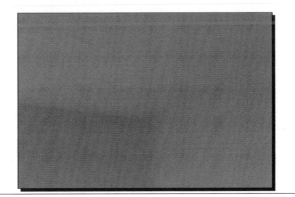

And if all that's achieved with just the Quickstart, imagine what you will be producing after reading the whole book.

This tutorial is an introduction to photo-realistic architectural visualization. I think you will be enthused by it when you see the quality of your own results.

Modeling the room

So, let's get started straight away. The room scene you'll be modeling here is simple and easy to produce in SketchUp; it's just four walls like the majority of rooms in the real world.

Time for action – model the room in SketchUp

1. Start by firing up SketchUp, then click the **Model Info** button (a blue circle with an **i** in it or go to **Window | Model Info**). Set the units to the values shown in the following screenshot. You can use inches if you prefer.

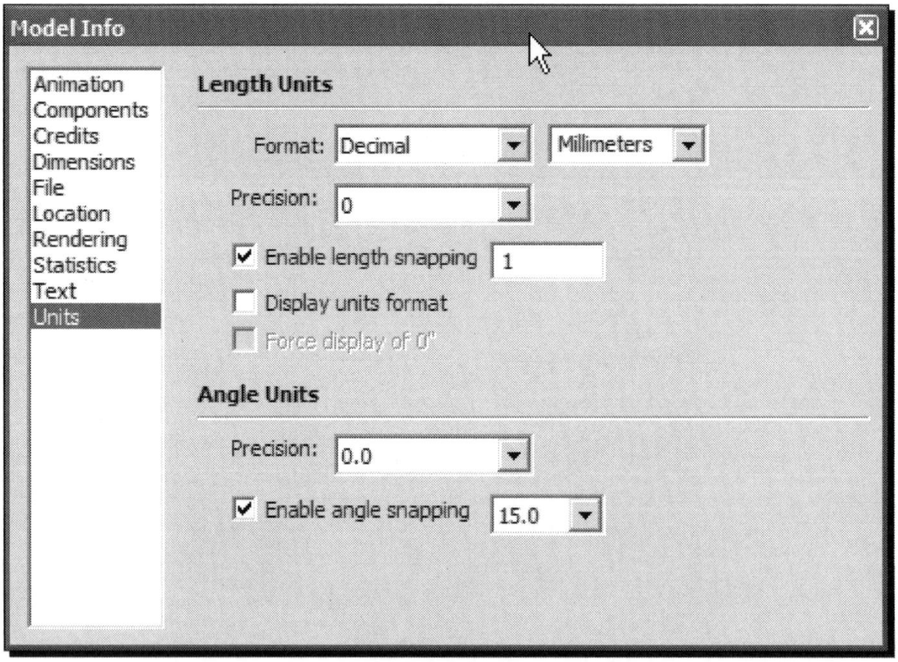

2. Close the **Model Info** dialog by clicking the red X and start modeling by selecting the **Rectangle** function.

3. You can snap to the **origin** and start there.

4. Draw a rectangle of any size. Click the left mouse button again to finish it.

5. Now type in **4000,10000**. This appears in the little text box at the bottom as shown in the following screenshot. Hit *Enter* and your rectangle will resize to 4000 mm by 10,000 mm (4x10 meters).

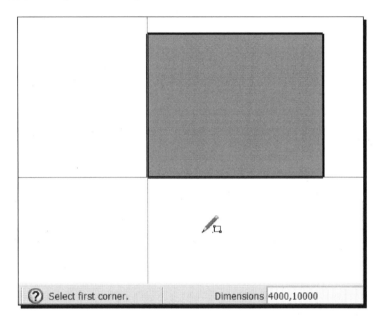

6. Rotate the view by holding the middle mouse button and moving the mouse.

7. Now click the **Push/Pull** tool and click the rectangle, moving the mouse up to extrude the rectangle into a box.

8. Type in **3000** and hit *Enter*. This sets the height of the room at 3 meters. You can see it in the following screenshot:

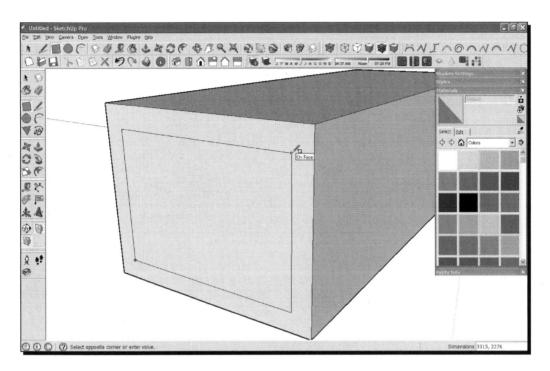

9. Draw a rectangle on the west facing side as shown in the previous screenshot. This is your window.

10. Now select and delete the face.

What just happened?

You've just created a basic room based on the inside dimensions. You don't need to create the building outside because you'll never see it. Rotate your view now until you're inside the room looking out of the window.

Composing the view

You're now going to set up the camera view and sun lighting. You might have noticed that there are very few actual camera buttons in SketchUp. That's because SketchUp is all about "what you see is what you get". If you see it on the screen, that's what you'll see in your render. In actual fact, all the complex camera stuff is taken care of in the background and the right settings will be exported to the renderer without you or me having to worry about it. You will find out how to set up scenes for maximum impact in Chapter 3, *Composing the Scene*.

Time for action – setting up the camera

1. Rotate and zoom the view so that you're more or less looking at the scene as shown in the following screenshot.

2. Click the **Walk** button or **Camera | Walk**.

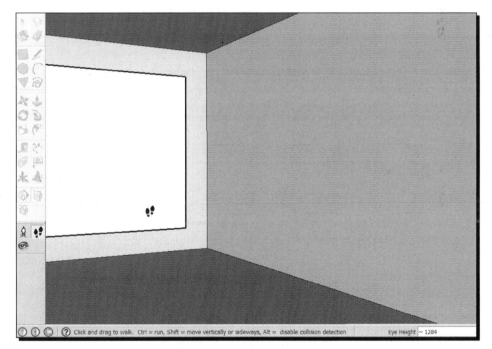

3. Type in your eye height in mm (say **1600**) then enter. The camera changes to view the room from that eye level.

4. Use the **Eye** tool to move your head around and compose the view you want, and use Walk to move in or out of the scene by holding the left mouse button and moving up or down.

Saving the camera view

Now that you're happy with the view you've created, you need to save it so that it can't be changed by accident, or while doing further modeling tasks. You do this by creating a scene tab, which will be imported into the rendering software as a camera view.

Go to **View | Animation | Add Scene.** A scene tab will appear at the top of the main viewing window.

Rotate your view now with the middle mouse button, then click on the tab. You are taken back to the saved view.

Time for action – setting up the sun

Let's get some direct sunlight in through the window to bounce off the wall and floor, just like a real-life setting. In SketchUp the sun only lights up areas directly and there's a sharp contrast between light and dark. But in the renderer (and real life) the sunlight will bounce into the whole room. You can read more on lighting in Chapter 8, *Photo Realistic Rendering*. Follow these simple steps now to set it up:

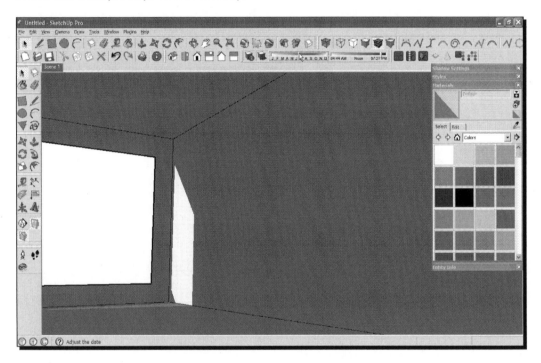

1. If you need to get the shadow buttons up on the toolbar, go to **View | Toolbars | Shadows**.

2. Click the **Display Shadows** button.

3. Move the sliders around until you get the effect similar to the previous screenshot.

4. If you can't get light to come in through the window, you may need to change the orientation of north (that is, the direction your building is facing). You can find out how to do this in Chapter 5. You could also select and rotate the whole room.

5. When you're happy, right-click on the scene tab and select **Update**.

What just happened?

You now have all the lighting you need for a daytime indoor scene. The following screenshot is what you would get if you did a quick test render in Kerkythea. As you can see, the whole room is lit by the sun, just as it would be in real life. You'll discover the quickest test render settings for Kerkythea in Chapter 8, but there's no need to go there now.

Add simple ceiling lights

No art gallery would just light its rooms by sunlight and turn visitors away on dull days. Happily, there's an incredibly easy way to set up lights in SketchUp and Kerkythea. Just draw rectangles and give them a light emitting surface!

1. With the **Rectangle** tool, draw a rectangle on the ceiling approximately the size of an ordinary fluorescent light.

2. Click the **Paint Bucket** tool.

3. Select a color you'll be able to recognize later from the **Pallet**. It doesn't matter what it is.

4. Click the rectangle (see the following screenshot).

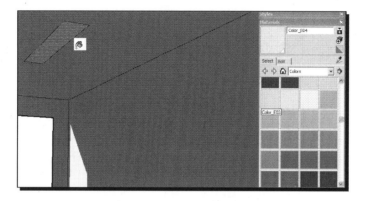

5. With the **Move** tool, click on the rectangle, hold *Ctrl*, move, and click to create a second light as shown in the following screenshot:

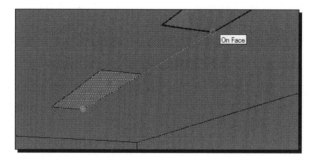

These colored rectangles will act as lights when we add a light emitting material to them in Kerkythea. They will light the room from three different angles to give pleasing shadows and depth to the scene. Now that wasn't so hard was it?

Materials

You'll now add some flooring materials straight from the ones included in SketchUp. In Chapter 5, *Applying Textures and Materials for Photo-Real Rendering,* we'll look at creating and obtaining many more materials from photos and online texture libraries. For now, let's stick with what's already there, so you can see how good a render you can get straight out of a basic, no frills, SketchUp model.

Time for action – timber flooring materials

1. Go to the **Materials** pallet and select **Wood** from the drop down box. If it's not visible already, go to **Windows | Materials**.

2. Select a material

3. Click on the floor. Try a few different ones until you find one you like best.

4. Now draw a rectangle on the floor for a carpet as shown in the following screenshot:

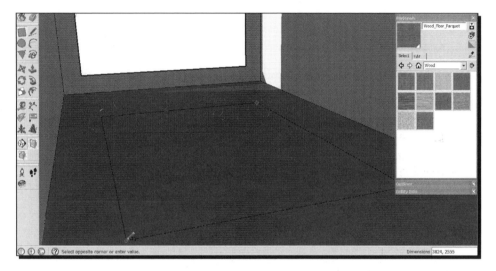

5. Use the **Push/Pull** tool to slightly elevate the rectangle.

6. Select a carpet texture and paint it onto the raised surface as shown here:

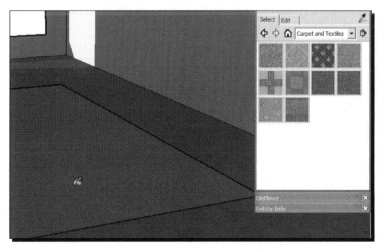

What just happened?

You've now got two textures in the scene that you'll be able to modify in Kerkythea to add highlights or reflections. The carpet will stay a matt finish. You'll learn how to add bump maps and other stuff to surfaces such as these in Chapter 8, if you want to. And you'll look at creating and applying SketchUp materials in more detail in Chapter 5.

Modeling the window

The scene looks fake with just a hole in the wall. Let's make a window using SketchUp's **Push/Pull** tool. It will help if you now hide the wall to the left of the window to allow you to view into the room more easily as you progress with the tutorial. You can un-hide it later.

1. Select the wall face to the left of the window, right-click and select **Hide**.

2. Use **Push/Pull** to extrude the side of the room with the window in it. This will give thickness to the frame.

3. With the **Pencil** tool, draw a line out from the bottom edge of the window, then down along the blue axis, back to the wall and back to the start as shown in this screenshot:

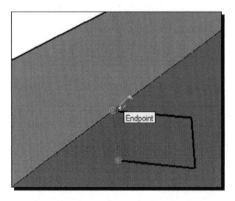

4. The lines will fill with a face as soon as the rectangle is completed.

5. Select the **Arc** tool. Draw an arc as shown, then delete the square corners with the **Erase** tool.

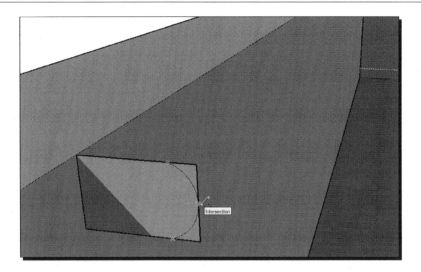

6. Use the **Push/Pull** tool to extrude the shape along the window first in one direction, then the other, to form a windowsill.

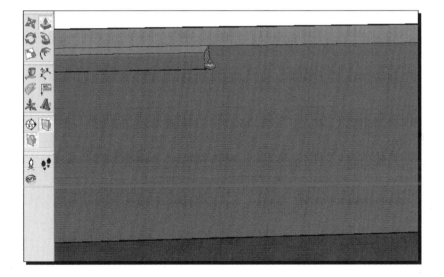

7. Select the **Rectangle** button and hover over the centre of the top of the window (see the following screenshot). When you see a **Tooltip** saying **Midpoint**, click and draw a square.

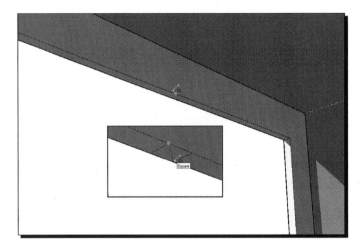

8. Use the **Arc** tool to round the corners facing the camera and delete the corners as before.

9. **Push/Pull** the shape to span the whole window frame.

10. Select everything you made so far (triple click), right-click and select **Create Group**.

11. Create the glass pane by selecting the rectangle tool. Click the **Midpoint** of one corner (as shown in the following screenshot).

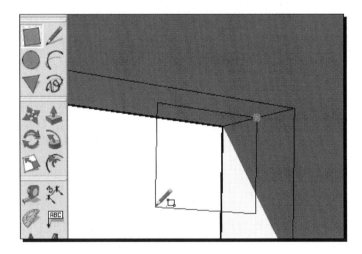

12. Rotate and pan to the opposite corner, find the midpoint and click again.

13. Select this rectangle and give it a glass material with the **Paint Bucket.**

14. If any wall faces have turned blue, select them now. Right-click and select **Reverse Faces**.

Here's the finished window:

Photo images

You're bound to have some images that will do as a backdrop for your scene. If not, just grab something from the Internet for now. All you're after is a fairly interesting view out of the window. You'll need some pictures that will do for the gallery paintings too. In Chapters 3 and 5 you'll look at where to find great images to use in your scenes from the Internet, and how to make the best use of them to set up your scenes.

Time for action – setting up the scenery backdrop

1. Go to **File | Import**, and tick the **Use As Image** box. Navigate to an image, click on it and click **Open**.

2. Zoom out in your model and click somewhere on the window to insert the image. Drag the cursor to size it and click again.

3. You have now inserted the image in the correct plane—the plane of the window.

4. Use **Move** to set it further from the window and alter the height position (see the following screenshot). Click on the scene tab at any time to check what you will see out of the window.

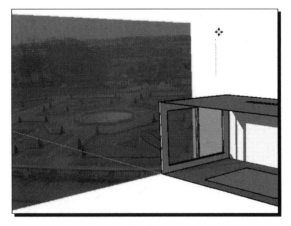

5. Use the **Move** function and hover over the edge of the image. You will see some red plus signs appear. Use these to rotate the backdrop if you need to alter the angle (see the following screenshot).

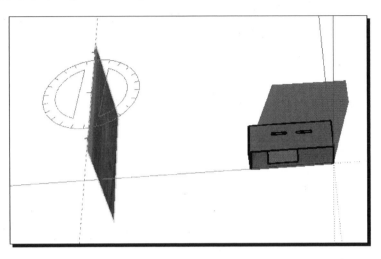

6. Explode the image (right-click and select, **Explode**)

7. Right-click on the image and select **Entity Info**

8. Untick **Cast Shadows** and **Receive Shadows**

Time for action – hanging digital art

For the artwork on the wall you can simply grab some images of your own or browse the web. It doesn't matter for this tutorial where you get them from. But if you have some art of your own, why not scan or photograph it and use it here? You can create your own 3D portfolio!

1. Go to **File | Import.** Now move the cursor to the wall and click. Stretch the image to the size you want and click again.

2. Repeat this for more images. Remember to click on the scene tab from time to time so that you can see what will or won't be in the frame when you render.

3. Now right-click on each image and select **Explode** (see the following screenshot)

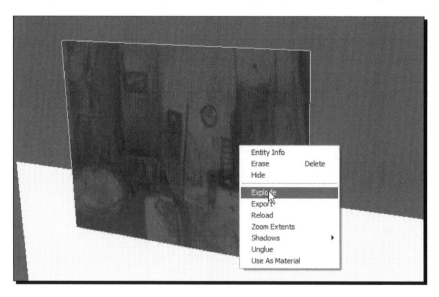

4. When you're done, use the **Push/Pull** tool to give the canvasses some depth.

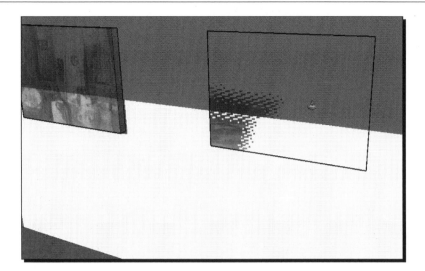

5. Finally, close the side of the room back up. Go to **View | Hidden Geometry**

6. Select the hidden wall. Right-click and select **Unhide**.

7. Click the scene tab to check the camera position. You should have something like this image:

Exporting to the render application

Install Kerkythea, the free rendering software which you will find on the website www. kerkythea.net. You'll also need to install the free SketchUp to Kerkythea exporter (SU2KT), which you'll also find on the website. Details about this and loads of other items up for grabs are in Chapter 2.

1. In SketchUp, go to **View | Toolbars** and make sure **SU2Kerkythea** is ticked.

2. Click the **Export model to Kerkythea** button. You'll get the dialog box shown in the following screenshot:

3. Change **Export options** to **Yes** for **Geometry** and **Lights**.

4. Click **OK**. Find a folder to save the file to and type in a file name, then click **Save**.

5. When asked **Open exported Model in Kerkythea?** click **No** for now.

6. Open Kerkythea and go to **File | Open**. Find your saved file, click on it and click **OK**.

7. The following screenshot shows what you should be presented with. All the buttons are explained in Chapter 8 but you can still produce a great render knowing no more about them than you learn in this Quickstart. That's because SketchUp has taken care of most things already.

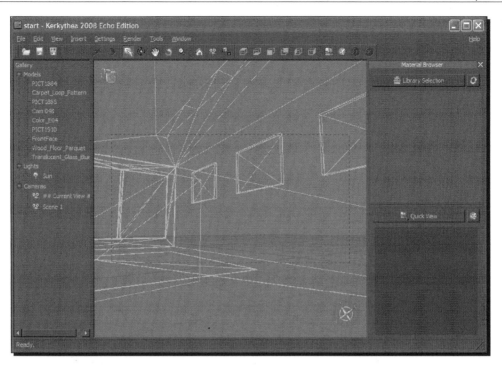

8. Hit *V* on the keyboard to view the scene in solid colors.

Modifying materials in Kerkythea quickly

If you were to render this scene straight away you would get something like the following screenshot:

This is rather nice, but there are a few things missing. Notice what still needs to be done for a realistic scene:

- The glass material needs reflections
- The smooth floor needs to be shiny
- The lights need to go on

But that's all you need to do. Kerkythea's lighting and shadows already make for a pleasingly realistic scene. Follow these steps now to add in these last few details.

Time for action – Kerkythea materials

1. Click on the glass window. A star appears in the list to the left, next to the name of the glass material you used in SketchUp.

2. Right-click this and select **Apply Materials | Basic Pack | Thin Glass**. This comes already installed with Kerkythea.

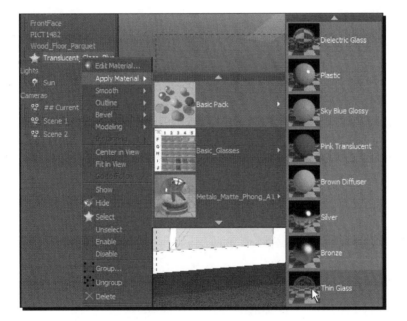

Diffused light

This is the easiest step of all, and it makes setting up photo-realistic scenes with indoor lighting child's play.

3. Click on the color you selected in SketchUp for the ceiling lights.

4. Right-click and select **Apply Materials | Basic Pack | Diffuse Light**.

Reflective floors

5. Select the floor material.

6. Right-click and select **Edit Material**. This takes you to the **Material Editor**.

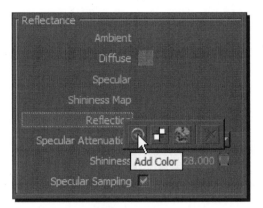

7. Right-click on **Reflection** and click the left button (shown in the previous screenshot).

8. Drag the cursor down the right-hand side of the triangle to select a dark grey (see the following screenshot). Click **Accept**.

9. You can alter these grey levels until you're happy with the preview image shown top left in the material editor. A dark grey is usually best.

10. Click **Apply Changes,** then **Close Editor**.

What just happened?

What you've just done is added qualities to your SketchUp materials that they didn't possess before. And usually these few steps are all that's needed to get a great render. It's really simple and really effective. The grey levels are Kerkythea's way of obtaining a value. It helps to think of it as a slider or volume control on your stereo: black is none, and white is maximum. You don't need to bother with the other colors in the triangle.

Rendering in Kerkythea

Now you're all set. If you've followed all the steps so far, the finished render is just a few clicks away!

1. Select the little green button (**Start Render**).

2. Select the preset setting labeled **07. PhotonMap – High + AA 0.3**.

3. Leave everything else as it is and hit **Ok**.

4. The render will progress and appear in the bottom right preview window.

5. At the top left corner of your screen you will see a percentage complete status. When it's finished click the **Image** button.

6. The image preview window appears. Click **Save**, type in a file name and click **OK**.

Here's your finished render:

Summary

This chapter was designed to give you a taste of how easily and quickly you can get great photo-realistic results with the SketchUp and Kerkythea combination. In particular, you've learned the basic steps towards:

- Modeling a simple indoor studio scene
- Setting up daylight and indoor lighting
- Applying photo backgrounds to add realism
- Enhancing SketchUp materials in Kerkythea for photo-realistic rendering

This is the basic framework for achieving successful renders of most interior and outdoor scenes. Congratulations! You're now able to apply what you've learned immediately in your own projects. The rest of the chapters in this book will take your skills a step or two further. You can dip in whenever you need some specific guidance, or follow the chapters in a course format.

In the next chapter, you'll find out how to create your own visualization and animation studio setup with free software and plugins, ready to make even better architectural visuals!

2
How to Collect an Arsenal Rambo Would Be Proud of

Have you ever watched an action movie and been moved to tears of joy when the would-be action hero suddenly stumbles upon a stash of armaments fit to kit out a private army? There's a rack of M60 machine guns on that barn wall; sixty boxes of ammo over there by the bale of hay; a table of handguns of every imaginable make, shape, and size neatly arranged over by the door; and to finish off the scene, there's always a special prize—the rocket launcher that turns weeny Wodger into a one man army. Cut to a scene outside the building: he appears through the door laden with his bounty; a smoldering cigar in his mouth.

Well, that's how you're going to feel in a minute!

In this chapter you will:

- ◆ Turbo charge your copy of SketchUp with terrain tools
- ◆ Set up your post-processing studio with GIMP
- ◆ Be given free access to the best rendering technology available
- ◆ Install some secret buttons that virtually turn SketchUp into 3D Max
- ◆ Witness how SketchUp and Google Earth work in tandem
- ◆ Set up an animation production studio

If it's not free, it's not worth having

Let's get one thing straight right now. This arsenal you're going to go get yourself is just lying around for free. No one ever expects the action hero to pay for it, so neither should you. In fact, if it's not free, don't bother with it. This book will show you how to create great looking architectural visuals for nothing. One of the reasons we're going to use free software is that it's sometimes better than the bought stuff. But that's not all; the most important thing is psychology. Let me explain.

Don't be beholden to your software

There's a subtle but very, very important psychological reason you should try free software. The reason is that the more you pay for software, the more you will feel compelled to use that software, rather than something better. This is suicide, because some other software is always being released better than what you've got already. And if you haven't bought any software yet, you end up spending all your time trying out, evaluating, and poring over product reviews rather than getting on with creating great visuals. With free stuff you just download it and launch right in.

So, don't be beholden to your software, or in other words, don't let it stifle your creativity. If you buy expensive software you will always be pressured to adopt the work-stream they have prepared for you. And that work-stream usually involves buying more add-on functions. Free software often lets you use it however you want to, without needing to buy more functionality to what you need it to do; in other words, in the most productive and effective way. With this book, we will discover what that is for creating architectural visuals.

How is free software so good?

Free software is so good because lots of people with lots of spare time contribute to it. Computer programmers, by and large, respond well to only two motivators:

- Respect
- Cheeseburgers

So, coding Blender or Kerkythea for free doesn't matter to them, as long as they can do it in their own bedroom surrounded by cheeseburger wrappers and get some credit for it. Remember, these guys might spend 8 hours of the day earning a living, 7 hours sleeping, leaving them 7.5 hours to create your arsenal of weaponry. (You don't want to know about the other 1.5 hours.)

Google software

Let's start with Google itself. Google SketchUp is free as long as you're not too bothered about importing/exporting CAD formats. Almost all of the tutorials in this book can be done, free of cost, with SketchUp. Once you have SketchUp (the free or the Pro version) installed, take a look at the other Google goodies that follow.

Google's component bonus packs

Google used to provide loads of great components readily available in their bonus packs. However, you now have to search and download them as and when you need to, using 3D Warehouse. Thankfully, there are options to save them all to your computer so you don't have to go online for them every time.

Time for action – restoring the collection to its rightful place

If you used SketchUp version 6 before you upgraded to version 7, you can import the component collections as follows:

1. In SketchUp 7, select **Window | Components**.

2. Make sure you're in the **Select** tab.

3. Click the details button to the right of the search box.

4. Select **Open or create a local collection....**

5. Browse to `C:\Program Files\Google\Google SketchUp 6\` and select the desired folder.

6. Click **OK**.

7. Click the details button.

8. Select **Add to favorites** so you can access the collection again.

Saving collections from the web if you don't have SketchUp 6:

9. Select **Window | Components**.

10. Click the **Select** tab and then click the little arrow next to the house icon.

11. Select a Bonus Pack category (such as **Architecture**).

12. Within this collection, scroll to a sub-collection and click.

13. Click the **Details** button then click **Save as a local collection**.

14. Navigate to the folder where you'd like to save the models.

15. Click **OK**.

16. Now click the **Details** button again.

17. Select **Add to favorites** so you can access the collection again.

18. Repeat this for any other collections you want to access off-line.

What just happened?

If you don't have SketchUp 6, you can still save the results of a component search locally to your computer. Using this method you can eventually find and download all the bonus pack collections. You can also input a special search string into the search box to only look for collections, not individual components. Just type in *is:collection* with your search. For example, film stage *is:collection*.

The main collections you should look for include:

◆ **Construction**

◆ **Film and Stage**

◆ **Architecture**

◆ **Landscape Architecture**

◆ **Mechanical**

◆ **2D People**

◆ **Transportation**

◆ **Shapes**

Google Earth

Believe it or not, SketchUp is joined at the hip with Google Earth. Didn't know that? I thought you'd be surprised. Just over a year before Google bought *@last software*, the makers of SketchUp, it also bought *Keyhole Corp*, the makers of Google Earth. Both Google Earth and SketchUp were then released for free. The development of the two technologies became inextricably linked, with SketchUp models being able to be viewed in Google Earth, and Google Earth terrain in SketchUp.

Geo location toolbars

Within the standard free version of SketchUp there are buttons which allow you to geo-reference your model in Google Earth; it's very easy to do and lots of fun. The buttons here can be used to import to SketchUp or export to Google Earth at a single click.

Within SketchUp just click the following to bring up the toolbar:

View | Toolbars | Google

Why do I need Google Earth?

Google Earth is really just an extension of SketchUp. Think of it as SketchUp on the web. Given that Google have also now released their own web browser—Chrome, it's a pretty good guess that the internet will go 3D in a big way some time in the future. The continual increase in the computing power available in a standard desktop computer, and the proliferation of fast broadband connections means that soon the average consumer could be exploring the world online entirely in a 3D browser!

What this really means to you as an architectural visualization creator is that the massive effort Google is putting into the Google Earth-Internet-SketchUp combo can be used to great effect when visualizing your buildings in their real world setting. You'll find out all about this in Chapter 5, *Applying Textures and Materials*.

 To get Google Earth visit `http://earth.google.com`

Once you've installed Google Earth it will automatically work with SketchUp. You can now import terrain into SketchUp using the menu buttons on the Google Toolbar. You can also export geo-referenced models into Google Earth.

SketchUp Pro, LayOut, and Style Builder

Although SketchUp Pro and the tools that come with it (LayOut and Style Builder) are not free, I'll give them a mention because a lot of you will already have, or be thinking of owning SketchUp Pro. LayOut is a stand-alone program and is explained more fully in Chapter 11, *Presenting Visuals in Layout*. With Layout you can easily import your SketchUp models and create presentation pages for print or onscreen rather like PowerPoint or Keynote.

SketchUp Pro enables you to import and export CAD data, which is a must when using SketchUp within a professional work-flow. You also gain the privilege of creating **dynamic components**, which work a little like Dynamic Blocks in AutoCAD.

Additional import formats with SketchUp Pro

♦   AutoCAD (`.dwg`, `.dxf`)

Additional export formats with SketchUp Pro

2D Formats:

♦   Portable Document Format (`.pdf`)

♦   Encapsulated Postscript (`.eps`)

♦   Epix (`.epx`)

♦   Autocad (`.dwg`/`.dxf`)

3D Formats:

♦   3DS (`.3ds`)

♦   AutoCAD DWG (`.dwg`)

♦   AutoCAD DXF (`.dxf`)

♦   FBX (`.fbx`)

♦   OBJ (`.obj`)

♦   XSI (`.xsi`)

♦   VRML (`.vrml`)

♦   AVI (Windows video)

♦   Mov (Mac video)

The Pro version of SketchUp is available as a free 8 hour trial from the main SketchUp website http://sketchup.google.com.

What's the best import/export file format?

Google has announced they are dropping .dwg and .dxf import capability from their free version of SketchUp. This was backed up by a statement that they prefer the Collada file format (.dae). You can probably take this as a good indication that Collada will go from strength to strength in the future. If you use CAD import a lot, it's worth finding out about Collada to see if you can use it in your workflow.

SketchUp's hidden features

There are certain features within SketchUp that remain hidden, or switched off, until you enable them. One of these is **Sandbox**. The great thing about the Sandbox tools is that they enable SketchUp to deal with curved surfaces and organic shapes. The tools in the Sandbox set are fun and powerful but sometimes crash the system. This shouldn't be a problem if you save regularly and don't try to model overly complex meshes (see Chapter 4, *Modelling for Visualization* for advice on **low polygon modeling**). You can see it in action in the following screenshot:

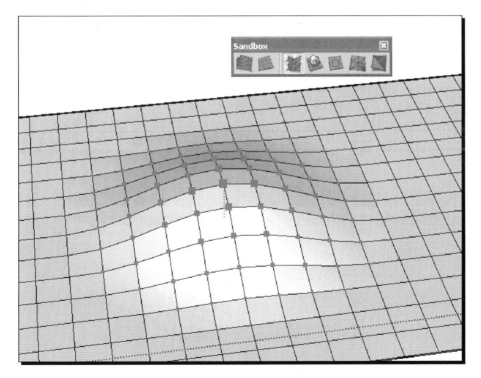

With Sandbox you can:

◆ Create terrains from map contours

◆ Instantly **stamp** any shape onto a terrain

◆ Push / pull a curved surface into shape using **smoove**

◆ **Drape** pictures or geometry onto a surface, such as maps or site layouts

◆ Use imported map data to create organic curved surfaces

Time for action – enabling the organic modeling tools

Follow the instructions below and then have a play at creating some hilly terrains. To enable the sandbox tools:

1. Select **Window | Preferences | Extensions** (for Mac, **Sketchup | Preferences | Extensions**).

2. Select the checkbox next to **Sandbox Tools**.

3. While you're there why not select **Utilities Tools** and **Dynamic Components** too.

4. Click **OK**.

5. To view the toolbar go to **View | Toolbars | Sandbox**.

What just happened?

SketchUp is all about simplicity. That's why when you first start the software, there are hardly any buttons on the screen. Believe it or not, most modeling tasks can be achieved with just six buttons! You've now taken steps to add some of the expanded toolset to your screen, which would have just confused a complete newbie if they had been there right from the start.

Use this process each time you install a new plugin to show toolbar buttons on screen. You can now arrange the buttons how you like them by clicking and dragging with the mouse.

 In Appendix B you can find a suggested screen layout. You might find this useful as a starting point.

Your image processing studio with GIMP

I became interested in computer art when I discovered the Acorn computer version of Paint at school. I was amazed by how I could zoom in to individual pixels and change their color! But things have moved on a little since then. Let's not stay in yesteryear. If you are one of those people who still use Paint on the Microsoft PC to do their image editing, don't worry. You'll be converted and you'll never look back.

If you have Photoshop (the commercial equivalent of GIMP) already, lucky you! All of the instructions for GIMP in this book should work for Photoshop too, so you don't need to install GIMP (unless you have trouble following the GIMP instructions in this book). Photoshop Elements won't do because it doesn't have layer masks.

Why do I need a professional level image processor?

Creating great architectural visuals in SketchUp is very digital image intensive. This is a good thing because it makes our lives easy as we will see later, as every digital image we use greatly diminishes the need for creating complex SketchUp geometry. So, we need to have the tools at our disposal that will quickly and easily manipulate all the different photos and textures that will go in to SketchUp, and all the images that come out. We will also be combining output from SketchUp with rendered images later on.

Should I buy a pen tablet?

The answer to this is probably "yes". If you're going to spend a lot of time doing Architectural Visuals you will probably find the finer control and comfort of a tablet over a mouse is well worth the investment. The Wacom A6-size tablet range received excellent reviews and should be sufficient for most people at under $70.

The importance of layer masks

While at university our Head of Department decided we ought to learn something about digital image manipulation to help us with our portfolios. Learning what Photoshop can do was one of those *Eureka!* moments. Until you learn about layers and masks, the door to digital graphics will remain firmly closed to you. Layers are what will allow us to composite multiple takes of the same scene together so that we get the best out of SketchUp native output. Using masks with layers is really where it's at.

Grabbing a copy of GIMP

Open source software is constantly being developed. So, there's usually a development version on the go with all the latest bells and whistles... and the latest bugs. So, the safe bet is to go for the **stable** version.

1. Navigate to the gimp website `www.gimp.org/downloads/`.

2. Click the download link on this page.

3. Save the file to `My Documents` (`Desktop` or `Downloads` folder on the Mac).

4. Navigate to the file using explorer (Finder on the Mac) and double-click.

5. Follow the on screen instructions to install it.

Have a go hero – unleashing the inner artist with watercolour brushes

The brushes that come with GIMP aren't really great for the non photo real methods we'll be looking at, so we'll download some better ones. These can be used later to create the sketchy style non photo-realistic (NPR) visuals found in Chapter 7, *Non Photo Real with Sketchup*. The methods you'll learn are all "broad brush" techniques that don't require any artistic talent to create great looking architectural visualizations, so try out a few until you find one or two basic brushes you're comfortable with (so you really needn't spend a lot of time).

[Try typing **free brushes gimp** into Google]

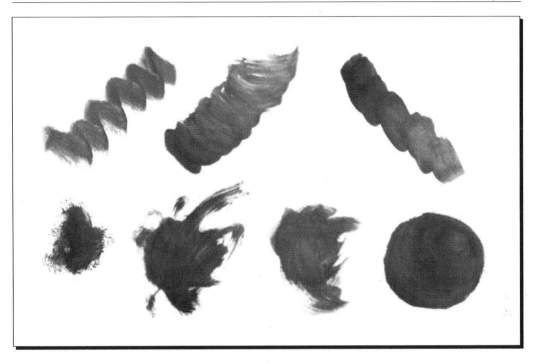

1. Go to `http://www.blendfu.com/`.

2. Type **watercolour** into the search bar. Select the Gimp download.

3. Save the ZIP file somewhere you can find it.

4. Extract the files in the ZIP folder.

5. Copy new brush files in the folder and paste them in your `GIMP Brushes` folder (usually `C:\Program Files\GIMP-2.0\share\gimp\2.0\brushes`).

On a Mac:

1. Navigate via finder to `volume/Applications/Gimp.app`.

2. Right-click and choose **Show Package Contents**.

3. Once shown, navigate to **Brushes**. Drag and drop all the brushes to this folder.

4. GIMP should automatically recognize the brushes when you next start it up.

Still stuck? Try this tutorial:
http://swimkid22.deviantart.com/art/Installing-Brushes-With-GIMP-33237659

Become a movie making genius—almost

Alright, we're not going to turn you into a fully clued up movie producer just yet. But you don't have to be one with SketchUp and the following software. One of the most painful experiences I had whilst researching this book was navigating through the maze of compression codecs, frame rates, aspect ratios, and other thorny issues that make digital moving image production such a nightmare. Well, I think I finally found some answers that might help you avoid reliving the nightmare. VirtualDub and MPEG Streamclip along with all the settings and work pipeline we're going to look at in Chapter 10 should leave you oblivious of the suffering you could have gone through!

Why can't I just use raw AVI output from SketchUp?

Raw animated output from SketchUp or rendering software will invariably be one of the following:

- Compressed beyond recognition with blotches, artifacts, fuzz, and fluff
- Have a massive file size
- Not viewable to those people who don't have the right viewer or codec

Following the easy steps in Chapter 10 with the software you're about to download will sort out all three problems. You will be completely amazed, for example, how far the file size comes down with no perceivable reduction in quality. I recently had a 300 MB AVI file which reduced to a 0.8 MB .mp4 file ready to stick on any website (via www.screencast.com) where anyone with flash viewer can see it (and that's virtually everybody).

VirtualDub

VirtualDub is the answer to most of our moving image woes. It's free, which is unbelievable as the next best available software is Adobe after effects or Autodesk Combustion, both retailing at around $1000. So, download it quick. VirtualDub will allow you to composite JPEG images together to form a video, with the use of a whole host of filters into the bargain.

Chapter 2

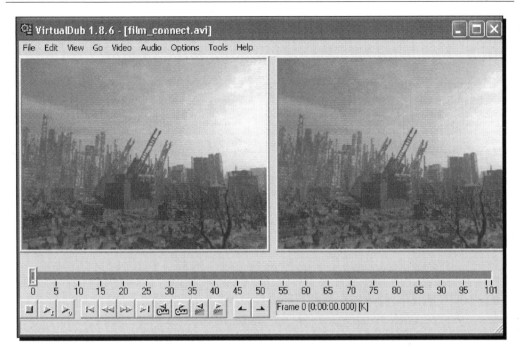

Time for action – installing VirtualDub

VirtualDub doesn't have an install program so you will have to save it somewhere and create a desktop shortcut to it manually. Here's how to do it if you have Windows:

1. Get the latest stable release of VirtualDub from www.virtualdub.org.

2. Save the ZIP file to your hard drive.

3. Unzip the file (right-click and **Extract**).

4. Move the whole VirtualDub folder somewhere safe on your hard drive.

5. Double-click on the VirtualDub folder.

6. Right-click VirtualDub.exe.

7. Click **Send to | Desktop** *(create shortcut)*.

MPEG Streamclip

MPEG Streamclip is the best video compression and conversion software I've been able to find. It also works seamlessly hand in hand with VirtualDub. MPEG Streamclip will output to all sorts of video formats and compression settings such as Quicktime, DV, Mpeg-4, and even has iPhone presets! For those of you who are worried about such things, you'll be glad to know it uses the popular `H.264` codec.

Obtaining MPEG Streamclip

To find it, go to `http://www.squared5.com/`. When you have downloaded the ZIP file, follow the same process as for VirtualDub

In addition to the download, you will also need Apple Quicktime installed before MPEG Streamclip will work. If you haven't got it already, you can find it for free at `http://www.apple.com/quicktime/download/`.

Unlimited upgrades: Ruby plugins

Have you ever played a multiplayer computer game, only to find your opponent canes you because they've chanced upon an unlimited weapon upgrades item? Or you've been about to slay your arch nemesis (you know, the other student in the next bedroom to you; the one who leaves broken crisps in between the sofa cushions just to annoy you?) when in the nick of time they find an invincibility pill? Well, this isn't going to happen to you with SketchUp.

The fact is, lots of upgrades exist for SketchUp that most people don't know about. If you've ever looked over the shoulder of someone who's been using SketchUp for a long time, you'll see lots of buttons you never came across before. And if you wait until they've gone for a loo break and secretly check out what's in their menus, there'll be twice as many menu items as in yours. So, sit back down before they catch you, and go to this website:

`http://www.crai.archi.fr/RubyLibraryDepot`

This is the place where you download anything else that you want to make SketchUp do things you didn't think it could! But be warned. Don't try too many at once or you'll just clog up your menu structure.

You'll discover several of these as we progress through the book. But for now just try out any that grab your imagination.

Time for action – how to install Ruby scripts

This isn't hard; really it isn't. The idea of "scripts" and "plugins" just sounds complicated. Give it a go and you'll soon reap the benefits.

1. Navigate to the script you want to download. I'm going for the **Smooth Animation** script.

2. Right-click and select **Save target as.**

3. Navigate to the SketchUp `Plugins` folder (usually `C:\Program Files\Google\Google SketchUp 7\Plugins`).

4. Hit **Save**.

5. Some plugins come with additional instructions or have to be released from a ZIP file.

6. Navigate to the folder where you saved the plugin and have a look at this now.

7. If there's a `readme.txt` file, open it and follow the instructions. An example of this is shown here:

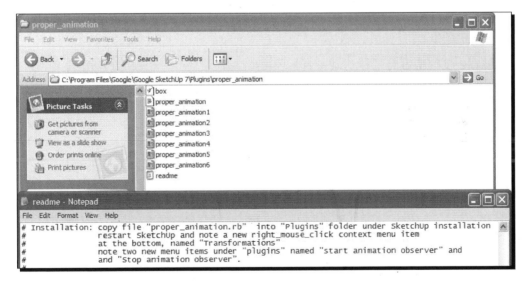

What just happened?

You saved and extracted a plugin file (and maybe a folder with associated other files as in the example above) into your `Plugins` folder. Now everytime you start up SketchUp it will detect and display the plugin too. Plugins will show up either:

◆ As menu items in the **Plugins** menu

◆ In other menus such as **Draw**, **Tools**, or **Camera**

◆ Using toolbars such as the **Sandbox** toolset

What rendering software?

SketchUp is ideal for creating photo-realistic visuals when used with rendering software. But what software should you go for?

Podium, IRender, and Twilight

Lots of readers will ask "why aren't you using the built-in SketchUp renderers such as Podium, IRender, and Twilight in the book?". The answer to this is that all of them, while being good in what they do, are simplified render applications. So, if you learn to render with one of these, you will not be taken seriously in the Arch-Viz world! Neither will you be able to transfer your skills as readily to other software. These programs might still be a good way to go if you want a simplified user interface and you wish to do all your rendering within SketchUp. Take a look in the appendix for a full roundup of what rendering software is out there, and how well it integrates with SketchUp.

High end rendering software

You don't need a "high end" rendering package (such as 3DStudioMax) unless you want to start experimenting with animating objects, people, water, clouds, and so on. If, after you start getting good results from Kerkythea and the methods described in this book, you want to venture into any of these areas, Vue or Cinema 4D would be a good starting point for your search. Take a look in Appendix A to compare them all and remember, you can obtain a discount on many of these software titles with this book!

Kerkythea: preparing to go photo real

You remember I promised you there would be an extra special prize in this stash? The flamethrower or rocket launcher that turns you into a one man army? Well, this is it.

Kerkythea is an open source software project. That means some guys have released the code for this rendering engine for free, and not only that, the ever grateful core users have built up a reputation for excellent support through their user forums. The important thing is that, because it's freely available, you can install it alongside SketchUp wherever you go. Gone are the days where you have to use whatever software your boss has a license for!

Why are we using Kerkythea in this book?

I've spent a lot of time evaluating rendering software in relation to SketchUp users, and believe me, they're hard to get to grips with. You might have had the same experience yourself. For this reason I believe it's important to get to grips with one main application, mastering one rather than dabbling with a few and never getting anywhere fast. Kerkythea is not immediately the easiest to use, but it has the powerful capabilities you need if you're going to grow with the software. Furthermore, the methods in this book use Kerkythea presets that make using photo real rendering a cinch. The render shown in the previous screenshot is done with SketchUp and Kerkythea.

Secondly, because it's free you'll never move jobs only to find you can't lay your hands on a copy. It also works on Linux which is important for high end renders where you wish to set up a render farm (more than one computer networked together to pool computing power in order to produce renders more quickly). You can do this cheaply with Linux/Kerkythea because you don't need to buy Windows or separate licenses for rendering software.

Thirdly, it integrates so amazingly well with SketchUp. You will see later on that cameras, lights, even materials are shared between SketchUp and Kerkythea. And that's a big deal!

Fourthly, it has functionality and user interface fundamentally the same as other industry standard rendering software, so whatever you learn in Kerkythea isn't wasted if you later want to move on to another package, or find you need to use something else at work.

 Some of the royalties of this book will be going towards Kerkythea's development as our way of saying "Thanks. Keep up the good work!"

Downloading Kerkythea

You can find Kerkythea as a free download for Windows, Mac or Linux at `www.kerkythea.net`

 Note: Un-install any previous version of Kerkythea you have on your computer before performing a new install.

Time for action – downloading and installing extras for Kerkythea

You should now download whatever goodies you can get your sweaty hands on at the Kerkythea website. These bits and pieces, such as materials, backgrounds, skies, and ready-made scenes will make life a lot easier for you later on. A little time spent here really pays off later.

1. Navigate to **Downloads | Materials and Models**.

2. Find materials you like and download them.

3. Open **Kerkythea.**

4. Go to **File | Install library.**

5. Navigate to where you saved the download.

6. Right-click and go to **Bookmarks | Set Bookmark.**

7. Click on the file and hit **OK**.

Install Library ✕

Directory: Kerkythea Rendering System ▼

..
Examples
Globals
ies
Language
Licenses
Locations
MaterialEditor
Models
n-k
RenderSettings

⚒ Set bookmark
✗ All Files (*)
1 C:\Documents and Setting

All Files (*) [ ] OK

File Filter: All Library Archives (*.zip) ▼ Cancel

What just happened?

This will automatically install the material library to Kerkythea. Because you set up a folder bookmark, you can now go back and download more libraries from the website and install them much quicker by returning to the bookmark.

Do it over and over again to install whatever you can find (Materials and Globals Studios are particularly important).

The marvel of SketchUp to Kerkythea

There's a final add-on that we absolutely can't do without, and that's the SketchUp to Kerkythea exporter.

This plugin provides some buttons within SketchUp that will instantly export the SketchUp model to Kerkythea and open the scene, complete with lighting, materials, and cameras. That's so wonderful I almost want to weep, but I'm a grown man so I'd better not.

But you can if you want to.

This piece of kit is one of the secret ingredients of this book. It makes our ultra-quick, ultra-easy method of producing great Architectural Visuals possible because it allows you to do most of the work in SketchUp. That's so good because it's many times easier to manipulate views, cameras and scenery in SketchUp than it is in a rendering application. So what would take you an hour now takes 10 minutes. Even better, it means that you only really need to spend time learning SketchUp, and we're going to make that a cinch with this book!

Installing the SU2KT plugin

1. Still on the Kerkythea website, navigate to **Downloads | Integration | SketchUp**.

2. Download the **SketchUp Exporter** .zip file.

3. Save it somewhere then extract the files and follow the instructions contained in the text file to install.

You'll find out how to use this plugin for best effect in Chapter 8, *Photo Realistic Rendering*.

Pop quiz

1. Why is it preferable to use GIMP rather than most simple image editing software?

   a. It's got a daft name

   b. It has layers and masks

   c. It allows you to work within SketchUp

2. What web address can you go to for loads of free plugins?

3. True or False: You should use high end commercial rendering software where possible because the image quality is better

Summary

So now you're all set! In this chapter you looked at how important it is to get free software as it won't stifle your creativity. You were also introduced to the following capabilities which will make your SketchUp Arch-Viz activities easy and more pleasurable:

- ◆ SketchUp's hidden organic surfaces tools
- ◆ Why a professional level graphics tool like GIMP is so important
- ◆ Google's component expansion packs
- ◆ Becoming a movie-making genius (almost) overnight
- ◆ How to find and install unlimited extra upgrades
- ◆ And the special prize—a fully functional pro renderer integrated with SketchUp

Congratulations! You now have a fully functional visualization studio. And best of all it hasn't cost you a bean. This set-up will save you an enormous amount of time later on. It sets you up with a seamless workflow that just works and works.

Now go to the next chapter to get started, or try out the Quick Start Tutorial if you haven't done so already!

3

Composing the Scene

Imagine you're a wildlife photographer. You're stalking a rare, brightly plumaged bird through the undergrowth. You lie in the grass for hours, centipedes and large spiders crawling all over your face and neck. Then when your body is stiff and aching, sun baked and drenched in sweat, the bird alights on a log with a fish in its mouth, and the sun is glimmering delightfully from the scales—you squeeze the shutter and success is yours.

Now imagine yourself instead in a vast empty film studio. It's bare. Everything is lit in the same uniform, bright, diffused, boring light. There's nothing to photograph except a skip full of ply-wood and canvas sheets. You'll have to make up your own scene. Go for it!

The importance of planning

This lack of subject matter is the reality for architectural visualizers! While a photographer creates their art from what's available in nature, using the natural phenomenon of light, the architectural visualizer is faced with having to create everything from scratch, just like a film or stage designer. And this is where it can all go wrong. Faced with so much opportunity, and so many possibilities, the visualizer becomes unfocussed from the job in hand. What will you show when you can show whatever you like?

- ◆ Close-ups of the building facade or views of the whole site
- ◆ Worm's eye view, person's eye level, or aerial views
- ◆ Photo-realistic or artistic watercolor
- ◆ Moving image or stills
- ◆ Flyovers or walkthroughs

- ◆ Shadow studies
- ◆ Sections through the building or individual wings or phases

It's a bewildering array of possibilities, and the temptation is always just to launch in and start modelling. Don't do it!

How to begin with the end in mind

Many people (often including me) start right out, modeling everything they see, in as much detail as possible, and simply run out of time. Their presentation is unfocussed and patchy, because having modeled everything, they sure as anything want to include it all in the presentation!

The better way to go about it, the vital ingredient to success, is to begin with the end in mind. Sketch each still. Storyboard each moving sequence. And then model only what you need to get these shots done. This way you conserve energy in the areas that don't need your time, and divert it to the areas that do.

There's more detail on planning for animations in Chapter 10, *Walkthroughs and Flyovers*. If you're designing a scene for animations (moving images) of any kind you should read that chapter too before you start modeling. If you're just doing stills, that chapter will also help, but isn't essential.

Think like a film set designer

Successful film and stage set designers save time with the following:

- ◆ Painted scenery backdrops
- ◆ 2D cardboard cut-outs swapped for 3D items
- ◆ Modeling high detail only for close up shots

You're going to learn how to think like a film and stage set designer. You'll use a backdrop image for whatever stays in the background and never enters into a close shot. That'll save you days of modeling time, and maybe hours of rendering time. You'll use 2D cut-outs for whatever you can get away with, rather than 3D geometry which eats up modeling and rendering time. And you'll only model in detail the close up features you choose to showcase. Once you've mastered these simple principles you'll be a top arch-viz artist.

You should now crack open a whole case of low alcohol ginger beer because you've just learned the key to successfully creating great looking architectural visuals! Now that you know how to use your time efficiently, you will always be a step ahead of others that don't do this. And you were already a step ahead because you've chosen to use SketchUp, which is the most powerful, streamlined and easy to use arch-viz software available.

Have a go hero – sketch visuals

Take a few sheets of paper and a thick pencil or marker and sketch each visual you wish to create. Sketch quickly and don't worry at all about making it look good. If you want to, include written information here about how you will achieve each item in the scene. Here's one example:

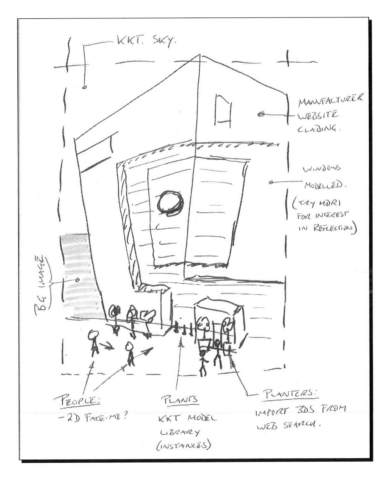

I've included basic positions of people and plants (entourage), notes on whether details will be modeled or textured, and information on where the background and sky will come from (in this case an image for the background and a basic sky chosen from within the rendering software). Draw a frame to help you compose the view.

Now you've sketched your main visual, how about some extra views? It's often good to give an idea of the building's context and maybe a close-up to show some neat features.

These will help focus your mind on what you want to show, and what you can leave out. You can see how we progress with this visual later on in the chapter.

In this chapter, you will learn how to set up a scene so that success is guaranteed later. You will discover:

- The four main ways to start your scene
- How to frame the scene using carefully chosen entourage place markers
- How to use theatrical fog effects to focus the eye on the subject
- How to be cheap—using ply-wood props and painted backdrops
- How to set up sky, sun, and shadows
- How to use perspective for the wow factor
- Lively camera angles to add interest

The four ways to set up an arch-viz scene

There are several ways to begin setting up our scene. All of these will help to anchor your scene in reality. It's like when the movie producer first steps onto location. He has to use more or less what's there—and quickly loses his wilder flights of fancy. So will you, with these methods:

◆ Photo-Match from a site photo

◆ Google Earth

◆ From a CAD file

◆ A scanned pen or pencil sketch

Any of these can be used in combination, and it is this flexibility that makes SketchUp so unique. SketchUp is as equally at home with accurate CAD as it is with pencil concept art. We're going to look at each of these starting points individually so that you can choose the best combination for your particular way of working.

Of course, you could just open up SketchUp and start drawing, but I wouldn't recommend that. Adopting one of these four starting points gives the scene a much needed context. In my experience this is vital to avoid aimlessly drawing anything that comes to mind.

Using a site photo

One of the best ways to bring across the concept of a new building is to put it into its existing setting. We can do this with a photo of the site as it is now before building commences. It's also one of the easiest ways of producing great architectural visuals because you don't have to worry about all the extra bits of entourage that need to be selected and arranged. They're already in the photo.

If you can get your hands on a decent camera, and the site's relatively uncluttered, this may be the best way to go. Here's an example image of a home about to undergo a renovation:

What you need for a Photo-Match photo

You're going to use Photo-Match to set up the SketchUp camera so that it matches the position and focal distance of the camera you used to take your photo. Before SketchUp version 6 we used to do this by trial and error, but since version 6, SketchUp has included Photo-Match, which automates the whole task for you. Using this feature you can create the kind of before and after photos so useful for renovation projects, such as this home extension. The realism the architect has achieved here wouldn't be possible without exactly matching the camera view.

But first some points about the kind of photographs you need to take:

- Sunny days with defined shadows work best when planning to use the scene for photo real rendering
- A 3-megapixel camera or better will do. Use a digital SLR if possible for best quality
- If you don't know much about composition, read up on it or get a photographer friend to take the pictures for you

For a before and after scene it's important to make a note of the following important details:

- Time of day
- Date
- Location sketch (to work out the North location)
- Take a reference photo of the sky
- Include some right angles in the frame

These allow SketchUp to recreate the camera and sun position. You might wish to use the sky photo to select a closely matching sky setting in Kerkythea for rendering (for example, clear, cloudy, or overcast).

Time for action – setting up a scene with Photo-Match

Photo-Match works by recognizing foreshortening in the frame. In order to do this, there have to be some buildings, walls, or other items with right angles in view. All you have to do is open the photo in SketchUp and line up some colored lines with these walls or other right angles.

1. Select a suitable site image. It can be your own photo or a scene you've downloaded from the Internet. If it's from the Internet check first whether it's licensed for commercial use.

[ Try www.sxc.hu or the attribution license search on www.flickr.com.]

2. Don't crop the image. Photo-Match won't work unless the centre of the image stays exactly where it was when you took the picture. So, some images downloaded from the Internet may not work either. If this is the case, just switch to another image and try again.

3. On the drop-down menu select **Camera | Match New Photo**.

4. Navigate to your photo and select **Open**.

5. Move the origin point to the corner of a building (or other feature) at ground level.

6. Click and hold the left mouse button to move the grips.

7. Align a green dotted line along an edge going off to the right.

8. Align the second green line in the same plane but further away from the first

9. Do the same with the red lines to the left.

10. Click **Done**.

What just happened?

SketchUp has now created a scene (the tab in the top left of your screen), which you can click whenever you want to come back to this view.

You have now set up the blue, red, and green axes to correspond to the real world up/down, in/out, left/right that you've captured in the photograph. Having done this you can now happily draw away in the scene, knowing that the model you create will always look right within the photograph. The depth of field, focal length, and eye height have all been taken care of. And that's a big deal, because doing this by trial and error would have taken far more time, and probably caused a lot of frustration!

You now know how to take just about any photograph and insert 3D content into it. Before the days of SketchUp this was only just possible; but best left to the experts. Having learnt how to do it, don't waste the talent. Use it as often as you can! Using this technique you can seamlessly fit your models into pre-made backdrops and save bags of time. You will come across other ways to benefit from this in Chapter 4, *Modeling for Visualization.*

Time for action – 3D drawing in a 2D photo

You can now test your new camera setup by drawing a simple box into the scene. If this looks right in relation to the photo, you know you've done the photo match correctly.

1. Select the **Pencil** tool.

2. Click on the origin (where the blue, red, and green axes meet).

3. Move up the blue axis and click.

4. Move along the green axis and click.

5. Move down the blue axis, hold *Shift,* and click on origin.

6. Click on origin again to complete the face as you can see in the following screenshot:

7. Select **Push/Pull**.

8. Push the face along the red axis to form a 3D box (see the following screenshot).

What just happened?

The perspective of this box should be in keeping with the house, wall, or other right-angled item you included in your photo. If it isn't, just click on the **Photo-Match** pallet, click the cogs symbol to edit the Photo-Match, and tweak the dotted lines. The best indication that you're right is when the blue axis lines up perfectly with the corner.

You've created a 3D box where the existing building is. Rotate the view with the mouse to view it. Notice the photo disappears? Don't worry, you can bring it back at any time by clicking on the scene tab that Photo-Match created at the start. You can now draw or add anything onto this scene; it will look correct if you place items into the scene in relation to that box, as you can see here:

Setting up a real world location and sun position

The most accurate way of setting up the physical location of the site is to import a location from Google Earth. This will set everything up automatically. However, you might find that this can slow your computer right down, as we'll see when we look at Google Earth in more detail. Another way of going about this is simply to set up the location, date and time of day using the menus in SketchUp. If you had previously noted down the time and date you took the photo, you can set this up now too.

Time for action – real life sunlight

1. Click on **Window / Model Info**.

2. Select **Location**.

3. Select the nearest **Country** and **Location** (city) from the list.

4. Close the dialogue box.

Checking North location

SketchUp defaults to North on the green axis. From the location sketch you drew when taking your photo match image, you will be able to work out which direction north is in your scene. You can use Google Maps or similar websites to check the site orientation if you need to. To change the North direction follow these simple steps:

1. Click **Window | Model Info.**

2. Select **Location.**

3. Under **solar orientation** check the box **show in model**.

4. Change the angle as necessary by keying in an angle by **North Angle.**

You've now set up the correct orientation and geographical location.

Setting up time and date for shadows

All that remains is to tell SketchUp what time of day and date the photo was taken. You can do this with the shadow dialogue box.

1. Click **Window | Shadows**.

2. Use the sliders or type in the date and time.

3. Click **Display Shadows**.

 Use this function to set up accurate shadow studies for all your projects. Also, when you go to buy a new house you can now check the sunlight each room will receive!

What Just Happened?

You have now set the location, orientation, time, and date of your site. This means that sun and shadows will behave just as they would if you were really there.

Check the shadow cast by the box. Does it match with the photo? If not you may have got the North orientation mixed up or forgotten to set the correct location. You can go back and change this now. You can also use trial and error on the sliders for date and time to match the shadows in the photo as closely as possible. This is the process you would have to adopt when using an image from the Internet because you don't know the time, date, location ,or North orientation.

Now that you've learned everything you need to know about setting up a physically accurate environment, let's look at other great methods you can use to set up a site in SketchUp. Don't forget, even though shadows and shading look quite cartoony now, when you export to a renderer these settings make up physically accurate sun and sky lighting.

Starting with a CAD site plan

If you are a CAD user and have an existing CAD drawing, either a proposed or existing site plan, you can easily import it into SketchUp and build up the 3D site from there. You will need a copy of a 2D CAD application such as **AutoCAD LT** or the free **DoubleCAD XT,** which can be downloaded from www.doublecad.com. In Chapter 4, *Modeling for Visualization,* you will also learn how to import and use CAD elevations (side and front views) to build up the detail.

Newer versions of SketchUp (free) may have the dwg/dxf import function removed. You may need to use an older or Pro version in this case.

Time for action – setting up a CAD site plan

1. Open the CAD plan in your CAD program.

2. Save a copy of the file (**Save As**) and rename it cadplan_xref.dwg or similar.

3. SketchUp can import DGW, DXF, or DAE (collada) files, so make sure you save in one of these three formats.

4. Delete all the lines, hatching, xrefs, dimensions, text, and blocks that you don't need.

5. You should be left with outlines of buildings, roads, and landscaping.

6. Select everything and move it near to the origin (0,0).

7. Hit **Save.**

8. Still in your CAD program, use the **Measure** tool on one side of a building and make a note of the measurement. This should be the measurement in the real world.

You now have a basic plan from which to begin modeling the environment around your building, and the building itself. Now you need to import it into SketchUp at the correct scale.

1. Open up SketchUp.

2. Modify measurement units if required, using **Window | Preferences | Template**.

3. Go to **File | Import**.

4. Select **AutoCAD Files** in the bottom drop-down menu.

5. Insert and move the plan where you want it.

6. Hit **Zoom Extents**.

7. Select all of the plan and turn it into a group if it isn't already.

8. Double-click on the group to edit it.

9. Select **Tape Measure** and measure the same thing you measured when you were in your CAD program.

10. If the measurement is different from before, you will need to scale the plan.

11. Type in the new measurement and hit *Enter*.

12. Select **Yes** to change the scale.

What just happened?

You now have the plan within SketchUp and scaled to the real world dimensions. This is important as the camera will behave differently at unrealistic scales. Also, light simulation in Kerkythea (the rendering software) simulates real world lighting effects, some of which depend on scale. Set up a top-down view now, so that you can revert to it later.

1. Click the **Top View** button.

2. Zoom until you get the view you need.

3. Go to **View | Animation | Add scene**.

Setting up a Google Earth plan

You've come across Google Earth already in Chapter 2. You can go there now if you haven't already and install it before you carry on in this section.

Time for action

1. Open Google Earth.

2. Navigate to a city you're familiar with using the search function.

3. Frame the view you want on screen.

4. In SketchUp hit the **Get Current View** button.

5. The view you framed in Google Earth is opened in SketchUp.

6. Trace over some buildings with the **Pencil** tool.

7. Use **Push/Pull** to give them some height.

8. Click the **Place Model** button.

9. Your 3D buildings appear in Google Earth!

10. In SketchUp, go to **Window | Model Info | Location.**

11. Notice the location has updated to the city you viewed in Google Earth.

What just happened?

You navigated to a real place in Google Earth and told SketchUp to adopt this location. This is important because now all your sun settings and North direction are right for that location. You also have context both with aerial photography and mapping.

You may have noticed that SketchUp can slow down a lot when operating this way. To avoid this you can take a screenshot of the Google Earth plan, save it as an image, and import this instead.

Time for action – using a Google Earth / Maps screenshot

1. Make sure you're in plan view in Google Earth, or using a mapping website.

2. Hit the *Prt Scr* key (Apple Key + shift + 3 on a Mac).

3. Open **GIMP**.

4. Go to **File | Create | From Clipboard**.

5. Go to **Save As** and save it as `filename.jpg`.

7. In SketchUp, go to **File | Import**.

8. Navigate to the image and click on **Open**.

9. Click where you want it and drag to a size about as big as the site.

10. Measure the scale key in the image and scale the image as you did with the CAD plan.

Maps on Google Earth, Google Maps, Multimap, and local.live, and so on, are copyright so the actual image shouldn't make its way into your visual unless you're sure it's allowed under the usage license. All you're doing here is using it as a base to model from.

Sketch plan

SketchUp works surprisingly well with sketchy details. So even importing a rough sketch plan or a scan of an old hard copy drawing you might have found lying around still works well.

1. Scan the page (200dpi or 300dpi scanner setting should be ample).

2. Save as .jpg.

3. Insert into SketchUp and scale as per the screenshot photo method above.

4. Draw over as you did with the map or screenshot in the previous section.

It's surprising how little detail you need to start drawing meaningful 3D visuals. Just try now to draw a very basic house and garden plan. Scan this into the computer, or alternatively find one on Google Image Search and use that. Can you see how easy it is to construct from sketches? The important thing here is that you've at least used something that was almost to scale to start from, rather than just starting to draw in 3D from scratch.

Fleshing out your site plan

Now that you've set up your site base using one of the previous four methods, you can flesh it out in no time. This process is called massing. The idea here is to give an overall impression of the 3D space that buildings occupy. Details can be modeled later on providing they will be visible in the frame.

Time for action – massing

1. Make sure your base plan is turned into a group so that you can't inadvertently change anything.

2. With the **Pencil** tool, draw over one side of a building.

3. Notice how the rubber band turns magenta to lock to the perpendicular (right angle).

4. In this way you can draw all walls at right angles to the first wall.

5. **Push/Pull** the surface up.

If you wish you can now triple-click on the building and turn it into a component to use elsewhere:

1. Triple-click on a building.

2. Right-click.

3. Go to **Component**

4. Us the Move tool whilst holding ctrl to quickly create boxes for all the buildings on your site.

What just happened?

You've added quick buildings to your site so that you get a good idea of how your new building fits in. You can model more detail or texture these buildings later if you need to. If you used Google Earth as a starting point for this you can export these buildings back there to get something like this:

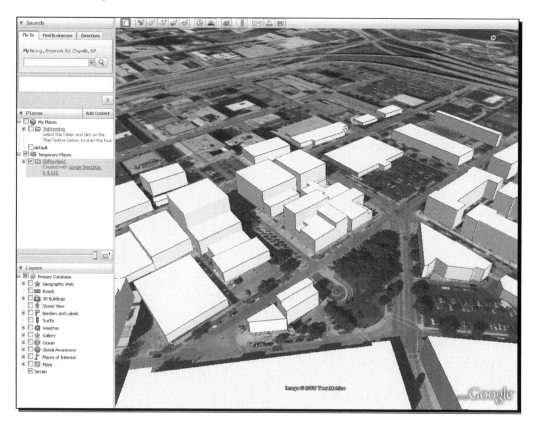

Setting up the camera to challenge and impress

Take a look at the following two examples. Which of the two do you find more stimulating?

The SketchUp camera view can be set up to simulate the human eye, a long range camera, or even a fish-eye lens. To you and me this means that we get great flexibility in the effects we can achieve when composing our scene. The two viewpoint here demonstrate that the same model need not convey the same idea. Here the first image is rather mundane and ordinary, but the second is aggressive and challenging. When setting up the view, experiment with the field of view and different angles until you have the striking image that will wow your clients.

Alternatively, depending on what you're trying to convey, you may like to go safe and conventional. The choice is yours.

Time for action – changing the field of view

1. Click on the zoom icon.

2. Hold down *Shift* and move the mouse up or down to increase or decrease the field of view.

3. Notice the **Info Box** (bottom right) changes to show the field of view value in degrees.

4. Now try typing in some different values and hit *Enter* each time.

The beauty of SketchUp is that the view changes in real time, letting you experiment to your heart's content. And field of view isn't the only tool you can use to break away from the mundane!

Think like a pigeon

Have you ever found yourself wondering what the world looks like to a pigeon walking around in the street? No? Well, I must admit neither have I until now, but let me assure you that the pigeon's view of the world is a very interesting one! Take a look at this sequence of three images, again starting with a standard SketchUp view of our model, and then how a pigeon would see it on the ground and in flight. Which of these gives the best impression of height?

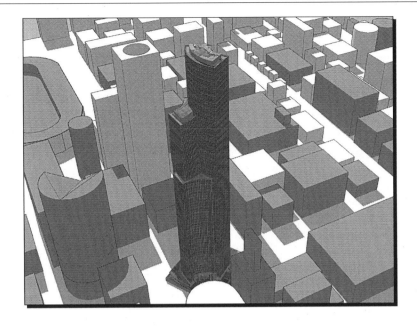

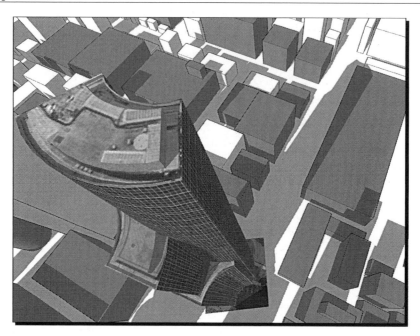

This just demonstrates how easy it is to show people buildings from a perspective they've never looked from before. And people want to be challenged in this way. Experimenting a little with viewing angles will pay off in the end with a gripping rather than a mundane image.

Here's some other things to try, which pigeons do regularly:

- Banking
- Tilting (hold *Ctrl* while orbiting)
- Flying right up close to the detail (usually with loss of feathers)
- Top-down views
- Panoramas

Other useful perspective tricks

Perspective means when far away objects look smaller and close ones larger. There are some neat little perspective tricks in SketchUp still to look at. These are:

- Orthographic
- Parallel projection (axonometric)
- Two point perspective

Orthographic and parallel projection

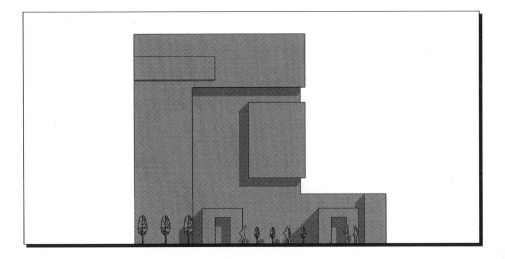

Turning perspective view off is generally only good for modeling when you need to see orthographic views (top, left, right, front, and so on). It's also good when you want to output these views to create 2D drawings. But bear in mind that there is no physical camera on earth that can achieve such a view, so when exporting to a renderer the camera info may be changed and won't render as you see it in SketchUp.

Now click one of the view presets to get the orthographic 2D views like you would on a drawing board. If you need to output some orthographic views for use in your presentation later, why not set them up now as scene tabs now?

Two point perspective

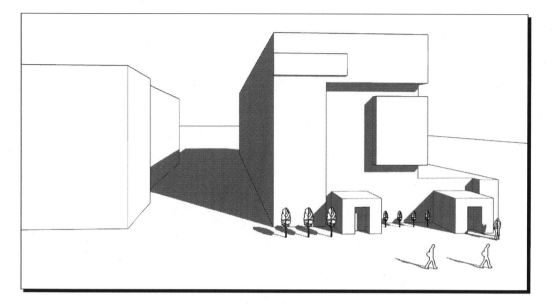

Two point perspective is what you may have learned to draw at school and also has its place. Again, it's not a real world view so exporting to a renderer might not retain the SketchUp view settings. In two point perspective all vertical lines in the model appear vertical on screen. You can pan and zoom using this view option, but if you orbit the view will go back to parallel or perspective.

Smoke machine effects (fog)

Have you ever finished a SketchUp model only to find yourself completely stumped as to how to finish off the edges of a scene? This is a common problem. In real life buildings aren't just surrounded by nothing. SketchUp now has a nifty little setting which allows you to simulate the image fading into the background, called fog. Other tricks which help with this are setting up photo backgrounds, as will be discussed in a moment. Of course, if you are using a photo match scene you don't need to worry about this.

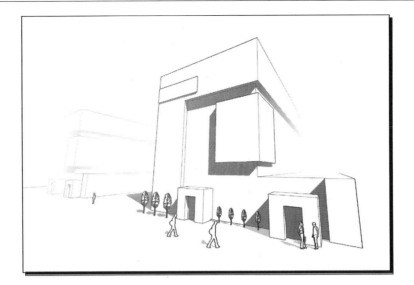

Time for action – obscure with Fog effects

Fog is like a smoke machine effect in film and stage, it adds atmosphere and covers over the bits you didn't have time to model.

1.   Click on your scene tab.

2.   Go to **Window | Fog.**

3.   Set the sliders to suit.

What just happened?

The first slider sets the foreground distance before fog starts to come into effect, and the second slider controls the distance until there's 100% fog. Note that the fog sliders automatically change as you orbit or zoom in and out of your model. This can limit its usefulness, and if you need more control over the effect then post-processing your image in GIMP is a better way to go.

Remember if you're going to render your model, fog settings won't be retained. However, you can still use your SketchUp view as a reference when adding fog or focal blur in GIMP or Photoshop. Focal blur is where the foreground and background are blurred to make them look out of focus. You'll learn this effect in Chapter 9, *Important Compositing and After Effects in GIMP*.

Saving days of toil with ready-made scenery

I once spent several days modeling scenery, people, trees, and streets full of buildings in order to finish off a view. The new building itself had only taken a day to model! In order to avoid this, most professional architectural visualizers make heavy use of paid for entourage: trees, people, cars, buildings, and such to liven up a view. But have you noticed they often look fake? You don't have to go down this route.

The answer here is to make constant use of the best thing ever to hit the architectural viz world—the digital camera!

Of all the important IT developments that have made 3D computer visualization what it is today, the popular availability of digital photos is the biggie right now. And the digital camera combined with SketchUp is a deadly combination that you're going to make fine use of in this book. You will have already come across the basic techniques you need in chapter 1. The rest will be discussed in more detail in Chapter 5, *Applying Texture and Materials for Photo Real Rendering*, and Chapter 6, *Entourage the SketchUp Way*.

Creating billboard scenery elements

Virtually any photo you take or find on the Internet can be turned into scenery elements. Take this one of wild horses for example. Would you have ever thought of using an image like this in an arch-viz scene?

But horse lovers need a home too! The rendered up version made it to the final of a rendering competition which was designed to show off the capabilities of Irender without doing any post-processing in Photoshop. All I did was cut out the foreground, mid ground, and background from the same image and set them up as you can see here:

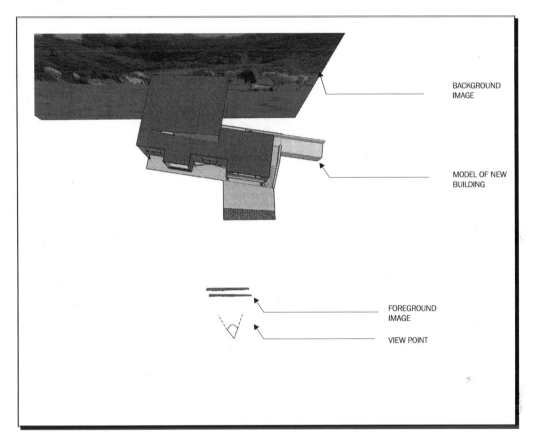

BACKGROUND IMAGE

MODEL OF NEW BUILDING

FOREGROUND IMAGE

VIEW POINT

All you need to remember when doing this is the further away from the camera the billboard image is, the larger it will have to be, so the individual cutouts will need resizing by eye. Here's how it came together. This is purely SketchUp output without any rendering. You can see the cutout edges in black.

Harnessing the plethora of online images

In Chapter 6, we will look at where best to obtain images on the internet to turn into entourage. But don't forget to use them here too.

Time for action – how to create billboard elements

1. Insert your image into SketchUp scene somewhere out of the way.

2. Right-click and select **Explode**.

3. Double-click to select, then make it into a component.

4. Copy it and rotate so it stands upright (90 degrees) using the **Move** tool with *Ctrl* pressed.

5. Place it where you need it. Scale as necessary.

6. Now go back to the first copy. Double-click to edit.

7. Click the **Plan** view.

8. Draw over areas to be clipped and hit *Delete*.

9. The in-place component automatically changes too.

What just happened?

When you import and explode images in SketchUp, they behave in just the same way as any rectangular surface with a texture applied to it. So, you can draw on it and erase sections. This can however be difficult when your image is in position, because it might be at a weird angle or obstructed by other items. Using this technique you have the image lying horizontally in the plan view so you can draw over it in a flat 2D view.

Here's what the horses looked like when they were clipped. As you can see, you could create whole scenes just with photos and no other modeling at all! But usually you would use this technique to insert a foreground image of foliage or people and a background image of, say, a city, or country scene.

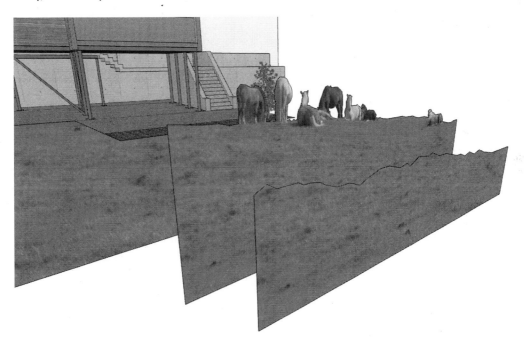

Framing the scene with entourage

Having set up your scene, your choice of entourage is now the most important decision you will have to make in the whole of the rest of the visualization process. Clever use of entourage will frame the picture, enhance it, and distract the viewer so that it will make or break your render. More than this, choosing the right kind of entourage can increase or reduce render times by ten or a hundred times.

Choosing your final entourage will be covered in more detail in Chapter 6 and you really don't want to have to worry about specifics until then. Choices on what trees to use, whether they will be 3D or 2D, downloaded from a website or created by yourself will all be decided later, and we'll discover together what the best options are for creating great looking architectural renders. But for now what you most need is creative flexibility. In Chapter 2 you looked at the importance of keeping a blank canvas and not allowing the software to dictate the bounds of your creativity. This is never more important than now.

The specifity trap

What is the specifity trap? Well, I may have made up the phrase, so you won't find it in any online lexicon. The specifity trap is when you bog yourself down in specifics far too early on in the design process. Using specific finished entourage at this early stage will force your creative brain to focus on that rather than the building. Worse, it will take lots of computing power away from SketchUp, particularly if you insert lots of 3D trees or people. It's like looking round for a house to buy and then arguing with your partner about the shrubs next to the front lawn, or rejecting the house because you don't like the colour of the living room wall. It really doesn't matter for now. You can paint the living room in that lime green color you like so much once you've bought the house! And the same rule goes for architectural visuals.

Definition: High Polygon Count

High Polygon Count means highly detailed 3D geometry. It refers to the number of faces (polygons) used to create the shape or geometry. The more polygons, the longer SketchUp takes to recognize what's there, and the more computing power it needs. This means that if you add a lot of detailed 3D entourage to your scene you might find moving the view around extremely slow and jumpy. You'll learn how to model "low polygon" in Chapter 4, *Modeling for Visualization*.

The answer is rough place holders

So the answer to all your problems here is to insert basic, rough, sketch-like entourage just to indicate, more or less, where a tree, person or car will go. You will change these place holders to something nicer later. It's really easy to do. Here are the benefits of working in this way:

◆ A non-cluttered work-space

◆ No high polygon 3D people/trees/cars to slow SketchUp down

◆ Creativity isn't stifled by concentrating on what doesn't really matter at this stage

◆ You retain flexibility to swap entourage later depending on what kind of output you go for (photo real, sketchy, watercolor, and so on)

If your composition doesn't look right with basic entourage, it won't look right with highly polished stuff either. But at least you can spot this early on and make big changes before you've put too much effort in.

Time for action – inserting entourage place holders

If you haven't done so already, frame your scene exactly how you want it and then go to **View | Animation | Add Scene**. This saves the view as you have it now so that you can keep going back to it. All you need to do is hit the tab at the top of the view window. Go to Right click and select **Scene Manager**, type in "final view".

Based on the composition you're aiming to achieve, insert any trees and people as follows.

1. Go to **Window | Components | People** and select a basic person (don't worry about other details for now—you'll replace them later).

2. Move the cursor into the view area and place the person somewhere near where you'd like them.

3. Click the view tab at the top of the view window and check whether the composition looks right.

4. Move the person around (watching the axis color as necessary) and repeat Steps 3 and 4 until you're satisfied.

5. Use the scale tool to grow or shrink the component as necessary until you're happy with the composition.

6. Repeat for each item of entourage, remembering to use the most basic items for now.

What just happened?

You will now have a fully composed scene: a sketched out canvas ready for you to fill in the boxes. At this stage, it's a good idea to print a black and white version of this for you to sketch over with any ideas. Also, remember to save the model.

Printing a test view

1. Click the black and white view icon.
2. Go to **File | Print**.
3. Select **Current View** and **Fit to page**.
4. Click **OK**.

Here is my version of the sketch we started with, complete with basic entourage and billboard backgrounds:

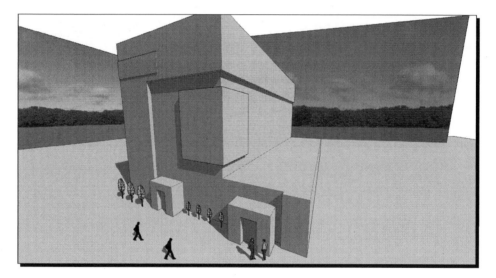

Summary

You have now completed the most important stage in creating great architectural visuals using SketchUp! And it wasn't hard was it? The piece of paper in your hand is proof that a great visual is on the way. If you completed the quick start tutorial in the first chapter, you'll know how easy the rest can be. In this chapter, you learned about:

- Thinking like a film set designer when setting up your scene
- The four main ways to anchor your scene in reality
- Accurate sunlight with location, orientation, time, and date
- Camera setup and how to achieve that extra "wow" factor
- Using photos for billboard scenery
- Using place marker entourage to quickly view and make adjustments

In the next chapter, you will learn how to model within SketchUp for great results quickly and easily. You will master the modeling methods and tricks that will ensure success every time. Remember, all you need to do is follow the tried and tested methods step-by-step. These individual steps are all baby steps. But at the end of the journey you'll be amazed at how far you've travelled. The reason other people consistently output unprofessional architectural visuals is not because it's difficult, but because often they haven't shown discipline early on in the project. By setting up your scene as you've now done, you've already distanced yourself from those people, and ensured that the rest of the process will be quick and easy.

4

Modeling for Visualization

No doubt you're already a dab hand at creating models with SketchUp's easy to use but powerful toolset. But what precisely is modeling anyway? It's any process you use to create objects or other geometry within SketchUp. Modeling is the making part of the visualization process. In this chapter, you'll learn the extra modeling techniques specifically required for architectural visualization. You'll look at:

- ◆ Swapping between low and high detail models
- ◆ How to model detail from CAD elevations or photos
- ◆ Low polygon modeling to increase computer speed
- ◆ Harnessing the power of components
- ◆ How to model the main building features for visualization

If you've already completed Chapter 3, *Composing the Scene*, you will have started your scene using one of four methods, or a combination of these:

- ◆ From a site photograph with Photo-Match
- ◆ From a scanned sketch or drawing
- ◆ Using an existing CAD drawing
- ◆ Using a Google Earth or other online mapping image

Using any of these methods will instantly give your model focus and context. If you haven't done so already, flesh out your main scene by placing boxes in place of all the buildings that give context but are not the main focus.

Time for action – creating the basic building shape

We're going to create a dummy building within the scene, save it as a separate model file, and then open it individually to start modeling the detail. This is firstly a good modeling technique, especially for large or intricate scenes, and secondly will also keep you from being distracted as you work on it.

1. Draw the basic outline of the building you will be modeling.

2. **Push/Pull** it to the maximum height (usually the ridge height).

3. Triple-click to select it all.

4. Right-click and select **Create a Component**.

5. Click **Set Component Axis**.

6. Set the origin at the corner of your building (see the following screenshot).

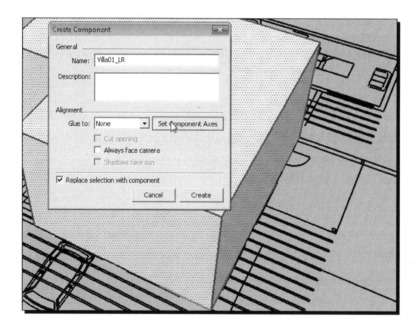

7. Set the red and green directions to line up with the edges of the building.

8. Now right-click again and select **Save As**.

9. Name it something relevant and suffix it with _LR.

10. Do this a second time. Suffix the first with _LR and the second with _HR (standing for **Low Resolution** and **High Resolution**)

What just happened?

Having done this you now have two versions of your building. You'll want to keep the LR version more or less as you see it now, and model the HR version to perfection (or near enough!). Why have we done this?

The reason for creating two versions of everything is simple. You want to stay as focused, uncluttered, and unencumbered with detail as possible while you're modeling and throughout most of the design process. When the time comes to output some great visuals, you'll bring all the detailed elements back in. The rest of the time you'll have the LR versions in place. Actually, this also makes massive sense due to the limitations of SketchUp. The lower the amount of polygons, the quicker you can maneuver around the SketchUp environment (see also the *Low polygon modeling* section later in this chapter).

Have a go hero

Have a go now at creating components of everything and saving them as LR and HR versions. It will help to keep a folder on your computer called "site components", or similar, to save them in. You can do it for everything from buildings and landscaping to furniture and road-signs.

Mobile file structure

When starting a SketchUp project it's a good idea to set up your file structure first. Start with a main folder for the project, and include sub-folders inside that for site components, input images, entourage, output drawings, and whatever else you need. When you transport your main model to another computer you can then grab the whole folder to keep the hierarchy intact.

Time for action – swapping high/low resolution versions

Now here comes the clever bit! Whenever you want to swap a LR with a HR version, just do the following:

1. Right-click on a component.

2. Click **Reload**.

3. Navigate to the HR version and click **Open**.

The scene updates with the HR version instantly. If you now double-click on SketchUp on your desktop to launch another SketchUp session, you can have two open at the same time. Now with the HR component opened in the second SketchUp window:

4. Modify the _HR component.

5. Save it.

6. Go back to the original SketchUp window that contains the main scene.

7. Load the HR component again using the steps above.

The scene updates with the changes you just made!

What just happened?

As you go along you will use this method to swap all the scene place holders you set up in Chapter 3 with final items of entourage (see Chapter 6, *Entourage the SketchUp Way*) and other scenery. Let's think of an everyday example. You have a large housing site with 40 house plots. Each of these has 20 bushes in the garden, made of the same component but scaled and rotated differently to give an impression of variety. Each bush may have (say) 3000 faces, giving a total of 2.4 million faces just for garden shrubs! This is how SketchUp ends up slowing down. Right-clicking on just one of these and replacing it with a simplified version (say a box) will change them all in one go and allow you to zoom, rotate and pan quickly again.

When importing Autocad files, blocks often import into SketchUp as components. This means if you have trees and the like, imported in your CAD plan, you can swap them out for 3D versions in SketchUp using the above methods. What's particularly good about this is that all copies of the AutoCAD blocks will update with the same SketchUp component so you can instantly turn all 2D trees to 3D in one stroke!

Carving out the detail

When visualizing with SketchUp the great benefit is that most of the detail can be introduced easily with textures and photographs. So, we don't need to be 3D CAD virtuosos to create great looking architectural visuals. In fact, the general rule of thumb when deciding whether to model more detail is—if in doubt, don't bother!

Here are some reasons to be lazy:

◆ You can always model more later if you really need to, but you can never retrieve the time you spent if you did too much

◆ Applying images and textures will work much better on flat simple surfaces

◆ The more complex your model is initially, the harder it is to change details later on

Modeling buildings in SketchUp is really easy. That's because SketchUp has been developed with the architectural market specifically in mind. You'll already have picked up lots of useful tips from the training videos on www.sketchup.google.com/training/videos.html.

Three ways to model the building

Open up your main building file (building name _HR.skp). You will notice that there's nothing else in the scene except for the building. We're now going to start modifying this simplified blocky building to resemble the finished article.

At this stage we really just need to focus on the major shape of the building. Often just walls and a roof will suffice. There are several main ways of doing this:

◆ From CAD elevations

◆ From a photograph

◆ By eye or measurements

Time for action – modeling detail from CAD elevations

Import and scale your CAD elevation using the methods you learned in Chapter 3. When you have inserted it into the model, turn it into a group.

1. Select the **Move** tool.

2. Hover over the CAD drawing edge. The rotation grips appear (see the following screenshot).

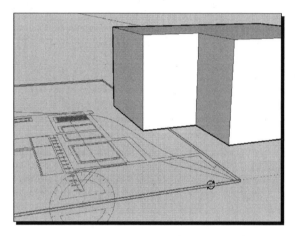

3. Click on a grip and rotate 90 degrees.

4. Move the ground level of the CAD elevation to origin level using inferencing: While clicking on the CAD elevation at a point in the ground, move up the blue axis and hold shift, then click at the base of your model as shown here:

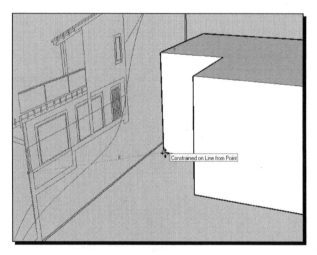

5. Line it up with the building outer edge in a similar way using inferencing.

6. Set up two or three elevations using this method so that you can model all sides of the building.

7. Select the **Pencil** tool.

8. Hover over the building face. Hold *Shift* to constrain the pencil line to this face.

9. Click wherever you need on the CAD elevation as illustrated here. Can you see how the line on the face (right) follows wherever you move and click the pencil?

10. Continue to draw outlines of the main features and **push-pull**, inferencing to another elevation or plan.

11. Remember to component-ize or group the main elements.

Here's a finished building done with this method, showing the CAD elevations set up at the front and sides.

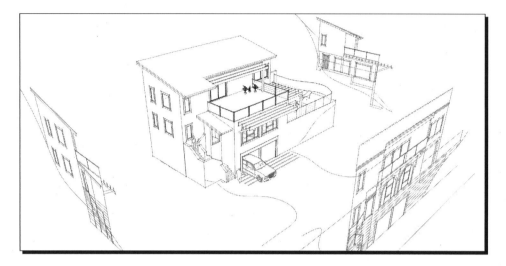

Time for action – modeling from a photograph

Use this method when you're modeling an existing building that needs modifications, creating building elements that already exist to include in your new building, or to model for fun, for Google Earth, computer game levels, and so on. You can use any photos you have taken more or less perpendicular to the building.

1. Start with your basic building block.

2. Go to **File | Import** then click **All supported image files** in the drop-down box.

3. Click **Use as texture**.

4. Select the image you want to use and click **Open.**

5. Click on the bottom left corner then top right of the side of the building.

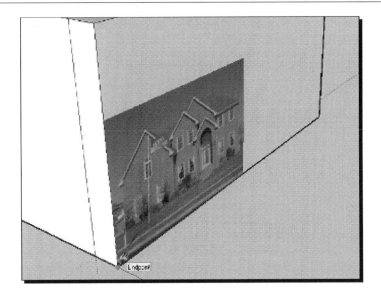

6. Right-click and select **Texture | Position**.

7. Click once on a pin to lift the pin up.

8. Zoom in to the corner of the building image and click to place the pin there, as shown in the preceding screenshot.

9. Repeat for all four corners. Usually you will need the two bottom corners and the upper corners just below the roof.

10. Click on a pin and hold the button. Now drag over to the corner of the face and let go.

11. Repeat for all four corners. You will see the image stretch more or less to fit to the face.

12. Right-click and select **Done**.

13. You can now push/pull to increase the building to ridge height.

14. Triple-click on the geometry and use **Scale** on the blue axis if necessary to reduce the height back to normal if this process has stretched the building.

15. Draw over the geometry and **Push/Pull** as necessary as shown here:

What just happened?

You just created the main shape of a building using only a digital photo. This is an excellent, easy method for creating simple buildings. The big benefit is that textures are retained on the model, making the texturing process easier later on. Here's the finished model with no more than some roof textures and windows added.

Have a go hero – modeling by eye or measurements

The third way to model your building is to draw by eye or using basic measurements. For visualization purposes nothing needs to be very accurate anyway. Just open up the _HR version of your building and start modeling. This method is the reason why SketchUp took off so quickly amongst architects. They just wanted a 3D sketch pad!

So, have a go at this if you haven't already. Use the rectangle tool and input the basic x and y dimensions on the keyboard (x,y) then use SketchUp's modeling tools to experiment creating basic building shapes. Review the training videos on YouTube or go to **Help** | **Help Center** | **Online Tutorials** to find what you need.

Use construction lines

Make use of the tape measure tool to set up basic grids or construction lines when modeling by eye. Select the tape measure, click a line and then type in the offset dimension to create a parallel construction line. Delete them when you're done.

Low polygon modeling techniques

You will already know the basics of modeling in SketchUp. If you haven't done so already, why not spend half an hour reviewing the great SketchUp tutorials on the website at `http://sketchup.google.com/training/videos.html`. These take you through all the main modeling functions of SketchUp. In this section, we will look at low polygon modeling techniques that are especially relevant for visualization, animation, and games end uses.

Did you know?

The beginners tip that makes the most difference to newbies is "create groups and components so all your geometry doesn't stick together".

What's low poly?

In SketchUp, everything you create is formed from a wire frame, over which is stretched a skin. You can see this process happening when you draw any shape with the pencil tool. The lines are the frame, and when a shape (polygon) is complete, the frame receives a skin (surface). These surfaces are actually all made up of simple shapes (polygons) which you can't see. Go to **View | Hidden** to see what I mean. Low poly modeling is where you create things in SketchUp while constantly striving to keep the amount of polygons to a minimum.

So what's the big deal about low poly modeling?

Have you ever downloaded a huge model from Google 3D Warehouse and found SketchUp becomes un-responsive? Low poly modeling makes the difference between the smooth, easy navigation around large scenes and a slow jumpy nightmare. That's because SketchUp has to calculate where all these polygons are many times a second when rotating/orbiting a view. This is even more difficult once shadows are switched on, because SketchUp also has to work out where shadows hit each polygon. Take a look at the following model. It's got 80,000 faces. It can really lock up SketchUp or at least make it hard to use.

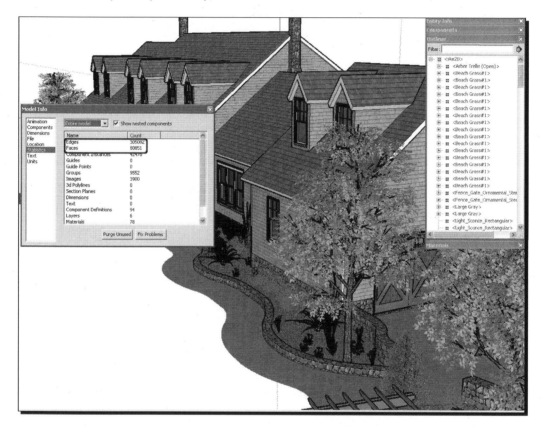

Removing the foliage shows us where the high number of polygons was. The model now shows 70,000 less faces (see the following screenshot). Foliage is often the biggest problem when downloading Google 3D Warehouse models. We'll look at purging large 3D Warehouse models further on in the chapter.

But things get worse. When rendering a photo real scene, physically accurate light, shadows, and reflections have to be calculated by the computer for each and every polygon you've modeled. If you don't take polygons into account this can add hours to your rendering times.

Having said all that, you really don't need to worry. With SketchUp, low polygon modeling is easy when you keep in mind a few simple questions.

- ◆ Will I see it?
- ◆ Can I replace it with 2D?
- ◆ Can I reduce the number of segments in an arc or circle?

Will I see it?

The first and most important question we have to ask ourselves when we start modeling is "will this be seen in the final image?". We've already set up the scene and view points in Chapter 3 so we already know what we'll see and what we won't. Ask yourself: If I only need this one view, does this house have to have a back to it at all? Will the interior of this building be seen when the windows are only a few millimeters in the final image? The trick here is to constantly click on the scene tab you've set up and check.

Can I replace it with 2D?

SketchUp has a most amazing 2D billboard capability called "face-me", which we've already touched on in Chapter 3. You can create a 2D component and set it to always face the camera. This is incredibly useful for keeping the poly count down, because a flat item has so few polygons compared to 3D. You'll create a face-me component from scratch in Chapter 6.

As well as face-me components, static 2D billboards can be created. You've already learned this skill in Chapter 3.

Can I reduce the number of segments in an arc or circle?

If you keep the above two things in mind, learning to model low poly curves and circles is all the extra knowledge you need. We'll look at this now to see how easy it is to produce low poly curved models.

Time for action – low poly curves and circles

All circles and curves in SketchUp are made up of straight lines. The default number of straight lines in a circle is 24.

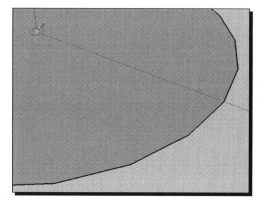

1. Draw a circle and zoom in to the edge. You can see a facetted edge as shown in the preceding screenshot. This is because SketchUp draws circles and arcs as a series of lines to create the curvature.

2. Now **Push/Pull** the circle to create a cylinder.

3. To find out how many polygons are being used to make up the cylinder go to **Model Info | Statistics**.

4. The number of faces will be 26. Now delete this cylinder and draw another circle. Select the edge only.

5. Right-click and select **Entity Info**.

6. Change the number of segments to *8*.

7. You will be able to see how many segments (straight lines) make up the circle. Extrude the cylinder and check polygons again. Faces now number just 10. Notice SketchUp still smoothes the curved surface even though it's hardly a curve any more.

What just happened

This method can be used for all circles and arcs to reduce the amount of segments wherever this will not impact on the final rendering. This means most objects, and especially any small or distant objects.

Making circles easy to snap to later

Keep the number of segments to a multiple of four. This allows you to inference (snap) to the quadrants of the circle or cylinder later, which can be very useful.

In a rendering program all the SketchUp faces are converted to multiple triangles. So, there will be twice as many polygons as there are square faces in SketchUp. The following picture shows three cylinders and their mesh in the Kerkythea rendering application:

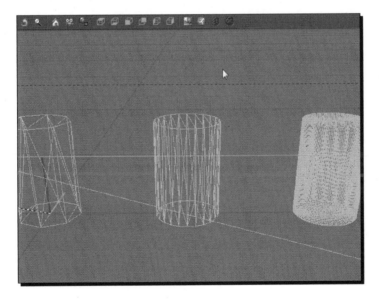

Notice from the following pictures that there is no visual difference between the 2nd and 3rd cylinders made from 24 and 128 sided circles respectively. The first one was just 8 SketchUp facets and though it looks bad up this close, it would still render fine for a small or distant object.

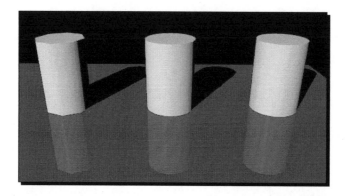

Have a go hero – low poly modeling in action!

Take a look at the following picture of a staircase handrail. It's got 1274 faces and looks really smooth.

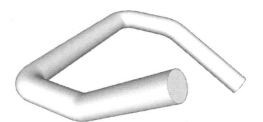

Draw the centre-line of this tube as follows:

 The sloping lines are 30 degrees up or down, which is achieved by using the **Rotate** function after you've drawn it all flat first.

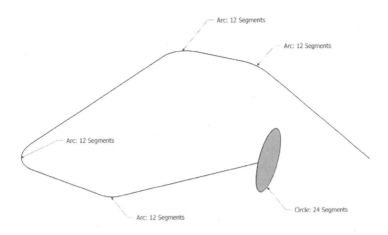

As you can see, all the arcs are normally 12 segments, and the circle 24 segments. Change all of these using **entity info** as follows:

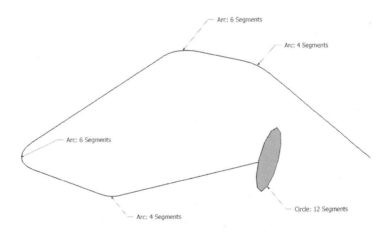

When you use follow-me to extrude the circle along the centre-line, you will now get a handrail which still looks smooth, but has a quarter of the faces. Use **Model Info | Statistics** to check how many faces there are now.

Using components to increase productivity

If you've come to SketchUp without any prior knowledge of 3D CAD, one of the features that will absolutely amaze you is **components**. When you create a component, you can copy it as many times as you like. These copies are linked to the original component and are called **instances**. If you change something in the original component, all the instances will also change! Likewise, if you change something in any of the instances, all the others will change too.

Imagine how much difference this single capability will make when modeling your building:

♦ Similar things only need to be drawn once

♦ Modifying one tree / roof tile / fence panel will update them all

♦ Components can be placed as place-holders and fleshed out later

You may also wish to use **groups**. This feature is more for keeping parts of geometry together in one place and separate from other geometry. Groups don't have the additional benefits of instances.

How to benefit most from using components

To benefit from components, we just need to think smart. In your mind, break everything down into its smallest common parts. So for example:

♦ Can the item be split in two and mirrored?

♦ Are there items of geometry within the component that can be drawn once and repeated (sub-components)? For example, panes in a window.

♦ Can I rotate, flip or scale instances of a single component to create different unique items?

♦ Can I randomly use the same component to create variety for no extra effort?

Have a go hero – dummy components to the rescue

What do you do if you need to modify a component that's hard to see or get to? Create an instance somewhere else in the model where you can see it better to modify it. When you're done, just delete it. You can also use this method when SketchUp's being a pain. For example, some modeling activities like **follow-me** don't work so well on small geometry. So, make a component, copy it somewhere where you can see it clearly, and scale it up by 10 or 100. Now you can edit it without any problems.

Also, have you noticed that the **Sandbox** tools only want to work on a horizontal surface? Have a go at creating a surface, make a component of it and then copy and rotate it as shown here. When you work on the horizontal copy the vertical ones update and are changed to create some undulating metal cladding.

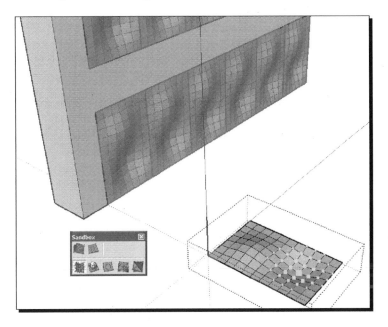

Using the Outliner for easy access

One of the most under-used features of SketchUp is the **Outliner**. Most people don't even know it's there! But, when using components heavily, it's a life-saver. Go to **Window | Outliner**. You should see something like the following:

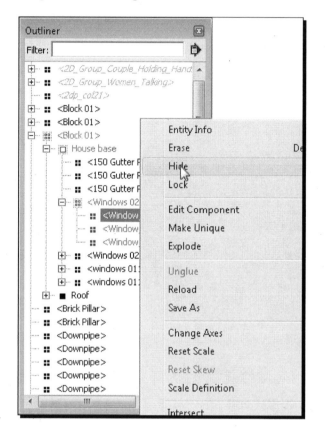

This is a list and hierarchy (tree) of components. Notice that you can click and drag these around. Click one now and drag it over another component. It nests itself underneath that component. In this way you can control how components nest within others. You can also:

♦ Select deeply nested components to edit without having to double-click multiple times on screen

♦ Right-click and enter the context menu to edit components and groups directly

♦ Reveal hidden items. You can't see them on screen when they're hidden, but they are there in the list

♦ Save and reload components

The outliner will become indispensable to you as you progress.

 Always close or minimize the outliner when using plugins as it can slow things down.

Why you should name components

Make use of the component naming fields as much as you can. When you create a component, name it something meaningful and different to other components. Depending on what renderer you use, this info may carry across to the renderer so that you'll be able to select and work on individual components within your renderer. You can access these functions from within the **Outliner**. Also think about what you will want to select once you've exported to the renderer. For example, components with different materials, foreground and background items, items you're not sure will make it into the final render, and so on. Selecting ungrouped or un-componentized items within renderers is always more difficult than within SketchUp. Many different renderers are listed in the Appendix along with info on whether SketchUp components are maintained once you import.

 Unfortunately, the SU2KT exporter for Kerkythea doesn't support groups and components at this time, but you can export using the .obj format if you have SketchUp Pro, which will retain component and group structure.

3D Warehouse components: Problems to be aware of

Using the 3D Warehouse will save you bags of time. But it's not a cure for all ills. When searching from the 3D Warehouse be wary of the following:

◆ Commercial (copyrighted) models passed off as someone's own work

◆ High polygon counts and large file sizes

◆ Sloppy modeling methods that won't allow a correct render

◆ Incorrect measurement and scale

The way to save problems later on is to use **Save As** rather than **Open in Model**. Open the component up once you've saved it, and take a good look at it using the Outliner (to see what's hidden) and **Model Info | Statistics** to check the number of faces. You'll get a good feel for this when you've done it a couple of times.

Time for action – purging 3D Warehouse components for your own use

Here's one foolproof way of purging components, but you'll probably work out your own version of it:

1. Select the component and click the **Explode** button several times.

2. Select everything.

3. Go to **Entity Info** and click the materials square.

4. Scroll up to the half grey half blue box (**Default Material**) and click.

5. If you have back faces showing (blue), right-click each one, and select **Reverse Face** to rectify this.

Now select groups of geometry, group and add materials and textures as you require. Remember, the less materials and textures you have here the less tweaking you will need to do at render stage.

6. Go to **Model Info | Statistics** and click **Purge Unused**.

7. Check the scale and change if required.

8. Move Geometry near to the origin if needed.

9. Save with a relevant file name in your component directory.

What just happened?

You turned everything back into geometry with the default material. This is important because you can now see which faces are facing in or out correctly. The outer faces should always be white, compared to blue for inner faces. Some renderers will completely ignore inner faces or give strange results, such as when viewing models in Google Earth.

When using 3D Warehouse components, bear in mind you'll want to apply library materials to it when in the rendering program. So, checking (and replacing) the materials within SketchUp first is vital. People posting components to the 3D Warehouse usually don't create components with rendering or low polygon techniques in mind.

Default material

Leaving geometry as the default material is often a good way to go because the component takes on whatever material you give it once you've inserted it in your scene. So, for example, a car with default material on the bodywork can be inserted multiple times in your scene but given a different body color. The rest of the materials in the component aren't affected.

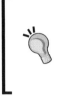

Quick material removal

If a component has too many materials attached, one way to quickly remove them is simply to open the component separately, and in the **Materials** pallet select the **In-Model** tab. Select and delete materials here without affecting sub-components and groups.

Taking it further: Challenging modeling tasks explained

We're going to look at some of the most common modeling tasks that you need to know about. There's no dark art to any of these, just good common sense proven methods of modeling, which you'll be able to use time and time again.

◆ Windows and doors

◆ Roofs, ridge tiles, and flashing

◆ Curtain walling

◆ Roads and pavements

◆ Masonry

Time for action – windows and doors

Don't model these if you can help it. Have a search on Google 3D Warehouse and see what you can get. There's a plethora of windows, so you should find exactly what you need. If not, Chapter 1, *Quick Start Tutorial,* introduces how to model a simple window.

Once you're happy with the window components you've obtained, you need to decide how to use them in the model. This will depend on the kind of Architectural Visuals you want to produce (which you've already decided on in Chapter 2). If it's non-photo real, it doesn't really matter how you place them. Just stick the components to the wall of your building. But with photo real you will probably want to see reflection on the glass, and also to see through it into the room behind. In Chapter 5, *Applying Textures and Materials for Photo-Real Rendering,* you're going to set up a photo textured room behind the window. For now, you'll place the window and create a cavity behind it ready for texturing later. The cavity is there to simulate the room behind the window without having to model it.

1. If the wall face is part of a group or component, double-click to edit it.

2. Draw a rectangle roughly the size of the room on the wall.

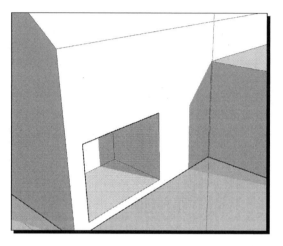

3. **Push/Pull** to the depth of the room.

4. Select all 5 inner faces of the room and create a component, leaving the **Cut hole in wall** box un-ticked, labeling it something relevant.

5. A face reappears in the wall.

6. Select your window component and place it on the face. It might cut an opening if it's been modeled correctly, or it might not.

7. Draw a rectangle round the window where it intersects the wall.

8. Delete the rectangle face.

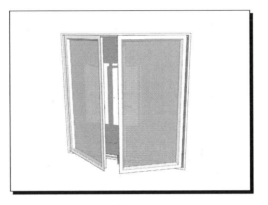

What just happened?

The reason we've cut a hole in the wall is that we can't be sure SketchUp's hole cut feature will work when the model is exported to a rendering program. Also we don't know whether the windows you downloaded from Google 3D Warehouse have this feature enabled correctly. Either way, this method will work. Repeat this simple process for each visible window. You usually only need to do this if you're aiming for photo real rendering later.

Now double check your window component and make sure the window pane has a material assigned to it that you'll recognize later. If not, label it "window_glass" or something similar. This is so that you can swap the material out in one go when you get to your rendering program. All the different types of windows in your scene should use this same material.

Roof

Roofs in SketchUp are a doddle as you probably already know. There are one or two important tricks to bear in mind, however:

- Make the roof a separate component.
- Push/pull the flat roof upward a little to create a 3D box first. This will make creating the pitched roof shape easier (see the following screenshot), and also forms the basis of fascias, and so on

♦ Model items such as gutters and drainpipes separately (and only if you need to).

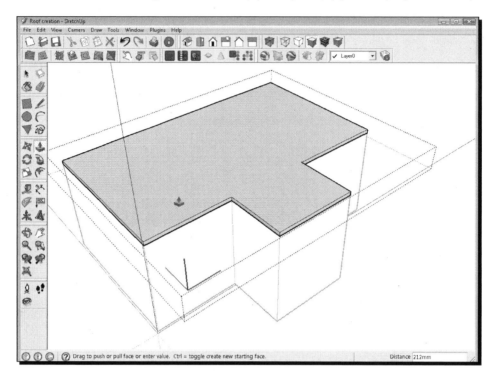

Some people advocate modeling individual roof tiles for added realism. This isn't necessary unless the roof is the main focal point of your visual. Any texture you create by photographing an existing roof is already far more realistic than modeling tiles, because of the variation in colour, weathering and size you will achieve. In Chapter 5, we'll look at how to create tiled textures from your own photos or pictures on manufacturers' websites.

You should probably make an attempt at valley gutter flashing and ridge tiles because this makes a big difference to the realism of a roof.

Time for action – flashing in a flash

Lead flashing at intersections of the roof is a breeze in SketchUp. Just follow these simple steps:

1. Select **Tape Measure** tool.

2. Click on a valley line.

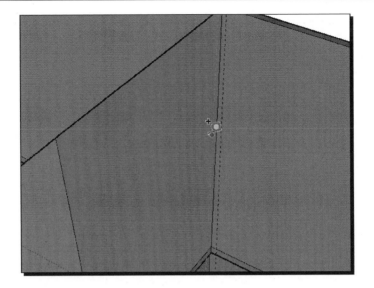

3. Click to one side as shown in the preceding screenshot.

4. Enter a suitable distance measurement. A construction line appears.

5. Repeat on the other side.

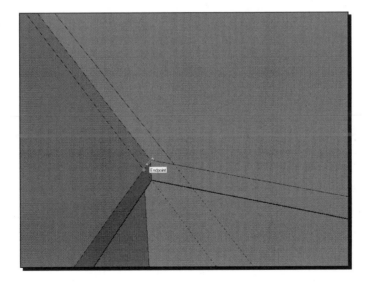

6. Draw over the construction lines using the **Pencil** tool, as shown in the previous screenshot.

7. Fill with a dark grey color with the **Paint** tool.

Time for action – modeling ridge tiles

Ridge tiles are a little more tricky because of the weird angles we get at intersections of pitched roofs. You're going to create a very basic ridge tile component and copy it along the ridge and hips (you can see this in the picture at the end of this section). Making it into a component means if you want to make the tile more complex later, you only need to modify one tile, and the rest will update along with it.

1. Find a tile manufacturer website or brochure if necessary.

2. In a new SketchUp file, draw the basic end shape of the tile.

3. Use as few polygons as possible (see also the *Low polygon modeling* section in this chapter). Click on the arc and use **Entity Info** to reduce the number of segments.

4. Finish the underside off flat as shown here:

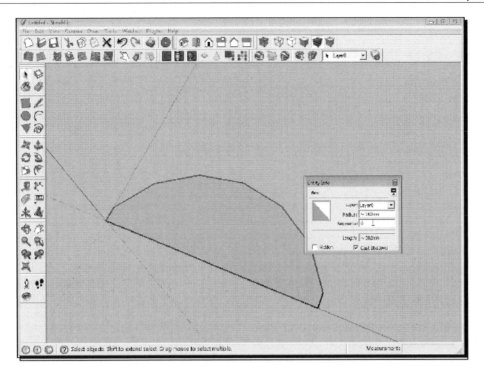

5. Scale the model if necessary.

6. Push/pull to the approximate correct length.

7. Move the middle of the bottom flat to the origin as shown in the following screenshot:

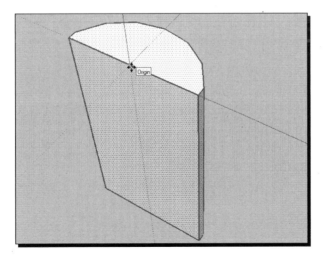

8. Rotate to lie along green horizontal axis (shown in the following screenshot).

9. Save the model.

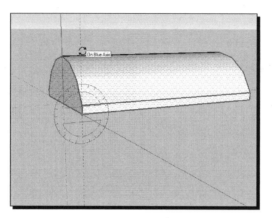

What just happened?

You created a simple ridge tile using the minimum geometry possible. You made it a closed form so that it renders correctly even though it won't be sat snugly on the roof. You also moved the tile to the origin (where the axes cross), so that when you insert it into your scene you insert it at this centered position. You're now ready to insert it into your scene to create the roof ridge.

Copying the tiles

In your building model, import the tile component and place it at the corner of the ridge. If this is a horizontal ridge, the tile may line up quite easily. With a sloping ridge (hip) it's much more difficult. Through a process of trial and error you will need to line up the tile to lie along the ridge, using **Move** and the rotation grips (shown in the following screenshot).

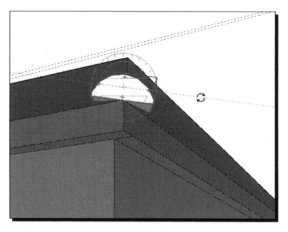

1. Select the tile.

2. Hit *M* for Move.

3. Click on the intersection of the tile and ridge as demonstrated in the following screenshot:

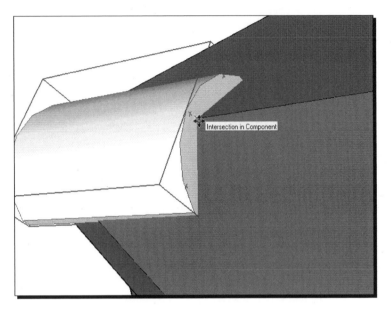

4. Hit *Ctrl* to toggle copy mode.

5. Click at the far end of the ridge to create the final tile.

6. Type "/" then followed by the approximate number of tiles (just estimate it) then hit *Enter*.

7. Change the number until you get just about the right fit (as shown in the following screenshot).

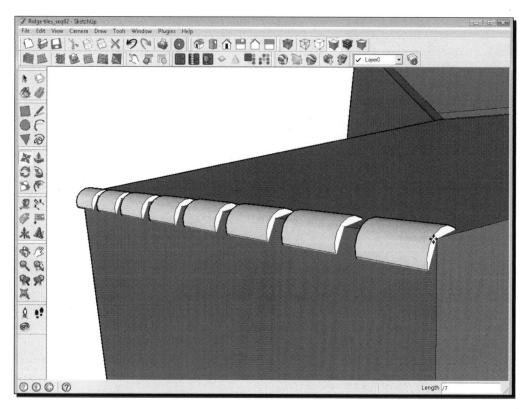

8. Double-click the first tile.

9. Push/pull the top face to resize.

10. Slight inaccuracy here is fine as it adds to the realism.

Have a go hero

After you've done one hip, create a component of the group of tiles. You should be able to copy, rotate, and flip this component to create the other hips. Lastly make a unique component out of any end tiles that need to be shaped, and shape the ends as shown in the following screenshot:

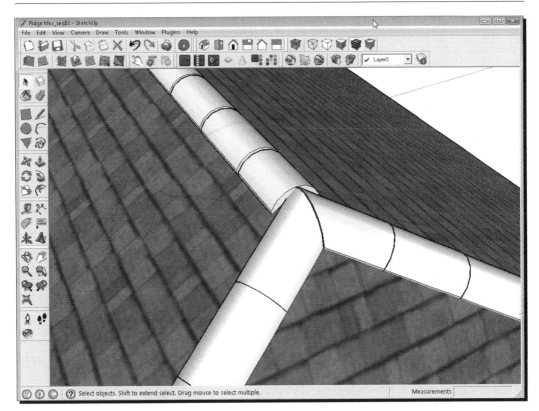

Try copying the component where you can easily access it. Also try creating a box or rectangle through where you want to slice the tile, and using **Intersect with Model** and **Erase** to cut it.

Curtain walls

Large expanses of glass may need some detail in the window mullions or other structure to look pleasing to the eye when producing photo real visuals. You learned how to do this in Chapter 1 by adding rounded corners, and it's also covered in more detail at the end of this chapter. Non photo real probably doesn't need this. Just remember to use components for the upright and horizontal members of the frame so that chamfers/fillets just need to be done once. Give the glazed areas a consistent material name as discussed earlier.

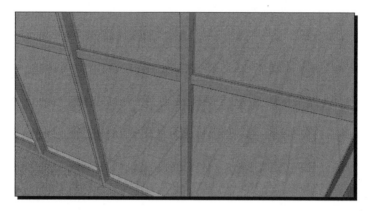

Creating large glazed areas

1. Create the glazing cavity the depth of the room or rooms behind (as shown previously for windows and doors).

2. Draw a rectangle onto the face of one side of the room to create the mullion shape.

3. Chamfer or radius the outer corners (remember to use **entity info** to reduce the number of segments). You can do this using the method you used in Chapter 1 or at the end of this chapter.

4. Push/pull to the opposite side.

5. Create a component and label it.

6. Copy and scale as necessary.

7. Repeat for the uprights and outer frame or use the component you just created.

8. Add a single rectangle for the glass and give it a material.

9. Turn the whole glazing frame into a component.

Roads

Roads are often in the foreground in visuals, but does anyone really want to see how great your tarmac modeling skills are? Hopefully you'll be able to obscure most of your road and foot-path areas with foliage, people or cars later. However, when modeling we need to take a couple of really easy steps that add a great deal of realism to our roads and paths. No one will notice when you do them, but they certainly will if you leave them out! Here are some features of roads you may not have thought about before:

- ◆ Pavements are always raised above roads
- ◆ Roads usually have curb-stones
- ◆ Paved areas usually have edging stones

Time for action – realistic roads and pavements

You're now going to lower the roads in your scene and add a curb or edging feature which can then be textured later on.

1. Trace round the edge of the road or pavement using the **Pencil** and **Arc** tools.

2. Select the edge and use offset tool to create edging (curb-stones, paths, verges, and so on).

3. Use **Push/Pull** to drop the road level down the blue axis.

4. Put a chamfer on the curb only if going for close-up photo-real.

Here's an example of these elements in practice:

Masonry features

Masonry features are best produced with image textures. But it will help at this stage to trace the edge of a feature and set it in relief a little with **push/pull**. The following screenshot is a work in progress model entirely done with this method and you can see how effective the raised detail on the pillars is when rendered. No other texturing has been added to this scene apart from the original photo.

Landscaping with sandbox: Watch your polygon count

If you have a CAD plan with proposed levels, you can easily draw around some contours and use sandbox to create landscaped areas. The only thing to bear in mind here when using sandbox for visualization projects is that the more detail you put in to the contours, the more polygons you get in the 3D mesh. So, use a few straight lines to approximate the contours.

The same goes for creating a mesh from scratch using the **from scratch** feature. Limit the amount of squares as best you can. SketchUp and your renderer will create a smooth curved surface between the mesh anyway.

Modeling for realistic highlights in interior scenes

Here's one final section on a very important trick for interior scenes. You've already read about this earlier in this chapter and when you followed the Quick Start Tutorial in Chapter 1. If you're modeling your scene aiming at photo-realistic presentation, you need to read this bit for instant added realism!

What's the problem with sharp edges?

If you model the basic shape of the box shown below and leave it at that, you'll obtain something flat and lifeless like the following image no matter how good your rendering skills:

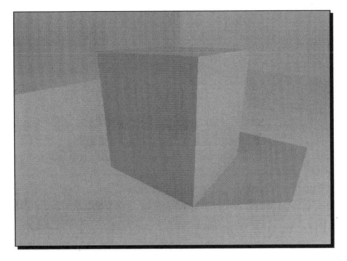

The problem here is that in real life, light bounces from corners and edges because they're always slightly rounded or chamfered. Even a knife edge has some imperfections if you look closely enough. So if you're modeling anything close up you need to add in this edge detail. If an object's further away from the camera you don't need to bother about it. In the following image, you can see the same box with some tiny chamfers at the edges. Can you see the difference in realism?

Time for action – how to add corner detail to your model

Here's how to achieve realism with radiused edges. I'm introducing it to you with a box shape but it's the same method for more complex shapes too. Start with a rectangle and push/pull it into a box as shown in the following screenshot:

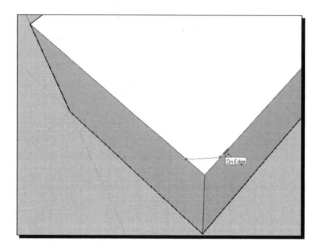

1. Select the **Arc** tool.

2. Draw across a corner as shown in the preceding screenshot.

3. Let the line turn cyan in color, showing there's a 45 degree angle.

4. Click on the edge.

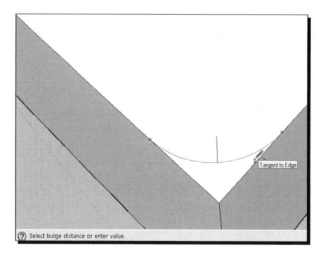

5. Move the cursor along the edge until the arc turns cyan and shows **Tangent to Edge** (see the preceding screenshot).

6. Click again.

7. Select the arc. In the **Entity Info** box change the number of segments to say 4 or 6.

8. Repeat for another two corners.

9. Push/pull them to create radiused edges.

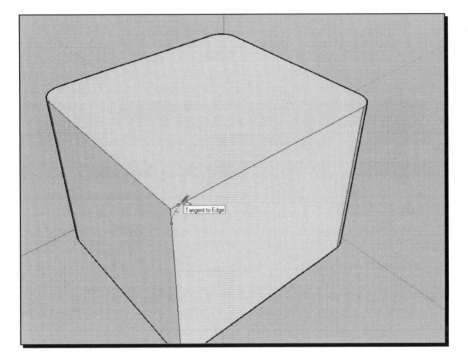

10. If you leave a corner without a radius, you can now radius the top face too.

11. Draw an arc as shown in the preceding screenshot.

12. Double-click the top face to select it.

13. Hold *Shift* and click it again to leave only the edges selected.

14. Use the **Follow-Me** tool and click between the arc and the corner.

15. The arc follows along the top edge as you can see in the following screenshot:

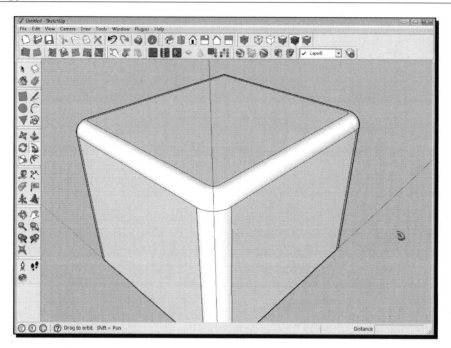

What just happened?

You've now learned how you can fillet or chamfer most objects to ensure they render more realistically. This is one of the most important modeling skills you need to create great Photo-real Architectural Visualizations with SketchUp.

Always keep in mind when you're doing this: do I really need this level of detail here? Chamfered and filleted edges make it a little more difficult to add textures later on, and are hard to remove once you've done it.

Easy edges with free plugins

Recently some helpful folk have created plugins which allow you to chamfer and radius edges automatically. This is unbelievably good news to all of us who have been doing this manually for years! You'll still need to know the above method because these plugins don't always work in every instance, and you also have more control doing it manually.

Have a go hero – the RoundCorner plugin

You can find the **RoundCorner** plugin by Fredo6 at the Sketchucation forum. Search for "Roundcorner Fredo6". Once you've downloaded it and followed the installation instructions, restart SketchUp and have a go. The functions you can try are:

- **Round Corner** (for fillets): Input the radius and number of segments
- **Sharp Corner**: The same as Round Corner but with a sharp corner where edges intersect
- **Bevel** (for chamfers): Input edge offset

A couple of tips to get you started: Remember to click outside your geometry when you've finished selecting your corners. It will show up as a green tick. Also, always save before you use any plugin just in case SketchUp decides to throw a wobbly. Here's a screenshot so you can see what you can expect:

Pop quiz

Have a go at answering these and recheck the corresponding part of the chapter if you're stuck.

1. What are the three main things to keep in mind for successful low polygon modeling?
2. How does a component differ from a group?
3. How do you reduce the amount of segments in an arc or circle?
4. True or False: When modeling for a photo-realistic rendered scene it is best to model as much detail as possible.

Summary

Believe it or not, you have now learned most of the extra skills you need to model for Architectural Visualization. Using these methods in various ways throughout the modeling stage will ensure that you have a render-ready scene. You will have saved bags of time by not modeling what you don't see, and you will have saved even more by thinking about the level of detail required.

You've learned how to use an amazing feature (components) to model things once and then utilize them many times. And you've seen how grabbing and cleaning models from the 3D Warehouse can enrich your scene through hardly any effort on your part. Furthermore, if you follow the good practice explained in this chapter, you'll not suffer from a slow computer and you'll always know just where your components are.

You're now ready to texture your model!

5

Applying Textures and Materials for Photo-Real Rendering

This chapter is mostly concerned with applying materials and textures for photo-real rendering with Kerkythea or other rendering software, or for output directly from SketchUp. If you're aiming for artistic styles such as pencil or watercolor, it is often better to use an untextured model, so skip this chapter for now and go to Chapter 6, Entourage the SketchUp Way.

We're now going to work through the various texturing processes together. Texturing is a simple process of applying the techniques mentioned in this chapter (and what you've learned already), piece by piece to your scene. You'll set up great looking textures one by one until your whole scene looks like the real thing.

In this chapter, you will learn about:

- ◆ When and why to use textures
- ◆ The process overview chart
- ◆ Using SketchUp's own textures
- ◆ Extracting great textures from your own photos
- ◆ Using photo-match to generate real life textures
- ◆ How to create seamless tiling textures
- ◆ Applying, manipulating, scaling, and editing materials
- ◆ Creating, storing, and sharing custom material libraries
- ◆ Image formats, size, and compression
- • Tweaking textured models for realism using GIMP

The methods you're going to learn are fun, quick, effective, and at the same time, possibly the most robust and versatile. These methods have been made possible because Google is so committed to modeling the whole world in 3D for Google Earth, that they have focused on making SketchUp the best in the world in quick building creation and texturing. Again, don't think that just because it's free (or cheap for the Pro version) it's not as good as other applications; it's better.

But first, should we be texturing at all?

How much realism do I need?

At this point you need to ask yourself this question: How much realism do I need? If you take a look at `www.bdonline.co.uk` for the latest architectural schemes, you'll see lots of sketchy visuals, some bad photo real, and some good photo real. On this evidence it doesn't appear to matter which you go for, but one thing is true—more realism is not necessarily better. A visual is a good visual as long as it conveys what the designer wants it to convey.

To texture or not to texture...

...that is the question. And the answer should usually be "no". Surprised? Well, maybe you should be. Because normally speaking we all place more value in the technique that takes the most time, that is, photo real. But as we can see from examples around us, investing more (time in this case) does not always equal a better visual. So, this paragraph is the last chance you have to change your mind and go for a simple native SketchUp output, a watercolor style, or other **Non Photo Real (NPR)** which will be less investment and perhaps bring you a better outcome for what you want. If that's the case, you can just skip over this chapter for now and go straight to Chapter 7, *Non Photo Real with SketchUp*.

So, what are the benefits of texturing? If done well, texturing can:

◆ Reduce the amount of detail you need to model

◆ Allow you to use lower render settings to get the same realism

◆ Increase render speed (especially important for animations)

◆ Allow almost photo real viewing in SketchUp without the need for rendering

These benefits are most pronounced wherever any movement is involved, for example, animations or demonstrations of real-time walkthroughs. That's because photo textures already have shadows, highlights, secondary light bounce, and all the other elements of realistic lighting built in already. The real world and your camera have been the rendering engine!

The texturing process flow chart

The process that I suggest you follow is shown in the following flow chart, and it shows how you can start with any of the base modeling techniques you learned about in Chapter 4, *Modeling for Visualization*, to end up with a superbly textured scene.

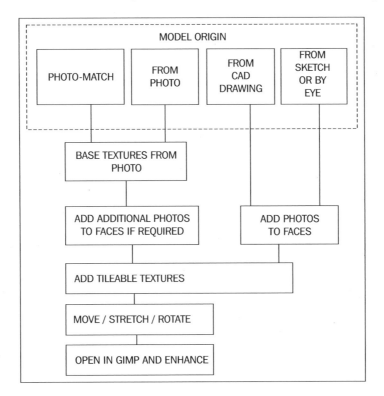

The mistake most newbies make is to go straight for tileable textures, and then leave it there, which makes for a sometimes dull and often unrealistic render. Also the same basic textures that come bundled with SketchUp keep cropping up in everyone's render!

Rule of thumb

If, after texturing, your model doesn't look like a photograph already in SketchUp it won't in your renderer either. If you get texturing right in SketchUp, the renderer will merely add soft shadows and more realistic illumination and anti-aliasing (soft edges), turning a great model into an exceptional render.

Beginning with basic photo textures

You're going to start by applying base textures which you'll build on later. It's like applying an undercoat when decorating, or if you're an artist, like laying down a water-color wash of some basic color. You can add these base textures using your own or other people's photographs, which will add a level of unparalleled realism to your renders or SketchUp output.

There are four ways to create these initial textures:

- From Photo-Match
- They are already present on a model created from a photo (method in Chapter 4)
- Using tileable textures
- Applying photos from scratch using SketchUp's great tools

Let's look at these individually in more detail now.

Starting with Photo-Match textures

If you've set up your scene using the Photo-Match function (Chapter 3, *Composing the Scene*) you'll already have a great basis for your texturing process. You can now project the photograph onto your model, like shining a projector onto the wall.

1. Click the **Photo-Match** tab.
2. Select the geometry you want to project onto.
3. In the **Photo-Match** window click the **Project textures from photo** button.
4. Orbit the model to see your textured creation!

Here is the Photo-Match model you saw in Chapter 3, *Composing the Scene*. Sang used it to create an extension to his house (he wishes he'd had a slightly larger budget).

You've now got a model which is already part textured, ready to add additional textures if necessary. Go ahead now and do this in the next section.

Textures from the photo modeling method

In Chapter 4, you have learned how to model from an image, which then resulted in a textured model. Similar to what we've discovered with Photo-Match, you now already have a partially textured model. The back of the model is still blank, but this might be fine if your scene is set up to be viewed from just one side. If you require additional textures on the back because, for example, you're going to animate the scene, you can add them using methods in the next section.

Using basic tileable textures

You'll learn all about these in a moment. For now, if you have started your model from scratch or from a CAD or scanned in plan, you can use SketchUp's textures to cover the model in roughly the right materials. You can also use the color fills. Do this also to fill in the gaps if you've used either of these two methods.

The closest you may have come to texturing is using the materials pallet (**Paint Bucket**) and the textures that come with SketchUp. And that's absolutely fine. The basic textures provided are very good and can be a good starting point. A word of warning though— because SketchUp is so popular many people can spot these textures a mile off. So at the very least you should modify them a little as you'll see later in this chapter (the final box in the process diagram).

Time for action – applying Sketchup's own textures

This is very simple. SketchUp comes with many repeatable textures already in the program. To apply these:

1. If necessary, double-click to edit the component or group.

2. Click the **Paint Bucket** tool.

3. Select a texture material from the **Materials** pallet.

4. Click on the face.

The texture is applied to the face. You now need to make sure the scale and orientation is correct.

Scaling textures

5. Click the **In Model** button in the **Materials** pallet.

6. Double-click on the texture you just applied to your face.

7. Here you can change the scale of the texture by typing into either of the dimension boxes shown in the following screenshot. Change the number until the texture looks right on screen.

Colouring textures

Still within the **Edit** tab of the **Materials** pallet, notice there are several ways to change the color of your texture. Changing these will only modify the texture within your model, not the actual texture library. So, go ahead and experiment with these!

◆ **Color Wheel**	◆ Click the mouse anywhere on the colored wheel to change the hue of the texture and use the slider for brightness value
◆ Hue, Lightness, and Saturation (**HLS**) ◆ Hue, Saturation, and Brightness (**HSB**) ◆ Red, Green, and Blue levels (**RGB**)	◆ Three different ways to achieve more exact colors. These can be edited using the three sliders or by inputting numbers.
◆ **Match Color of object in Model**	◆ Click on this icon then select a basic color from an object within SketchUp
◆ **Match color on screen**	◆ Same as above but you can select anywhere on your computer screen. Excellent feature if you're copying a photo or matching a model to an existing scene.
◆ **Colorize** checkbox	◆ Use this if you have a particular hue that you wish to use on the texture. It ensures that all the colors throughout the texture are locked to the hue you have selected (like a grayscale image using that hue instead of gray)

What just happened?

You've applied SketchUp's own textures to your model. Often it then becomes necessary to scale the texture because it doesn't look quite right. Bricks and paving, for example, are more or less the same size, but may vary from country to country. Timber textures, for example, could be many different scales to simulate different wood grain. And coloring the same textures slightly differently gives us the scope for many more materials using the same basic textures.

When you type a figure into either of the scale boxes the texture resizes at the same time on screen. The number in the box you didn't type in changed too because the x and y directions are locked. That's to keep the texture in its original **aspect ratio** (the ratio of x and y sizes). If you want to edit these values individually, just click the chain icon first.

Using Google Street View

Using photos grabbed from Google Street View is a new amazing way to texture models. Use it to find buildings or building features similar to the ones you're modeling, then grab images straight from there. Here's an example of a roughly textured model using just Street View images. It needs lots more work if you're going to use it in the foreground, but could conceivably be good enough in the distance or in a quick moving animation. This took just five minutes to create:

Time for action – travel the world for real textures!

1. For this exercise you need an active internet connection because SketchUp will be accessing Google Maps, part of the main Google website.

2. Draw a rectangle, **Push/Pull** it and click on the front face to select it.

3. Right-click and select **Get Photo Texture**.

4. A window opens and connects you to Google Maps. You can now type in an address in the text box at the bottom of the window.

5. Type in an address near you.

6. Use the mouse to place the little yellow man in a street. If Street View images are available these streets will turn blue.

7. In the top window, navigate around using the arrows on the road until you find a house with a garage.

8. Double-click on the side of the house or garage to zoom in. You will have
a view like this:

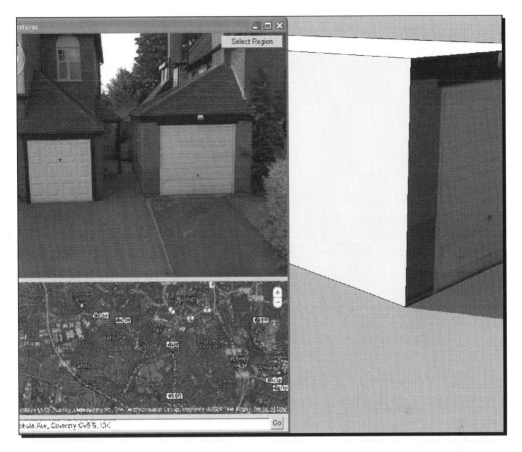

9. When you've zoomed in enough, click the **Select Region** button.

10. Move the blue pins around to enclose the area you wish to capture. Here I'm grabbing the front of someone's garage.

11. When you're done, click **Grab** (or **Cancel** to reselect a better view).

12. Your SketchUp model updates with the texture!

What just happened?

Google have done all 3D artists a massive favor. All the buildings in the world are available to you as long as Google sends a photo car along the road it's on. To put it in perspective, you can browse the biggest buildings texture store in the world... the world itself!

Use this method to quickly grab building textures for elements of your design that are standard features in common with other buildings. If there's anything particularly new or complex in what you're creating, you can spend a little more time modeling it from scratch.

Moving on from basic texturing

You've now got a part textured scene (from one or more of the above methods) which is ready for detailed texturing. You will now already be able to see whether your scene works as it is or whether some changes need to be introduced to make the composition work. Go ahead and make these changes at this stage before you spend too long on texturing. The following two sections will explain these texturing methods in much more detail:

◆ Whole photograph based texturing
◆ Tileable textures

You will learn how to manipulate the textures you've already got, enhance them, and add new ones.

Applying whole photographs as textures

I think by now you have experienced why SketchUp is so revolutionary for arch-viz. You don't need to rely on texture creators any more, because you can just use your own photos in Photo-Match, create seamless textures, or utilize Google Street View to pop the real world into your models. You can now further capitalize on this by experiencing how you can find and use any photographs to texture your model.

You've already learned most of the skills you need for this in previous chapters. Use these same techniques now to cover any blank face with realistic textures from photographs.

Where to find texture photos

Now here's the thing. Ask yourself this honest question: Does the building you're creating have any building materials, cladding, or features not already used in other buildings? So why model or texture these from scratch? Exactly. Somewhere on the Internet, or in your neighborhood there will be a photo you can use.

Here's some examples of places to look online:

◆ **Flickr**: Go to the **Advanced Search** option to search by geographical location. Tick the boxes for:
   ❑ **Only search within Creative Commons-licensed content**
   ❑ **Find content to use commercially**
   ❑ **Find content to modify, adapt, or build upon.**
◆ Also try www.flickr.com/map
◆ **Stock.xchg**: Go to www.sxc.hu
◆ Paid for photos from "Royalty free" photo sites such as www.Istockphoto.com and www.BigStockPhoto.com

But don't be limited to the Web. Some of the best texture images will be your own. Even taking photos with your 2-megapixel phone will often give you better textures than what you can get online, because at least you'll be taking them square on, and getting what's local to you.

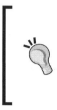

Go through all your old photos to find some that feature buildings and other areas of texture. Copy them into a `textures` folder somewhere on you computer for ready access when you need them. When you have spare time go through them, and crop and straighten them with GIMP. There's more on this in the *Tileable textures* section.

Time for action – set up a fake room

Here's an example of how to utilize images in your scene. When rendering a building with large windows, all we need to do is set up a billboard image of a room, such as this one, behind the window. Someone on Flickr took the photo for me. Thankyou!

But what if you're making an animated flythrough and the camera passes by the window slowly? The image behind the window won't move right at all. The answer is to mock up a quick Photo-Match room. Have a go yourself!

1. Start with a new model.

2. Find a suitable picture of a room.

3. Start the Photo-Match as before and select the photo.

4. Because it's a concave room, rather than a convex building, select the **Inside Grid** style as shown in the following screenshot:

5. Set up the Photo-Match as you did in Chapter 3 but use the back wall and the right / left hand walls.

6. Draw a rectangle to cover the back wall of the room and **Push/Pull** it towards you until it fills the screen.

7. Delete the face filling the screen.

8. Triple-click the geometry, right-click, and select **Reverse Faces**.

9. Click **Project Textures from Photo**.

10. You should have something like the following screenshot:

11. Scale as necessary to get a more correct room size if you have discrepancies in your Photo-Match (as you can see, the Photo-Match on mine created a super long room!).

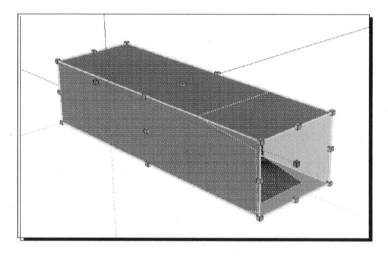

12. Add in any extra colors or textures if you need to spruce the room up a little using the **Paint Bucket** tool.

13. Now save the scene and remember what you called the file name.

14. In your building model, insert the room as a component behind each window and flip if necessary, depending on where you'll be viewing from (see the following screenshot).

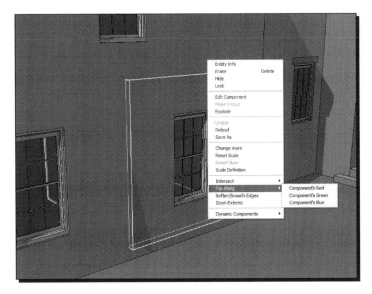

What just happened?

You now have a room behind each window that will behave more or less correctly on camera, The reason for all this is that when you have a moving camera in an animation, things further away from the camera appear to move slower than the foreground. So, if you have set up a room with just a flat image behind the window, it'll look all wrong. This method allows you to quickly make a photo-realistic room which behaves in the right way with a moving camera, without the hassle of modeling everything in there.

These fake rooms are great for night scenes where room interiors are much more visible in contrast to the dark outdoors. Set up a light in the room (find out how in Chapter 8, *Photo Realistic Rendering*) and see the result.

Have a go hero – creating balsa wood film scenery props

You know the drill. Maybe it happened to you just last week. Your expedition space ship lands on an unexplored planet. You've heard a distress beacon and have come to investigate. There's a crashed alien vessel over there, and the beacon's coming from the middle of it. Backed by lots of creepy film music you set out with your reluctant team. They're all likely to die bringing back an alien for your science officer to experiment on, but hey, you're the hero and they can't kill you off in the first scene, right?

This next part of the process you're going to work out yourself. The level of success you reach is directly proportional to how much danger you're willing to put yourself through. Or in other words, how far outside your comfort zone are you willing to go? I've been raving for most of the book so far about the revolutionary way in which SketchUp allows you to handle digital images, but you'll only ever really benefit from this if you throw the traditional workflow out the window and embrace the SketchUp one.

Based on what you've learned so far, surf the Internet or explore your own image collection. What's the *biggest* thing you've modeled, or need to model, that you can get rid of and replace by a simple image? It's "oh so dangerous", "oh so alien", but if you don't let the alien fix itself to your comrade's face and bring him back to the lab, how will you ever learn the alien's secrets?

1. Find a picture depicting part of your model or scene.
2. Start a new SketchUp model.
3. Import the image (**File | Import**) and draw around the area you want to keep with the **Pencil** tool.

4. Create a billboard 2D cutout, or a face-me component with it, like the one in the following screenshot (but maybe lose the leopard-skin...)

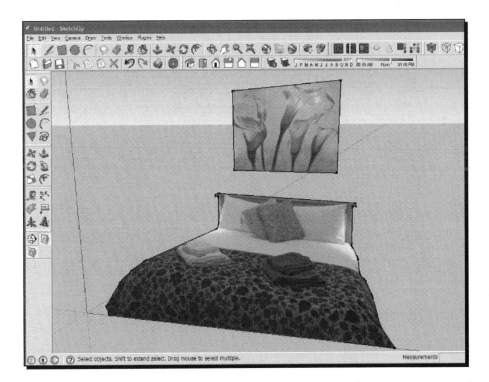

5. Alternatively, create a quick photo match like you did with the room:

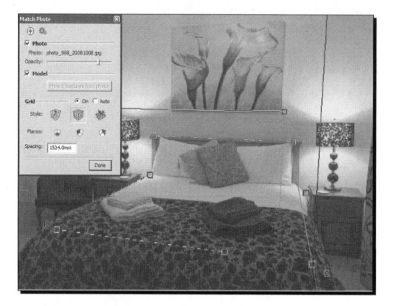

6. Draw in some rough geometry:

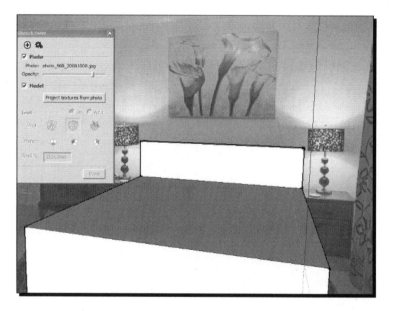

7. Project the textures.

8. Save as a component and insert the component into your scene.

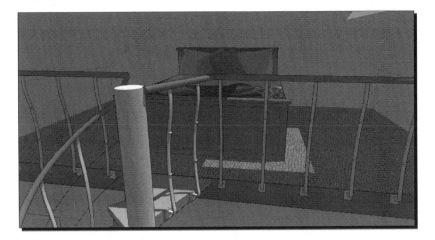

Using, finding, and creating tileable textures

In this section, you will learn all about beautifying your scene further with tileable textures. These methods can be used in combination with all of the other methods you've learned so far. Some of the following section applies to any texture, whether tileable or not.

Manipulating textures

Much of the time you will want textures to match your geometry fairly exactly, such as when applying brick to a wall close-up. We want mortar joints to line up with edges. Once you have sorted out the basic scale of the texture, you can now rotate, move, and scale with the mouse.

You learned the method of manipulating the photograph of a house in Chapter 4 by using the push-pins. We'll now look at the other ways of doing this which are useful for textures.

Time for action – exact texture placement

1. Select a face with the texture already applied.

2. Right-click and select **Texture | Position**.

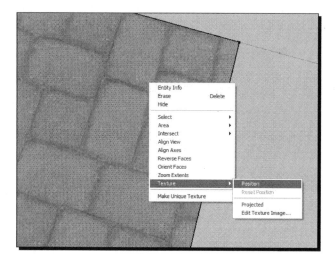

3. Click and hold one of the pins and move the mouse as follows:

4. Use the red pin to move.

5. Use the blue pin to scale the texture (shown in the following screenshot).

6. Use the green to scale or rotate.

7. Use the yellow to distort the texture.

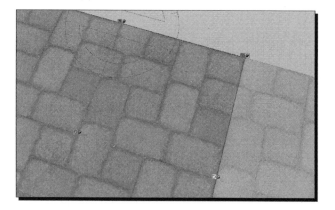

8. Play around with these. At any time you can reset to where you started or undo what you just did.

9. Right-click and select **Reset** or **Undo**.

What just happened?

You had a feature with edges (a rectangle) to which the texture needed to line up exactly. The different color pins all do slightly different things, and can be used to manipulate the texture to fit correctly onto the geometry. You can do this with any texture, whether it came from a photo or a tileable texture. Editing a texture in this way only affects the face you're working with.

Now notice the other features listed in the right-click menu:

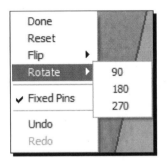

- ◆ **Flip | left/right** or **up/down**
- ◆ **Rotate | 90**, **180**, or **270** degrees
- ◆ **Fixed Pins**

The Fixed Pins feature is easy to miss here. What does it do?

Free Pins mode

If you un-tick the **Fixed Pins** menu item you will notice the different colored pins are replaced by all-yellow pins. This is **Free Pins mode** and lets you stretch the material at each pin wherever you want it. This is very useful because you're not constrained by the red, blue, green, and yellow functions previously described. Each pin behaves in the same way. It's like an elastic sheet stretched between four posts.

Again, play around with this a little because it will set you in good stead for what we're going to do later on.

Pop quiz – applying and editing basic textures

You now know how to apply, edit, and colorize textures you found bundled with SketchUp. Once you've created some yourself in the next section you'll be able to use your own textures in just the same way! But first, a little pop quiz. Answers are at the back of the book but you probably won't need them.

1. What does the chain symbol at the side of the dimension boxes do in the edit textures pallet?

2. How do you exit the texture position feature?

3. True or False: Match Color on Screen works anywhere on your computer screen, even outside the SketchUp program window.

4. What menu item do I need to enter the Free Pin mode?

Creating your own tileable textures

Learning how to create your own tileable texture materials for use in SketchUp is one of the most useful skills you can learn. And it's quite fun too! Here's two methods using GIMP. First, you'll learn how to prepare an image for use as a texture, and then you'll learn two method's of making them tileable (in other words, seamlessly repeatable). You'll pick up the first method in minutes and use it all the time.

Time for action – correcting perspective

Often your source photos will not be taken square on to the texture. That's not a big problem. Just follow this method in GIMP or other powerful image editing software such as PhotoShop.

Keystone correction cameras

Some digital cameras have an automatic feature called "white board capture" built in (such as the Casio Exilim range). This is a fantastic way of skipping this step and will save you lots of time if you're using textures regularly. It works with any rectangular surface.

1. Start with a photo taken as near square to the surface as possible.

2. With the **Rectangular Selection** tool, select the area to be used as a texture. A square is easiest.

3. Select the **Perspective Tool** (shown in the following screenshot).

4. Drag one of the corners out until you feel the perspective has been corrected.

5. Release the left mouse button to see what you have done, you can see the straightened version in the following screenshot:

6. Repeat as necessary. Use the dotted line of your selection as a guide.

7. When you're done, click **Transform** in the perspective dialog box to apply the effect permanently.

8. You now have a perspective corrected area of texture. Use the **Crop** tool to crop the texture within the area you corrected.

What just happened?

You selected a square area so that you could see where the edges of the area were. Using the **Perspective Tool**, you corrected the perspective in the photo to make sure the image lined up with the edges of the selection box. This is a trial and error process, and during it the image remains malleable for as long as you need. When you're happy, just press the **Transform** button to fix the changes. Even then, you can still go back to the original by selecting **Edit | Undo**.

You did all of this simply because textures are always applied to real surfaces, so have to be near enough flat textures. Now that you've done this preparation, you can go ahead and turn it into a seamless texture:

Time for action – tiling method one

This method is great for random textures such as:

- Grass, leaves, or other ground cover
- Water and sky
- Concrete and asphalt

It's not so great for repeating regular textures like brick, roof slates, or ceramic tiles.

1. Open your photo in GIMP. I'm using a dry stone wall photo.

2. Click the **Crop** tool.

3. Select **Fixed | Aspect Ratio**.

4. Type in **1:1.**

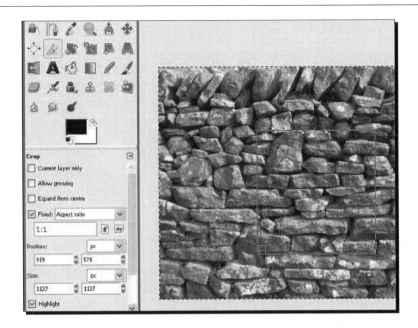

5. Drag a box over the photo. Notice you've fixed it to be a square box as you can see in the screenshot, but it can be any size.

6. When you're happy, hit *Enter*.

7. Go to **Filters | Map | Make Seamless**.

8. Then go to **Image | Scale Image**.

9. Enter a value for the image size **(1024 pixels or less)**. Select **Cubic**.

10. Click **Scale**.

11. Select **File | Save a Copy**.

Here it is with the filter applied:

What just happened?

You applied the **makeseamless** filter to your texture image. This will allow it to tile in SketchUp without you seeing the join between the tiles. You reduced the size of the image before you saved it because SketchUp can currently only handle sizes of max. 1024 x 1024 pixels. There's more on the best image size to use later on in this chapter.

Time for action – tiling method two

But if you still want to create a better texture from the outset, there's a second method. It takes a little longer (or a lot longer to get it perfect) but the results are cleaner. It's here if you need it.

1. Open your original straightened texture in GIMP.

2. Crop square as done previously, but make sure the size is an even number.

3. Open the Layers pallet by clicking **Windows | Dockable Dialogs | Layers**.

4. Click the **Duplicate Layer** icon (at the bottom).

5. Right-click the new layer and select **Edit Layer Attributes**.

6. Rename it **Texture**.

7. You now have a texture layer which you will modify, and a base layer which you will use as a reference.

8. Click the **Texture** layer in the **Layer Pallet** to select it.

9. Go to **Layer | Transform | Offset**.

10. Click on the **Offset by x/2, y/2** button and select **Wrap Around,** then click **Offset**.

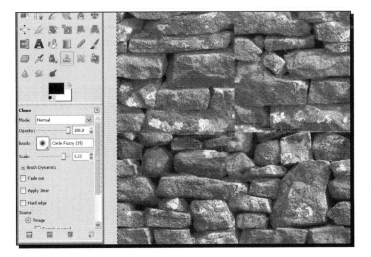

11. The idea now is to paint over the edges which have been wrapped into the middle.

12. Click the **Clone** tool.

13. Turn off visibility for the texture layer (the eye icon).

14. Select the base image layer in the **Layer** Pallet.

15. Hold down *Ctrl* (*Cmd* on the Mac) and click somewhere on the base image.

16. Turn on visibility on the texture layer and select it in the **Layer** pallet.

17. Start painting. Areas of the base image will clone onto the texture image.

18. Select a fuzzy brush for this and increase the size if it makes it easier. You can see my settings in the following figure. The dotted circle is the brush I'm using.

19. If you prefer you can *Ctrl*-click inside the texture image instead and use parts of that to clone over the middle area.

What just happened?

This method has much more flexibility than the previous method and can yield more pleasing results with a little practice. But don't get too bogged down with getting this perfect. Using a two layer approach allowed you to sample (clone) from the original image to paint over the offset image. Folding the image in on itself using offset x/2, y/2 ensured that the image would tile seamlessly.

Let's now apply this texture to a scene and save it to your own texture library.

Time for action – importing a texture into SketchUp

You're now ready to use this modified image in SketchUp to create a material. Once you've done this, you can use it again and again.

1. In the materials pallet, click the **Create Material** icon (top right). On the MAC right-click and select **New Texture**.

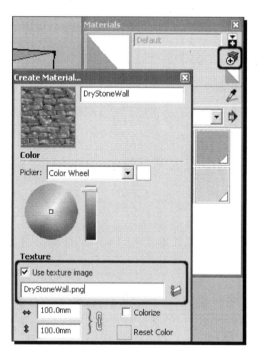

2. Type in your material name.

3. Select the folder icon.

4. Navigate to your image file.

5. Click **OK**.

6. Your new material should appear in the **In Model** tab.

7. Create a rectangle of say 1m x 1m using the **Rectangle** tool.

8. Select your material and paste it onto the surface.

 Don't worry if the texture doesn't look perfect or if you can see a repeating pattern. This can be edited when we get to the later steps of texturing (see the diagram at the start of the chapter). The important thing at this stage is to cover large areas of your model with realistic photo textures as fast as you can.

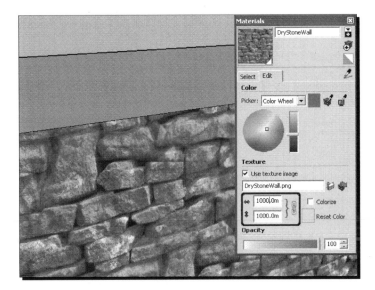

9. You'll be able to see if it scales right. Modify by typing into the first text box until the scale looks ok (see the preceding screenshot).

10. You can modify the x and y scale separately by first clicking the chain symbol.

Saving a material to a library

Congratulations! You've now created a new material in SketchUp. It's an achievement that will make SketchUp texturing much easier and more versatile for you from now on. And once you've done it a few times you'll realize it's not that hard at all. Using these methods you can create a library of real world textures for ultra-real architectural visuals.

Now the last thing you need to do is to save the texture, and make it easily accessible for later use. You can even share with others.

 If you'd like to share your textures with others, why not go to `http://forums.sketchucation.com/`, select Components, Materials & Styles and upload them for everyone to use? Sharing your hard work in this way makes texturing easier for everyone else too.

Time for action – saving the texture

1. Right-click on your material icon and click on **Save As.**

2. Navigate to where your SketchUp program is stored.

3. Find the **Materials** folder.

4. Create a folder called **My Materials** or something similar (see the following screenshot).

5. Type in a material name and hit **Save.**

6. In the **Material** browser navigate to **Materials | My Material** to find your new material!

Materials		
Asphalt and Concrete	Water	
Blinds	Wood	
Brick and Cladding	New Folder	
Carpet and Textiles		
Colors		
Colors-Named		
Fencing		
Groundcover		
Markers		
Metal		
Roofing		
Sketchy		
Stone		
Tile		
Translucent		
Vegetation		

File name: MyMaterial

Save as type: Material Libraries (*.skm)

What just happened?

You just created a texture from your own photo or one you downloaded, inserted it into SketchUp, and saved it into your new library. This is the bedrock of texturing! If you used the first method, you'll notice that once you've applied the new material to your model you may see a repeating pattern. When covering large areas this doesn't look too great. Even so, most of the repeating pattern will usually either be obscured by other objects in the scene, or edited out when you tweak textured faces in GIMP later.

You're now all set up. Everything in your model has basic textures applied. Whatever doesn't need a texture just has a color applied to it.

You can now progress to the final stage in the process diagram.

Advanced image considerations

I haven't mentioned image file types such as JPEG or PNG because it hasn't mattered so far to the fundamentals of texturing. But there are some tricks which make a huge difference to the size of your SketchUp files, and therefore the speed at which you can model and render your scene. We're going to quickly discuss the salient points and then come up with a method which will allow you to benefit from the various options you have.

Texture size

As you may already know, digital images are made up of pixels. Pixels are dots (more like squares) of color, and each image is made up of a grid of these dots. So, for example an average computer screen has around 786,000 pixels in a rectangular grid measuring 1024 x 768 pixels. A digital camera might take pictures of 8 mega pixels, or 3264 x 2448 pixels.

Now, the number of pixels in an image makes a big difference to image quality, but also file size. Here's a screenshot of the same texture saved at different sizes—800, 1425, and 200 square. Can you see what a difference in file size there is between the first and third?

Name	Size	Type	Dimensions
DryStoneWall02.png	1,507 KB	PNG File	800 x 800
DryStoneWall02_LR.jpg	142 KB	JPEG Image	800 x 800
DryStoneWall.png	4,196 KB	PNG File	1425 x 1425
DryStoneWall02_ULR.jpg	23 KB	JPEG Image	200 x 200

File type

Secondly, file type matters a lot. JPG saves files in a much more compressed format than PNG as you can see from the first and second files. The JPG is one tenth the size of the PNG! And don't even begin to think about using TIFF or BMP! The problem with JPG files is that they lose information every time you save them, because every time you save a JPG it compresses it a bit more. JPG compression is so successful because it throws image information away—but that's a bit ruthless isn't it?

Compression

When saving an image in JPG format, you will be presented with this box.

Moving the slider will change the quality of the image from very compressed (bad quality, low file size) to no compression (very good quality, large file size). The trick is to get a balance between low file size and image clarity.

The way forward with size and compression

So, we should just save every texture in a compressed JPG format at a small image size right? Well, no. Not unless you want your textures to look like this one. Can you see the blurred and jaggy artifacts the compression has introduced? This is what saving JPG at low compression settings does to an image. This is fine for distant objects, but not close up. So, what do we do?

Here's the deal: Save three versions of textures, then follow the following workflow:

PNG at large size (say 800 x 800 and above).	This can be reused and resaved again and again without loss of quality.	Use on all close-up surfaces where the surface will be further altered using "Edit Texture Image" in SketchUp (explained later).
JPG at large size and adequate compression (say 80 quality)	This cannot be resaved.	Use on all close-up surfaces that will stay as they are.
JPG at low size and high compression (say 200x200 at 50 quality)	This cannot be resaved	Use on surfaces far from the camera

This way we have all bases covered. Here's the workflow:

1. Save the image as PNG format and import into SketchUp.

2. In GIMP, go to **File | Save as Copy** as a JPG and name it the same as the PNG except type "_LR" on the end of the filename.

3. In GIMP go to **Image | Scale Image**.

4. Change the drop-down box to Percent and select **25%**.

5. Go to **File | Save As** and reduce the **Quality** slider to **50**. Name the image with "ULR" or "SML".

Import the third image into SketchUp as a new material and multiply the scale by four so that it matched the hi-res version.

Here's the model again with our own hi-res texture applied. Much better!

Modifying textures in GIMP for added realism

Now for the final step. Once a surface has any texture applied to it using any of the methods we've looked at, they can be edited within any image editing software. This is handled from within SketchUp so you don't need to mess around exporting and importing images. It works with any flat surface.

Time for action – telling SketchUp to link to an image editor

Before you try to modify textures using image editing software, you need to tell SketchUp which one, and where to find the program.

1. Go to **Window | Preferences | Applications**.

2. Click **Choose**.

3. Navigate to the directory where GIMP is stored.

4. This is usually `C:\Program Files\GIMP-2.0\bin`.

5. Select GIMP and click **Open**.

What just happened?

You have now set up SketchUp to open GIMP each time you need to edit a texture image. You could have chosen any image editing software such as Photoshop or Picasa.

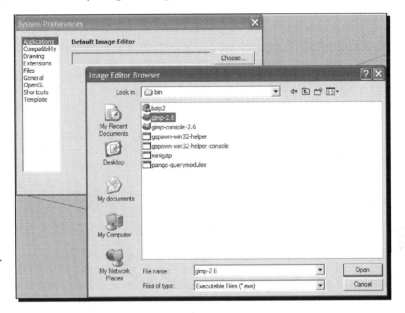

Time for action – making unique textures for surfaces

Before you can open an entire surface texture in GIMP, turn it into a unique texture for that face.

1. Right-click on a surface.

2. Select **Make Unique Texture**.

3. Right-click again.

4. Select **Texture | Edit Texture Image.**

5. GIMP opens up with the texture ready for editing!

What just happened?

You just created a separate texture image for the face you selected. This creates an image based on the face, and detects any cropping and holes, such as window openings. If you don't do this GIMP may open a tiled texture and edit that instead, which will change that texture wherever it is used in the model.

Editing textures in GIMP

You now have the textured image of the entire face you selected open in GIMP. You can now modify whatever you wish. When you click **Save** and go to SU, the image will update in SketchUp.

As you can see from the texture I opened below, the image here is only 178 x 337 pixels. That's a little too small to do anything with. You can see the poor quality of the texture. So instead I'm going to go back to SketchUp, apply a standard brick pattern, and re-open the texture in GIMP.

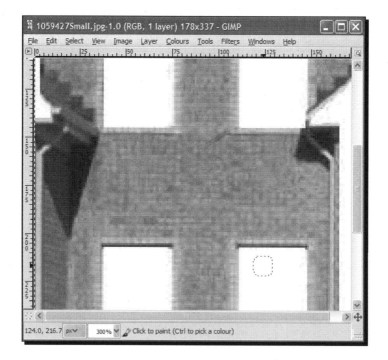

As you can see from the following screenshot, I now have a larger image of 1071 x 2048 pixels to play with. Much better! This is because each SketchUp brick tile is 250 x 250 pixels and GIMP opens the texture using that size data.

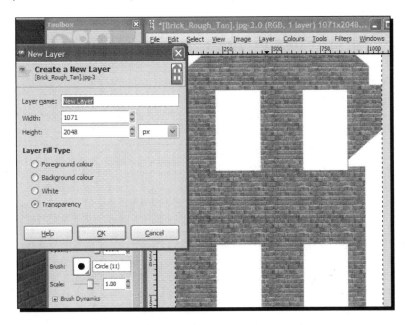

Time for action – adding some muck and variation

Hats off to the SketchUp folks for creating such a clean texture, but in real life we wouldn't expect it to be so uniform. You're going to apply some variation within GIMP now.

1. Create a new layer: **Layer | New Layer**.

2. This will create a see through layer over the top of the original. You can now modify this without being afraid of spoiling the original.

3. If you can't see the Layer pallet, press *Ctrl + L* (*Cmd+L* on the Mac).

4. Click on the new layer to select it.

5. Select the **Fill Bucket** and select a texture or gradient fill.

6. Click in the image window to fill.

7. Now go to **Filters | Render | Clouds**.

8. Experiment with any of these options.

9. You might now have something like this:

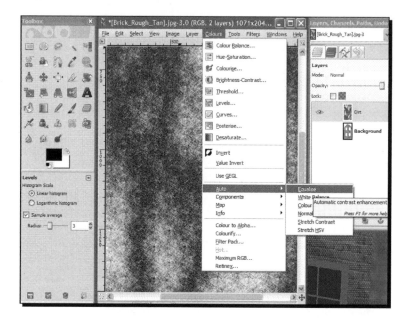

10. Go to **Colors | Auto | Equalize** to stretch the range of contrast (see the preceding screenshot).

11. Now take the **Opacity** slider down to say 10 (**Layers** pallet).

What just happened?

You have now overlain some simple random variation on the texture, as there would be in real life. You can do this for all your textured surfaces one by one, or just the ones nearer the camera. At this point you might like to add anything else you want to the texture, such as the hanging flowers in the next exercise.

Time for action – how to add extra elements to a texture

1. Open a photograph that contains the extra elements you require.

2. Select around the area as shown here:

3.   Go to **Edit | Copy**.

4.   Go to your original image and select **Edit | Paste**.

5.   In the **Layers** pallet, right-click on **Floating Layer | New Layer**.

6.   Use the **Move** and the **Scale** tool to get the pasted image in position as demonstrated in the following screenshot:

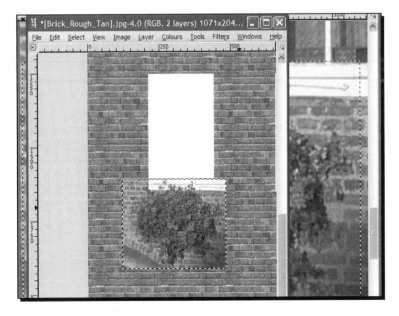

7. Select the original layer in the **Layer** pallet.

8. Right-click and select **Add Layer Mask**.

9. Click on the mask to select it.

10. Select the **Paintbrush** and make sure black is showing in the Toolbox pallet..

11. Paint out all the background bits you don't need as you can see in the following screenshot:

> There's more about layer masks in Chapter 9, *Important Compositing and After Effects in GIMP,* where you will get to grips with GIMP in much more detail.

12. Go to **File | Save a Copy** to save a master copy somewhere as a GIMP `.xcf` file.

13. Hit **Save** then click **Export** when prompted.

14. Your textured face will update with the changes you made, like this:

What just happened?

As you have been dealing with layers, all this detail will be lost when you save and go back to SketchUp, because the image is saved as a JPG or PNG, which don't accept Layers. Hitting **Save as a Copy** before you save and close can be a real time saver. Saving as GIMP .xcf or Photoshop .psd will retain all the layer info, and won't lose any detail either, so you can come back to it and make edits as many times as you like.

Have a go hero – adding extra detail

Now it's your turn. See how much difference you can make by adding little details where it matters. Try adding a soldier course of bricks to your windows by taking a texture from an existing photo. I've given you a clue how to do it in the following images:

Know when to call it quits

I've been known to spend ages texturing and then finally deciding that I didn't like what I'd done anyway. I changed it to some tiled texture and it was adequate. So, we shouldn't get drawn into games like adding cats to a window sill.

Summary

I think you're now fully clued up in the dark art of SketchUp texturing. As you've seen, SketchUp has some amazing tools to help you along the way. Now that you've made the best use of textures you can rest assured your model will render beautifully.

In this chapter on texturing, we covered:

- When to use and when not to use textures. Sometimes it's best just to leave this stage out completely and go for an NPR look (see Chapter 7).
- Using tileable textures, and a couple of ways to make your own. Don't forget to keep taking photos and keep a library for future use.
- Using Photo-Match to greatly speed up the texturing process and allow you to use digital photos wherever you want.
- How to tweak materials in GIMP to finalize and add realism. This is all accessible within SketchUp linked to GIMP.

We also discussed lots of other stuff, all of which combines to give you the wherewithal to create quick, great looking textured models that are ready to render or output straight from SketchUp. You can now go to the following chapter on Entourage, which is a weird name for people, cars, and trees... or you can go straight for the Photo Real Rendering in Chapter 8. Yippee!

6

Entourage the SketchUp Way

When pitching a great design to a client, your pitch will stand or fall on the presentation of architectural visuals. But your visuals will stand or fall on the entourage. So, in fact, a promising design can be marred by bad entourage. Entourage of saleable quality is hard to create. Obtaining in-focus photos of trees, with the right light, the right background, then clipping round them to remove all background elements can take forever. And that's why buying quality entourage will significantly lighten your wallet.

In this chapter, you will find out a way to find, create, and use entourage that you'll be happy with. If you don't have the money to spend, you'll learn how to create your own. We'll look at some of the best resources you can use to do so quickly and easily. You'll also learn how to use this entourage within your SketchUp workflow.

In this chapter, you will learn:

- ◆ Where to find high quality free photo real furniture models
- ◆ How to overcome problems with foliage
- ◆ How to create 2D people to use again and again
- ◆ Where, in your workflow, to use entourage to obtain the best results

The "notice hierarchy"

The notice hierarchy is a term I think I've made up on the spot, but wherever it comes from, it's not a bad way to describe something you've probably experienced: If you walk into a room there are certain things you'll notice first. If these things are missing, you'll notice something else first, and so on. Here's my take on the order of the "notice hierarchy":

1. People
2. Animals
3. Decor
4. Furniture
5. Lights
6. Carpet
7. Pictures
8. Any other objects

This might not be entirely accurate but hey, I'm only a part time behavioral psychologist ok? What's interesting though is that you can choose exactly where the viewer (the client) looks for his first impression. And we all know first impressions count, right?

So, what would you rather your multi billionaire client see first when showing them their new apartment development?

- A smiling, relaxed young couple
- A toaster

It's all about transporting the viewer into the image you've created. So, when you show people inhabiting the space in the same way the client would wish to, you've put the client into the scene. Neither men nor women, rich or poor, think nostalgically about the great bread toasting they did this morning.

But, actually, there's an even more important consideration. You may have looked at the list above and thought "I'd put an axe wielding maniac at the top of that list". And you'd be absolutely right. The fact is, no matter how good your render, or how good an impression your entourage makes, if there's a single piece of really bad entourage in the scene, it gets noticed first.

The first aim: Don't be bad!

So, the very first aim of entourage is—don't ruin your scene completely! And so sometimes the best advice is "leave it out completely". Some of the best visuals show a building on an open background, like this one by REVI21ON. Would you want to spoil it with entourage?

If you make sure you always use entourage sparingly, you are more likely to spend time finding good quality entourage to fill the spot.

Be the marketing exec

Here's a little quiz. I hope you do well in this one because it'll show whether you've grasped what creating great architectural visuals is all about:

Pop quiz

◆   When creating an architectural visual for a new commercial development, what kind of image should you strive to create?

1.   Showing the best workmanship.

2.   Whatever the client asks for.

3.   A realistic depiction.

4.   A dream.

The answer, surprisingly, is (4) a dream. You are a salesperson, and all the most effective architectural visuals are sales documents. If you treat them as such you will never go wrong. Think about this for a minute and internalize what it means. You need to pull out all the stops to create the vision of their dream space. And the easiest way you do this is not by getting every minute detail of the building right, but with well selected and placed entourage. Entourage brings life to your scene.

In the rest of this chapter, we'll go through how to use entourage to help you make that impact.

Choosing entourage

Let's evaluate your choices at this stage. I suppose there's little difference between all these choices in the final visual, but obviously some types of entourage will suit you more than others. But be warned, it's easy to drift aimlessly on the internet trying one thing after another. To help you, I've included a quick reference table or two so you can compare the relative merits of each, side by side.

At which stage do I introduce entourage?

There are three options here, illustrated in the first column of this table:

Design stage	Difficulty to use	Quantity available	Formats
SketchUp	Easy	Low (but growing)	`.skp`, `.3ds`, `.dwg`/`.dxf`
Renderer	Medium	High	`.3ds`, `.obj`
Post production	Difficult	Medium	Images

Broadly speaking, the level of difficulty experienced with entourage will increase the further along the process you decide to introduce it. So, as already discussed in Chapter 3, *Composing the Scene,* it is best to set up entourage place markers at least in SketchUp right at the start. The disadvantage of introducing detailed entourage (high polygon, detailed textures) into SketchUp is that it tends to slow the program down to a snail's pace. The way to get round this is discussed in this chapter when we look at swapping high/low detail entourage.

Many visualization artists leave entourage to the last moment, introducing it in the post-processing stage in Photoshop or GIMP. The reason for this is that it used to be difficult to set up 2D billboard style entourage in modeling or CAD software. That's not the case now with SketchUp. So, there's really no need to learn all the skills required to do this successfully in Photoshop. If you already have the skills and a library of images, you might still like to do it this way.

What I suggest is to introduce entourage in SketchUp and at the rendering software stage. The two work so seamlessly together that you will be able to keep both programs open, using the best features of each to populate your scene. While most entourage can be introduced in SketchUp, extra file formats can be imported into Kerkythea that are not supported by SketchUp, such as the popular .obj format.

What's my acquisition strategy?

An acquisition strategy is the posh way of saying "be consistent". This is unlike me, who has a bit of everything on my computer in lots of different file formats and visual styles, and software for creating this or that spread over several hard drives so that I can never find it. It pays to decide on the best way of acquiring entourage for you, and then stick to it. The broad choices are to buy it, find it on the Internet, or make it yourself.

	Quality	Suits your workflow	Money	Time
Buy	High	Not always	High	Low
Find	Medium	Not always	Low	Medium
Make	Med/Low	Yes	Medium	High

So, how much time or money do you have to spend? And what quality do you expect? It might seem wise always to buy entourage, and this is true to the extent that you will have more time to work on design. But bought entourage doesn't always fit your workflow, and you might be able to get exactly what you want with a little searching or time spent making it yourself. For example, trees are usually sold as either 2D images for postproduction or high polygon 3D. You might prefer 2D face-me cutouts. Making entourage, as you will see from the tutorial on 2D people, is not so difficult for some types of entourage. And you can also use software to make it easier for you, such as tree creators or people makers. For others, such as vehicles, it's best left to the experts.

What about subscription sites?

Subscription sites may offer a good way forward, but before signing up check whether they're geared towards your workflow (that is, SketchUp) and the output you require (photo real rendering or NPR). There's nothing worse than seeing an almost photo real tree in a photo real scene, or a realistic person in a watercolor style scene (remember the axe wielding maniac?). What's clear is that there's no panacea for all entourage needs, and you're allowed to have some fun finding out what's best for you.

Have a go hero

Look around on visualization forums such as `www.cgarchitect.com` to see where others are finding their entourage. In particular, look in gallery sections of forums, and if you see anything you like, why not post a question to see how the artist did it?

2D or not 2D, that is the question

Here's a table showing what entourage is available for each category: people, trees, vehicles, furniture, and backgrounds (such as city scenes). For each of these there are pros and cons for 2D or 3D, based on availability, quality of the outcome, and ease of use. In addition there are the types of output to consider. When aiming for stills, 2D will usually be the best way to go if it's available. 2D isn't resource hungry (unlike high polygon 3D trees) and actually more photo real than 3D when the entourage is made from photos. You'll learn how to make photo-based 2D entourage in this chapter. But for animation the decision is more difficult. Sometimes 2D entourage will look like, well, like a cardboard cutout.

	Availability		Suitable for Animation		Cost		Software to help	
	2D	3D	2D	3D	2D	3D	2D	3D
People	Yes	Yes	Yes	Yes	Med	High	N/A	Poser, Daz, Makehuman
Trees	Yes	Yes	No	Yes	Med	Med	RpTreeMaker	Vue, ngPlant, Xfrog
Vehicles	No	Yes	No	Yes	N/A	Low	N/A	N/A
Furniture	No	Yes	No	Yes	N/A	Low	N/A	N/A
Backgrounds	Yes	Yes	Yes	Yes	Low	Med	Vue Easel/Esprit	Vue/Bryce

 For a brilliant flythrough video using 2D face-me entourage, see one of the two Uniform (UK) entries at `http://vimeo.com/awards` (it's the one with 2D comic scenes in it).

Furniture

When creating interior views the furniture you choose is of paramount importance in establishing the look and feel of the image. While people are not used to discerning build quality of architecture, they are very well equipped to discern good or bad furnishings. That's because everyone buys furniture, and everyone spends most of their lives in rooms. And so, when looking at an interior visual most of the impact will be created by the furniture, not the room itself, as you can see in this image:

This fact gives rise to the continual need for good 3D models of furniture, much of it branded. And as design houses want their designs to show up in interior visuals, they often find a way to provide free models to us. It's just a matter of finding them.

Accessing the 3D Max furniture back-catalogue

Before SketchUp came along, most visualizers used 3D Max to create architectural visuals. So, there's years and years worth of content sloshing around the world in the old 3D studio Max 3DS format. And guess what? Lots of it is good stuff, free, and you can insert it directly into your renderer.

Have a go hero

In a minute you'll find out some of the best places to get this free stuff, but first you should give this a go yourself and see how well you do. We'll cover it in more detail later.

1. Insert basic or 3D Warehouse models into your SketchUp scene as place markers.

2. Do all the tweaks and changes in SketchUp until you get the visual composition you're happy with.

3. You now know what entourage you need for your scene. Search the Internet for it (try .3ds or .obj format).

4. Import each item into your renderer on its own to do a quick test render (you might be able to figure out how to do this from Chapter 1, *Quick Start Tutorial*).

5. Decide whether to use it or not, and repeat steps 3-5.

6. Once you're ready to render your scene (learn more about this in Chapter 8, *Photo-Realistic Rendering*), insert each item into Kerkythea and scale, rotate and move it around.

7. Perform tweaks to materials if necessary (such as color changes).

Hey presto! You have a room filled with succulent furniture. I didn't know you had such expensive taste!

Go easy. Some of the best interior renders I've seen show an empty room with just one visually interesting chair in it and great lighting.

List of websites

Once you've done your own search, try these great free sites too. Remember to save and catalogue the best stuff you find, because once its on your hard drive you'll find it impossible to find again later. With file names such as `1234asdf4qwe.zip` being commonplace, don't say I didn't warn you!

Try these websites for furniture models:

- `www.3dfilter.com`
- `www.Archive3D.net`
- `www.Turbosquid.com`
- `www.Dlegend.com/html/free-3dmodels.html`
- `www.Mr-cad.com`
- `www.3delicious.net`
- `www.Resources.blogscopia.com`

To further explore what there is on the net, free or paid for, you can go to a list of links at `www.3dlinks.com` and select **3D Objects | Commercial Objects** or **3D Objects | Free Objects**

And of course there is also Google 3DWarehouse itself, but beware, many models in there are not produced for photo real rendering.

SketchUp furniture models

There are bags of SketchUp furniture to choose from in the 3D Warehouse, and the amount of good quality gear is going up all the time. Most of the stuff there should be absolutely fine for SketchUp-based output and NPR output. If you're going to export your scene to a renderer, make sure you check out the section on 3D Warehouse components in Chapter 4, *Modeling for Visualization*.

People cutouts

We're going to learn how to make 2D face-me people that can be used both in photo-real rendering and NPR. Using this method you can build up a stock of people that you can use no matter what the required output. Here are the applications for this type of entourage:

◆ Black and white with sketchy edges

◆ Colored with sketchy edges

◆ Textured within SketchUp

◆ Photo real rendered

The following pictures of the same man correspond to these four output types:

So, you can see this entourage works with every type of output. There are many ways of creating entourage, but this is possibly the most versatile. This is because:

◆ It works with any rendering software

◆ There is no alpha channel to mess up within the renderer (the alpha channel is covered in Chapter 8)

◆ It has a correct scale, and no resizing is needed

◆ It casts detailed shadows

◆ It can be inserted within SketchUp

◆ It is easy to make with any skill level

Time for action – how to create 2D people components

1. Open the image of a person in GIMP.

2. Go to **Filter | Unsharp mask** if necessary to enhance sharpness.

3. **Crop** the image near the person using the **Crop** tool to take away excess image. Do this by dragging a box round the person then press enter when you are done.

4. **Save as** a PNG. This is a non-lossy format (refer to Chapter 5, *Applying Textures and Materials for Photo-Real Rendering*).

5. In SketchUp, go to **File | Import** select **All Supported Image Types** in the drop down box.

6. Select the image (make sure the **Use as image** button is selected).

7. Click **Open** and place it in SketchUp.

Scaling the person

8. Select the **Tape Measure** tool and click under the feet and on the top of the head.

9. Now type in the approximate height of the person. Just take a guess.

10. Click **Yes** to resize the model.

Tracing the outline

11. **Camera | Parallel | Projection** and then click the **Top View** button. You should see the image flat on your screen.

12. Zoom in using the mouse scroll button.

13. Select the **Pencil**.

14. Click on the edge of the person and trace round them.

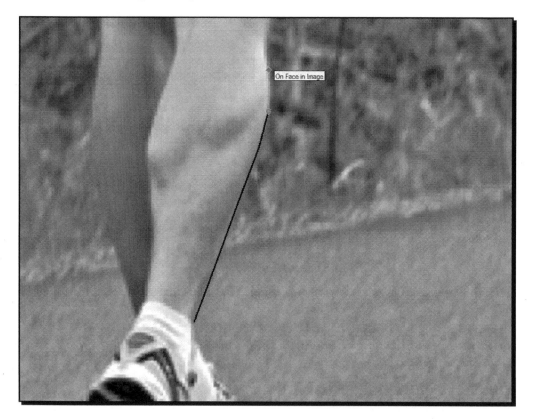

15. Make sure **On Face in Image** shows each time before you click (see the previous screenshot).

16. You will find it best to get the lines well within the edge of the person so no background shows on the cutout.

17. You will now have a completed outline like the one shown here:

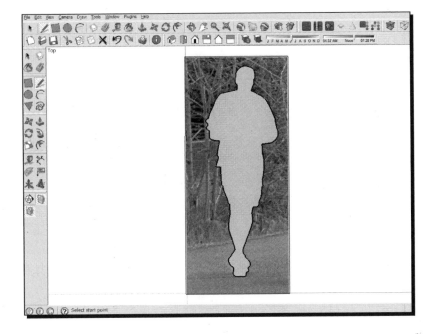

Applying the photo texture

1. Select the cutout, right-click, and select **Reverse Face** to get the white face uppermost if necessary.

2. Select the image, right-click, and **Explode**.

3. The photo is now projected onto the cutout person.

4. Erase the background around the person.

Checking for halos

A halo is the glow you see around some entourage making it look fake. It appears when the background in the photo was light, when the background in your scene is darker.

1. Turn off edges: Go to **View** | **Edge Styles** and untick the **Profiles** and **Display Edges** options.

2. Export a 2D image, open it, and check around the edge of the person for a halo effect.

3. Change the background to black: Go to **Window** | **Styles** | **Edit** | **Background Settings**, click on **Background** and change the color to black.

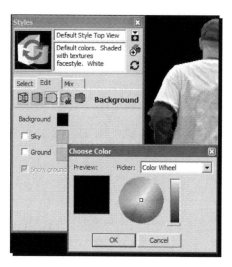

4. Check around the edges again. If any edges need adjusting, turn edges back on and redraw those lines.

What just happened?

You've just created a 2D person cutout which you can use as face-me components in SketchUp. The photo you used has been projected onto the cutout so that it's good enough for photo-real rendering. Now click on the **Hidden Line** view button and you'll notice there's no detail apart from the outline. There's still a little work to do if you want to use this entourage for NPR visuals.

Have a go hero – drawing the innards

You can now add some detail in the inside of the person, such as edges of clothing, hands, neck, and hair. Once you've done this your entourage can be used for any of the SketchUp styles. Here's the basic plan to get you started:

1. Using the same method as before, trace in some internal details.

2. Create a copy of the cutout person.

3. On the copy, fill in blocks of colour using the **Paintbucket** tool.

You'll now have two versions of the same person. The left one can be used for photo real, and the right one for artistic or sketchy styles including the methods in Chapter 7, *Non Photo Real with SketchUp*.

Time for action – creating the Face-Me component

1. Triple-click on the first copy you made.

2. Create a component and label it "label_PR".

3. Select **Always Face Camera**.

4. Select **Set Origin** and place the origin where the feet touch the ground.

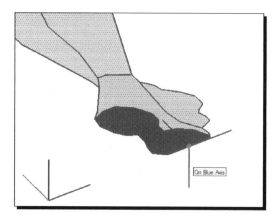

5. Place the red axis along the horizontal and click.

6. Place the green axis along the perpendicular so that the blue axis lines up with the centre of the person (see the preceding screenshot).

7. Right-click and select **Save As**.

8. Repeat with your second copy and label it _NPR.

Switching between PR and NPR versions.

9. In your scene, right-click and select **Reload**.

10. Select the PR or NPR version and click **Open**.

What just happened?

You made a component from the 2D cutout and told SketchUp where the axis should go. This means that when inserting the component in the future, it will always appear with the middle of the feet at the cursor. This eases placement dramatically. Even more importantly, because a Face-Me component rotates to follow the camera, you've told it where the centre of rotation is. You've labeled your components PR and NPR so that you can easily swap between components whenever you wish, depending on what output you plan to use that day.

Vegetation

We've already looked briefly at vegetation in Chapter 3, *Composing the Scene*, and talked about how important it is in the effectiveness of a visual. Hopefully, you've already included some great vegetation in your scene by cutting 2D billboards from photos. But for some applications, especially when aiming for animated output, you might need some other vegetation.

Non photo real sketchy trees

In NPR scenes, cartoon style trees look great. You can create these easily yourself by starting with a tree photo and tracing round it as you've just done with the Face-Me person. But this time why not use much larger strokes?

Have a go hero

Below is an example of a Sketchy tree. Have a go at making one now from a photo. Then follow the earlier steps to create a Face-Me component.

Want an automatic veggie maker?

RpTreeMaker from Render Plus allows you to create 2D trees from within SketchUp and place them into the model. It saves a PNG with alpha mask on a 2D Face-Me component. An alpha mask is a black and white image of the tree showing SketchUp and Kerkythea where to clip the image. The down-side of this is that Kerkythea doesn't always detect the alpha mask. This can be overcome by saving the PNG from within SketchUp and telling Kerkythea where to look for it within the **Materials** screen. You will find out how to do this in Chapter 8, *Photo-Realistic Rendering*.

ngPlant is a free 3D tree maker that works similarly to RpTreeMaker. It's a little harder to get to grips with.

Vue from e-on software has to be the top choice for vegetation. The foliage engine within Vue creates an infinite variety of different random trees and shrubs at the click of a button. Depending on how much you spend, you can gain greater control over this, and even create your own species. For any outdoor scene with a large amount of foliage it's well worth looking at Vue, as its render engine is built specifically for handling the massive polygon count created with lots of 3D vegetation. Some versions of Vue now have SketchUp import capabilities, so the workflow for this should be quite simple. Vue is regularly used in movies to simulate forests or entire ecosystems.

Vehicles

Lots of people are fascinated by cars, boats, and planes, so there's always a large amount of hobbyists who've taken it upon themselves to model their favorite vehicle in SketchUp. These models end up in the 3D Warehouse, where even more enthusiasts modify them and upload them again. So, you should be able to find any vehicle you need.

Watch out for fussy models

The thing to watch out for here is over fussy models. If you need thirty different cars for a road scene, and each of these has forty different materials assigned to them, you're going to have a nightmare in Kerkythea. To avoid this, go for the good quality models given away for free by some of the commercial model libraries, or spend some time in SketchUp reducing unnecessary materials or polygons before you export to your renderer.

2D vehicles

But don't assume you need 3D high polygon vehicles for your renders. You can often do just as well using the same methods as the 2D people you've just learned. Here's a coastguard helicopter found on www.Flickr.com, made into a 2D face-me component, and rendered in Vue to get the nice sky and lighting. In the following screenshot, you can see how the component was made out of the photo shown next to it:

Summary

In this chapter, you looked at the challenges and solutions for using entourage in your scenes that will enhance, and not detract from, the visual appeal.

Specifically, we covered:

◆ Where to find entourage and what to look for

◆ When to choose 2D or 3D entourage for best effect

◆ How to create your own high quality 2D entourage which will work for all types of image output

◆ When to buy, when to make your own, and when to scrounge around on the Internet for free stuff

We also discussed at what stage in the workflow you should use entourage, and came to the conclusion that in most cases, inserting stuff either in SketchUp or in the rendering application is preferable than at the post processing stage. You'll find out how to add extra entourage in Kerkythea in Chapter 8

Now that you've learned enough to get your scene populated with entourage, you can get on to the real fun stuff about creating the visualization images themselves – which is the topic of the next chapter.

7

Non Photo Real with SketchUp

As the name SketchUp suggests, SketchUp does sketchy styles extremely well. You can get pleasing visuals straight out of the box by hitting a few buttons, and you can take things further by exporting to an image processor such as GIMP. In this chapter, you will learn how to do both of these. In the process you'll learn the tools to help you experiment with your own styles too. The skills you need for this are found in the three main artistic image classes:

◆ SketchUp's own sketchy styles
◆ Watercolour style output (the Dennis technique)
◆ Black and white pencil drawings

The Dennis technique is illustrated in this image by Dennis Nikolaev to give you an idea of what's possible with this chapter.

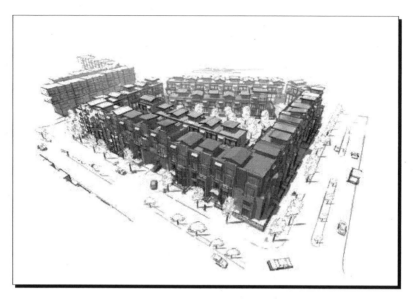

SketchUp's native output

Let's get started immediately with some sketchy output. SketchUp has some fabulous built in sketchy styles that you can always fall back on when you haven't the time or inclination to do anything more adventurous. And just because they're quick and easy to use, doesn't mean they're not great. Other CAD software developers would kill to get automatic output this good.

Keep a settings diary

Often when you discover a great look in SketchUp—the best combination of styles, shadow, face, and background settings—you never remember how to recreate it next time. So, why not keep a list in the back of your desk diary or even start a SketchUp notebook especially?

All you need to know to get great looking sketchy output from SketchUp is how to access, and maybe modify, the built-in styles. These styles completely control how you view every aspect of what you see on screen:

- ◆ Background color or image
- ◆ Overlay or watermark
- ◆ Sky and ground

- Line thickness and texture
- Line jitter, extensions, and endpoints
- Face style and opacity

All these settings are covered in detail in the online help you can access from **Help | Help Center**.

Time for action – editing SketchUp's built-in styles

For the purpose of this book on Visualisation, we're going to look at what you specifically need to know to create architectural presentation drawings. You can then experiment to find out the rest if you want to.

1. Make a start by opening any SketchUp model.

2. Go to **Window | Styles**. This opens the **Style** pallet.

3. In the **Style** pallet, go to **Assorted Styles | Brush Strokes and Canvas**.

4. The view of your model changes to reflect the style you selected.

5. To modify this style, for example, click on the **WireFrame** button in the **Face Style** toolbar as shown below:

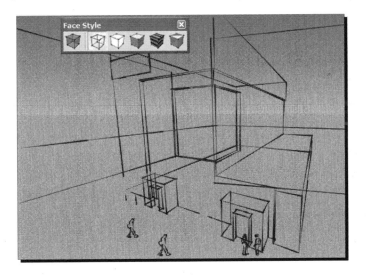

6. This only changes the view temporarily. Now click on the **In Model** icon in the **Styles** pallet.

7. Hover the cursor over the thumbnail top left in the **Style** pallet, and notice the message, "update style with changes".

8. While you're watching it, click the thumbnail.

What just happened?

Did you notice the thumbnail had a refresh arrow on it, which disappeared when you clicked? I never noticed this arrow for a long time because it's so easy to miss. But now you've seen it, you'll always keep your eye on it. When you clicked it, your update to the style was saved in the model. But don't worry, this won't affect the original style in the main style pallet. If you do wish to save this modified style for use in other models, you can do so by right-clicking and selecting the **Save As** option.

But why is this important? Well, SketchUp used to save all such style settings when you set up or updated a scene (the tabs at the top of your editing window). In later versions, after styles were introduced, every scene simply has a style associated with it which only changes when you select a new style, or edit the one you've got. Confused? Really all you need to be aware of is that any style changes you make must be updated in the way you just learned, if you wish to keep them that way. Otherwise, as soon as you hop from scene to scene you will lose your changes.

Have a go hero – get some style

So, why not have an experiment now with styles? Start with a simple model you drew, or download one from the 3D Warehouse. Now set up five scenes with different views and styles. Experiment with settings in each of the styles you've set up. Then save your changes to a new style if you like the result. Feel free to experiment, because when you reload SketchUp you won't have ruined any of the default styles.

Saving 2D images in SketchUp

Before SketchUp, when people still used CAD to produce presentations, all sorts of workarounds had to be developed to get decent visuals from CAD. Mostly all you could do with CAD was output 3D line art images, or 2D elevations, plans, and sections, then rework these in Photoshop (mostly just to add color). This was an art in itself. Now with SketchUp you output exactly what you see on your screen, as this is usually what you also want to see in a presentation. Why didn't anyone think of that before?

Follow these steps to save your onscreen image to use in a presentation, on the web, or however you want.

Time for action – 2D graphic export

Before saving a 2D image, I'd recommend creating a scene tab. If you have one set up already, but you changed shadows or the view in any way, right-click on the tab now and select **Update**. This means if you need to resave the same view again, you can. The camera angle and other view settings will still be there whenever you click the scene tab.

1. Maximize the SketchUp window (top right of the window).

2. Set up your scene with styles, shadow settings, camera angle, and field of view (you learned about these in Chapter 3, *Composing the Scene*).

3. Go to **View | Animation | Add Scene**.

4. Go to **Styles** pallet. Click **In Model** and **Update Style with Changes**.

5. Go to **File | Export | 2D Graphic**.

If you have the Pro version of SketchUp, you will be able to export in the following extra 2D CAD and Vector file formats. Some of these are a must when working within CAD or Illustration—Autocad (DXF, DWG), Portable document format (PDF), Encapsulated Postscript (EPS).

6. Select PNG if you plan to work further on the image, or don't want to lose detail.

7. Alternatively, select JPEG if you need a low file size and don't plan to modify the image further. You can move the quality slider after clicking on **Options** to alter the file size. High can produce an image five or six times the filesize of low.

8. Click **Options** and set the **Width** to 3000. This is standard for techniques in this chapter but will give a large file size.

9. The **Height** will change automatically to suit. This depends entirely on the shape of your main view window.

10. Click on **Anti-Alias** if you like softened edges. Usually you will want this box ticked.

Screen limitations to be aware of

As SketchUp exports what you see on screen, the shape of the output depends on the shape of your SketchUp window. So, if your window is roughly square, it will come out roughly square when you export. When you maximise your screen, it will come out roughly the shape of your monitor. But even then, it is affected by how many toolbars you have at the sides and top. In short, if you want output with consistent number of pixels in x and y, you need to keep your screen consistent.

That's a basic overview of how to output sketchy styles from within SketchUp. But as a pro architectural visualizer you will need something more polished. In the rest of this chapter you will find out how to combine several of SketchUp's styles within GIMP to give even better results. These are called **non photo real (NPR)** visualization techniques.

The Dennis technique

The Dennis technique is the quickest and most fun of all NPR techniques yet developed for SketchUp. The skills you'll learn here will allow you to experiment and develop your own particular preferred style or technique.

The method gained a huge following after an architect calling himself Dennis on the SketchUp Pro forums posted the following image "up for review" in the gallery section of the forum. He agreed to provide us with a run through of his method, and having done this he proceeded to mentor and encourage those of us who were trying to copy it. The Dennis technique was born in a 400+ post thread!

It turns out that the big trick, or secret if you like, behind the Dennis technique is speed. You need to be quick in everything you do. Quick, rough mouse movements. Quick decisions on whether you like what you see, or to erase it. The whole process should take no more than half an hour once you're used to it, and that lack of time investment will make you willing to be bold and use flourishes you wouldn't usually. "Getting it right" is not the idea here. In fact, it spoils it. You can see why by looking at this close-up of Dennis' original.

This close-up shows the roughness which actually provides the desirability of the image. It's as if watercolor has been applied to a hand drawn pen and ink drawing. Follow the steps here exactly so that you gain an idea of why each step is required. Once you've done it like this once, you can add your own embellishments.

Time for action – setting up the Dennis technique in SketchUp

This picture shows a dwelling in SketchUp. I've taken this one from the 3D Warehouse. It might be easier for you to do the same, rather than using your pride and joy project, simply because you'll be defacing it beyond recognition and this can be quite upsetting! Choose a really simple model like this one:

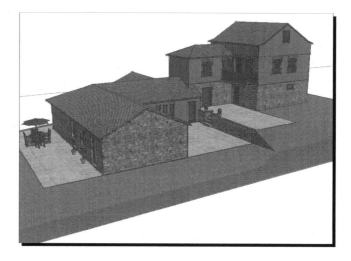

First you will set up the three pages which you will export to GIMP. They are:

- Color wash
- Lines and shadows
- Lines only

1. Maximize the window so that you keep the window size consistent.

2. Compose your scene, if you haven't done so already.

Color wash

1. If you have selected any styles other than the default one, go to the **Style** pallet now and select **Default Styles**.

2. On the main toolbar, click the **Shaded with Textures** view style button.

3. Open the **Style Manager** and press the **Create New Style** button (the one with the + in it).

4. Go to **Edit | Edge Style** and turn off **Display Edges** and **Profiles**.

5. Click the **Background Settings** button in the **Style Manager**.

6. Turn the **Sky** off. Set the background to blue, and turn the **Ground** on.

7. Click the thumbnail image at the top left of the style manager to update the style.

8. Turn shadows on and experiment with time and date settings until you like the result.

9. Go to **View | Animation | Add Scene.** This fixes the camera, style, and shadow settings to the scene.

10. You may get a message like the one below. Click **Save as new style** and hit **Update Scene.**

Warning - Scenes and Styles

Warning! You are creating or updating a scene and have not saved the changes you've made to your style.

What would you like to do with your style changes?

- ⦿ Save as a new style.
- ○ Update the selected style.
- ○ Do nothing to save changes.

☐ Please don't show this again. I will manage style changes on my own.

[Update Scene] [Cancel]

You should have something like the following screenshot, just colors, textures, and no lines. We'll call it the Color wash layer.

Lines only

1. In the **Styles Manager**, select a sketchy style with a white background. I've used the **Sketchy Charcoal** style here.

2. Make sure **Shadows** is off. Now create a new scene tab

Lines and shadows

1. Turn shadows on and create the last scene. You can mess around with some of the edge settings here if you like.

Optional selection layer

Optionally, you can now also create a flat colored version which you will just use for masking/selecting areas of color in GIMP. Use the **Shadows** dialog box at the settings shown below.

Untick the **Antialiasing** box in **Save Settings**. This is useful when you get more advanced with GIMP as you can select areas of color to work on. You might want to do this to simulate real watercolor where you would apply one color at a time.

Exporting the scene tabs

1. First save your SketchUp model. This means you can come back to it and re-export the images-later if you need to.

2. Go to **File | Export | 2D Graphic**.

3. Select *.**png** from the drop down list.

4. Type in **3000** into the **Width** field (refer to the previous screenshot). The **Height** will adjust automatically.

5. Type in a file name and hit **Save**.

6. Repeat for each of the three views you just set up. I suggest you us these filenames: ColourWash, LinesShadows, and LinesOnly.

What just happened?

You now have the three views set up which will be opened in the GIMP image editor (You should have this downloaded and installed already from Chapter 2, *How to Collect an Arsenal Rambo Would Be Proud of*, or if you prefer you can use Photoshop). A fourth optional view is there just to help you select areas of color if you want to. Setting up scenes (page tabs) first, rather than just manually exporting views is important. This will allow you to come back and make changes to your model and re-export the images at exactly the same camera angle, shadow setting, and style setting as before. You made sure the style settings won't change by clicking refresh in the style pallet. Putting a flat blue color in the background allows you to select and replace the sky with an image in GIMP.

Keep the screen the same

Annoyingly sometimes, SketchUp outputs images exactly as they are on screen. So, you might save a file, change or maximize the size of the SU window, and find that it saves a completely different view. To combat this, use the same computer and always maximize the SketchUp program before saving an image.

Now on with Dennis's magic formula!

Time for action – setting up GIMP for the Dennis technique

You should have a ColourWash, LinesShadows, and LinesOnly; PNG images all of the same size.

1. Once you've opened GIMP, go to **File | Open**. Select the ColourWash image and click **Open**.

2. Now go to **File | Open as Layers**.

Hold down *Ctrl* and select the other two images and open them.

All three images will now open in GIMP as layers. Layers can be seen by opening the **Layer** pallet. If it's not open already, do this now, go to **Window | Recently Closed Docks | Layers, Channels, Paths, Undo-...**

Your screen should now look roughly like mine. If you need to reorder your layers, you can click and drag them with the mouse.

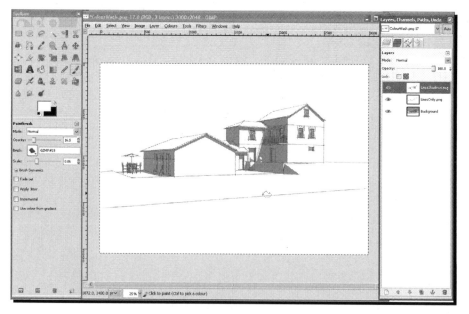

3. Click on the ColourWash layer in the **Layer** pallet, then click **Duplicate Layer** button at the bottom.

4. Click on the eye icon for the other layers so you can see the new layer.

5. Select this new layer by clicking on it in the **Layer** pallet.

6. Select the magic wand from the main pallet and change **Threshold** to **1**. Click anywhere within the blue sky area to select it.

7. Hit **Delete**.

8. The sky is now transparent ready for you to insert a sky image behind it. Go to **Select | None** to reset the selection area.

9. Now you need to simulate the inaccurate random characteristics of paint and pen.

10. Go to **Filters | Distorts | Ripple**.

11. Alter the settings as shown here:

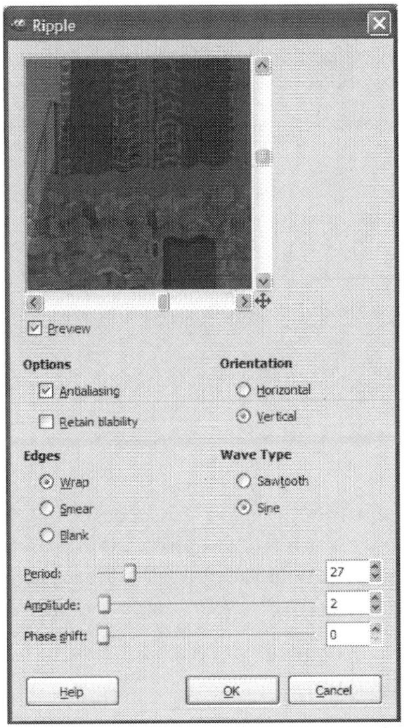

If your image has repeating textures these won't look too good. So, try using the Oilify filter instead. All we're trying to do here is introduce some variation. You can experiment with many of the filters to achieve your own version of this effect.

12. Click the **LinesOnly** layer and change the layer mode to **Multiply**. You should now have something like the following:

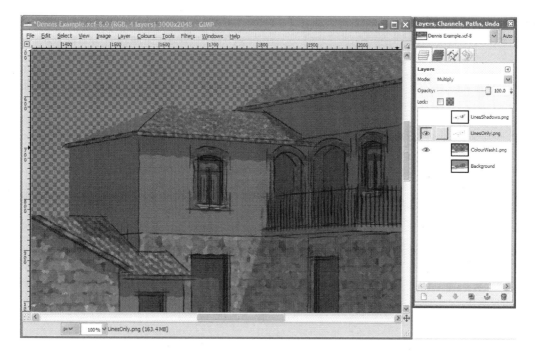

What just happened?

A lot has happened so far and I hope you're not too mind boggled! If you're new to GIMP then please give yourself plenty of time to get used to it. You'll find it to be worth it in the end. So far, you've set your images as layers in GIMP. GIMP layers work like see through sheets on an overhead projector, or tracing paper if you prefer that analogy. We stack one on top of another and mask bits out from each so that the final image we get is a composite of all three. The layer stack you've got so far is shown here. The LinesOnly layer has been set to Multiply, which will project only the lines onto the Colourwash layer, as shown in the following diagram:

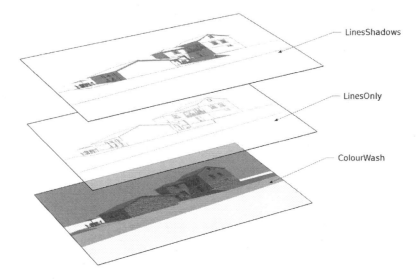

LinesShadows

LinesOnly

ColourWash

Using layer masks in GIMP

Layer masks are a key feature of pro image software, and the main reason we're using GIMP instead of, say, Photoshop Elements. A layer mask is a black and white image associated with a layer. Wherever you paint black on the layer mask, you will be able to see through the layer. And wherever there is white, you will not be able to see through. You'll also be using layer masks in Chapter 9, *Important Compositing and After Effects in GIMP*.

You're going to use layer masks now to create holes in the LinesShadows layer. This will allow "paint" through from the two layers below. You'll be able to see how it all works by following the procedure that follows. Don't worry, you'll get to grips with it really quickly because there's nothing to it!

Time for action – using layer masks for the Dennis effect

1. Click the eye icon on the LinesShadows layer to switch it back on.

2. Right-click this layer and select **Add Layer Mask**.

3. Select **White** (full opacity) and click **Add**.

4. Select the mask (the white rectangle that's appeared beside the layer).

5. Click the **Paintbrush** icon.

6. Select a large rough brush. Don't select anything too round or smooth. I like the "Galaxy, Big" brush that comes with GIMP.

7. Hold down *Ctrl* and rotate the middle mouse button to zoom in a little on the focal area of the drawing.

8. Quickly and roughly paint in the most important areas.

9. In the **Paintbrush** pallet, change **Opacity** to around 50.

10. Paint in some more areas.

11. Reduce Opacity to 20% and paint over any larger areas of color to simulate a watercolor wash effect. Go over some areas more than once to build up color.

Here's the image so far. It doesn't look great, but then it doesn't have to! You don't need a lot of skill for the Dennis technique, which is why it's so popular.

And below you can see the rough brush strokes I've made to produce it. The black areas are the focal point where I used 100% opacity. You can see in the various shades of grey where I used the 50% or 20% opacity brushes.

Now, I'm feeling the pain with you here. I'm just following the method as I write it, so you're not getting a dressed up version. I'm no artist either, just a CAD guy, maybe like you are. If I can do it, then you can too. And do I look worried at this stage?

Don't answer that...

What Just Happened?

You've been punching holes in the sketchy black and white top layer to allow the paint through from the layers below. Doing this quickly tends to give the best "watercolor sketch" effect that we're after. And it also saves loads of time. Bear in mind that you're not actually deleting anything here. You can simply go back with a white brush on the mask and reinstate whatever you like, or neaten it up if that's what you want. We've also left lots of uncolored areas in there to give the pencil sketch feel. If in doubt, look back at Dennis' originals earlier in the chapter.

Dennis's help forum: While writing this book I managed to track Dennis down. True to the generosity he showed back in 2005/2006 when he first showed us the Dennis technique, he has agreed to tutor fans of his method on his website, as long as you're nice to him. His site can be found at www.archmodeling.com. Click the Forum link.

Time for action – using a sky image in GIMP

The web's full of stunning sky photos. Just grab one you like, and follow these steps to insert it into your composition. Or why not just point your camera upwards on a sunny day?

1. In GIMP go to **File | Open** and select the sky image.

2. This will open a new GIMP window. Working in this has no adverse effect on your first window.

3. Go to **Filters | Artistic | Oilify** and increase **Mask size** and **Exponent** until you get an oil paint effect similar to this:

4. Go to **Select | Select All**.

5. Select **Edit | Copy**.

6. Switch back to your Dennis window.

7. Just in case you're still editing a layer mask, click any layer icon in the **Layer** pallet.

8. Now go to **Edit | Paste**.

9. Right-click on the **Layer** dialog and select **New Layer**.

10. Move this new layer just below the ColourWash1 layer in the **Layer** pallet.

11. Select the bottom layer (ColourWash), and use the magic wand to select the sky area again.

12. On the top layer, click the mask and roughly paint in some sky as before.

What just happened?

You inserted a sky image into the main scene and turned it into a layer. This was put just below the color wash layer which had the sky deleted previously. So, only the sky area shows through this layer. You then used the magic wand on the original sky area to create a selection. Anything you now do will only affect this selected area, so there's no way of painting over the building.

Time for action – creating the vignette layer

The vignette layer is where you focus the eye into the image and take away edge distractions. The idea here is to start with a completely white mask, and gradually reveal only the areas you really need to see. It's very minimalist, but that's what sketchy visuals are!

1. Create a new layer, and select **White**.

2. Create a layer mask as before.

3. With a large brush and opacity at 20%, just reveal the largest extent of what you need to see. Leave a good white border around the edges.

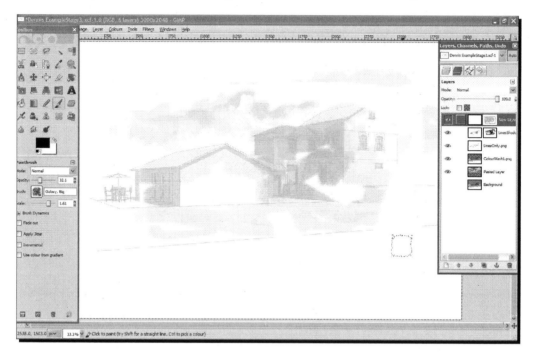

4. Go over the inner areas you want to highlight again.

5. With a 40% opacity brush, half the size of the first, uncover some of the focal areas bit by bit – but be sparing.

6. Change your brush to white full opacity and paint out all the areas that are irrelevant or distracting.

Modifying the final composition with new SketchUp output

My final image is shown here. It's not great, mostly because the textures weren't great in the first place, but much better than before. Repeating, mechanical textures like this look really fake in the Dennis method. I also don't feel the lines are sketchy enough, and I may have been too heavy handed with the main colored area. So, what can I do about it? Lots!

Using layer masks has allowed you to apply lots of effects to the images whilst not damaging the underlying images. So, you can just go in and swap them with some better ones! You can also go back to any of the layer masks and reveal more or less of each layer, neatening things up as you feel the need. Nothing's ever lost.

Have a go hero – modifying the Dennis technique

This can be challenging because it's open ended. But you're up for it. So experiment!

Go back to your SketchUp model and try out another sketchy lines style. Choose a really scruffy one if you can find it, and modify some settings yourself too. Re-export this image as a PNG file to use as new LinesOnly layer. In GIMP, insert the layer as before, and move it next to the original one in the **Layer** pallet, but turn off the old layer using the eye icon. How does it look? Now change some colors and textures in SketchUp and export a new color Wash image too. Replace the ColorWash layer with the new one and re-do the oilify or ripple filtering if you want to. Modify some of the layer masks too and see what you get. Save the results of each change as an image and print them next to each other: write notes next to each so you can get the effect again next time.

Here's my final image. In the following screenshot you can see the layer stack I ended up with. You can see the duplicate LinesOnly and ColourWash layers which I've switched off. Also I went for a combination of two pencil styles in the end. Remember, only the layers with an eye next to them contributed to the final image.

Richard's sketchy pencil technique

By now you've probably learned all you need to know about creating non photo real artistic compositions using SketchUp and GIMP. All the skills are contained in the Dennis technique you've just mastered. But let's look at a pencil only method that takes these techniques a little further still. This method relies on artistic judgment and skill just as little, because most of the pencil look is created automatically. It's developed from a technique we named the "Richard method" because of a guy on the original SketchUp forum who first proposed it during Dennis's thread. Here's Richard Jeffrey's wonderful pencil image:

Time for action – setting up Pencil sketch technique

Create scenes in SketchUp corresponding to the following images and export them as before. They can be based on any black and white sketchy line style from the style pallet. All the settings listed below are modified in the style manager pallet:

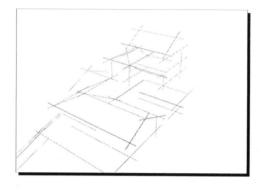

- ◆ The Heavy Construction Lines layer, consisting of:
  - ❑ Large line extensions
  - ❑ The low detail slider
  - ❑ No shadows

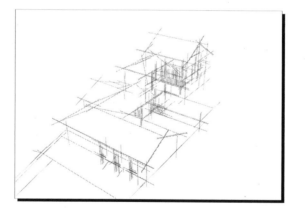

- ◆ The Light Construction Lines layer, as before but it consists of:
  - ❑ The higher detail slider
  - ❑ No shadows

These first two layers are created using the **Level of Detail** slider with high **Extension** values, as you can see in the following screenshot:

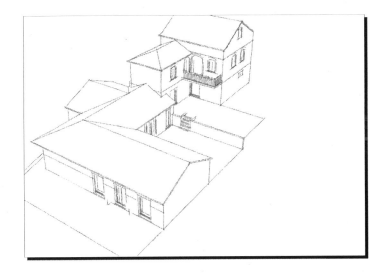

◆ The Outline layer:

❑ Use an unmodified sketchy lines style

❑ No shadows

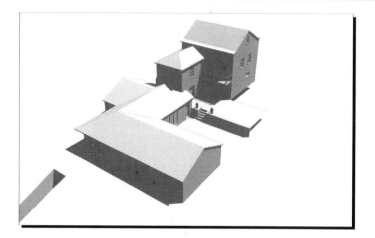

- ◆ The Pencil Shading layer:
  - ❑ Shadows on
  - ❑ Select the monochrome face style
  - ❑ Turn edges off

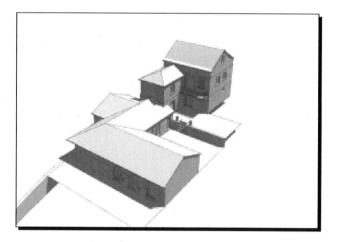

- ◆ And finally the Dirty Hands layer:
  - ❑ It's almost the same as the previous one
  - ❑ It's different because sketchy edges are switched on

1. Open all images as layers in GIMP, as you did with the Dennis technique.

2. Select the Light Construct layer.

3. Go to **Layer | Transform | Offset**.

4. Move slightly by several pixels (see the following screenshot) to give the lines a construction line feel.

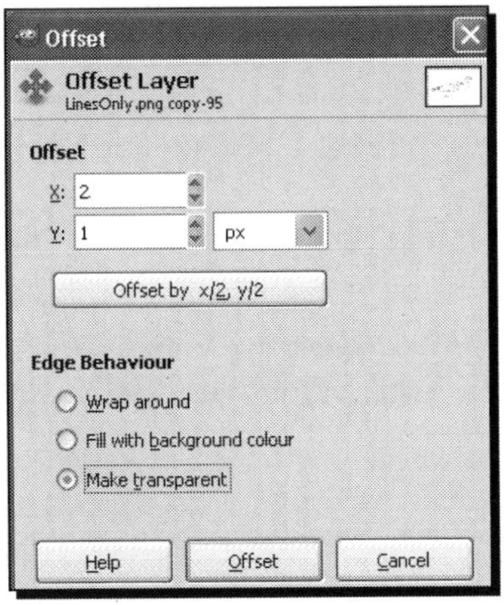

5. Alternatively you can use **Filters | Distorts | Lense Distortion** on this layer.

6. Set the layers in order as shown in the following screenshot:

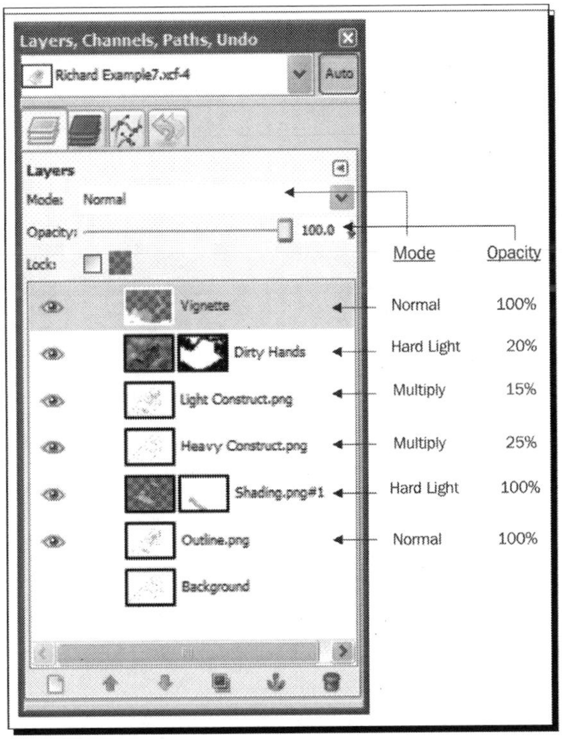

What just happened?

You set up layers to simulate the different pencil marks you would expect to see in a pencil drawing. The Light Construct layer simulates the many feint construction lines done at the beginning of a sketch. They're offset or distorted slightly to give the idea that they were drawn over a second time. The Heavy Construct layer is the same, but has fewer lines and heavier line weight. The normal, shading, and dirty hands layers will be worked on to create the main image.

So, let's start working on these.

Time for action – creating pencil shading in GIMP

1. Select the Shaded Pencil layer.

2. Select the **Select by Colour** tool from the main pallet.

3. Set **Threshold** to **1**.

4. Go to **Filters | Blur | Motion blur**.

5. Set **Length** between 10 and 20, and **Angle** to however you like it to simulate the direction of your pencil strokes.

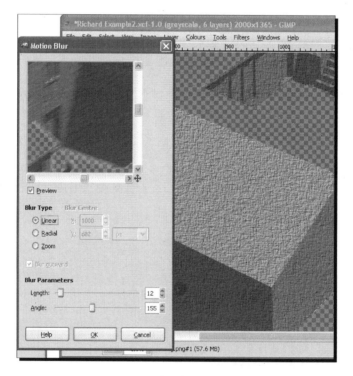

6. The contents of the layer are blurred in the direction you specified.

7. Select this layer in the layer pallet. Select the move tool and move it back approximately within the sketchy lines (use the arrow keys).

8. Select **Colours | Brightness/contrast,** then increase brightness and contrast a little until it looks like pencil shading.

9. Set the longer blend mode to **Hard Light** or **Grain Extract** as preferred.

10. Now mask out any areas where you don't want this shading to be, like you did in the Dennis method. You can see me doing this here to take away the shading from the windows.

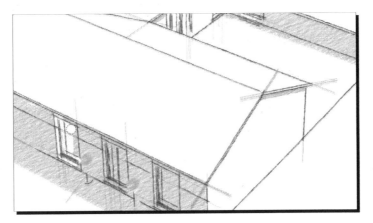

What just happened?

You just took a shaded image from SketchUp, added noise, and blurred it to simulate pencil shading. The layer was then set to Multiply (to allow all the shading to show through) or Hard Light (to allow only the shadows to show through). I've gone for Hard Light on this image.

Add some grunge: the Dirty Hands layer

Just as the Dennis technique had a magic step, so does Richard's. The following might not seem like much, but it makes all the difference. Master this and no-one will be able to tell it's not genuinely hand drawn.

1. Import your Dirty Hands image in GIMP as a layer.

2. Move it to the top of the layer stack and select it.

3. Go to **Filters | Render | Clouds | Difference Clouds**.

4. Use the default settings and click **OK**.

5. Go to **Filters | Noise | RGB noise**.

6. Leave settings as default and click **OK**.

7. Roughly mask or erase anywhere you don't want any smudging. You can see this in the following screenshot (all the hatched areas are masked/erased).

8. Set layer opacity to 15-20.

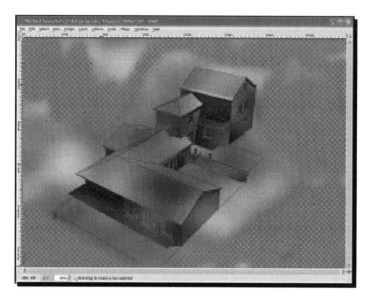

Finishing touches

1. As with the Dennis technique, add a Vignette layer to finish the composition.

2. Save a copy in GIMP .xcf format to allow you to edit it further some other time if desired. This format retains all the layers and masks.

3. Go to **Image | Flatten Image** (this will remove layers and masks).

4. Go to **Filters | Artistic | Apply Canvas** to get the paper affect.

5. Choose a depth setting to your own taste. You can see here how the paper grain shows up the smudged graphite just like when you do it by hand.

6. Save this final image as a PNG file.

Here's the completed image:

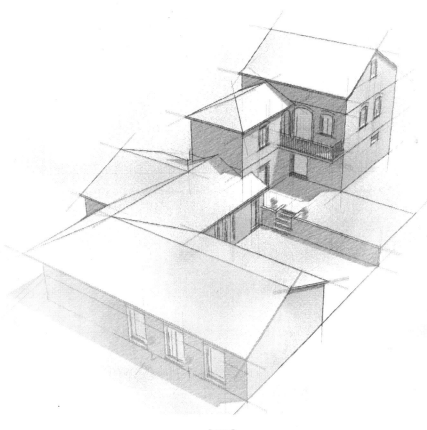

Pop quiz

1. Why is it important to set up scene tabs before exporting images?

2. What does the Vignette layer do?

3. Is it more important to be quick, or accurate with the Dennis Technique?

4. When you make changes to a style, how do you make the changes permanent?

Summary

In this chapter, you have learned all the basics you need to create artistic visual styles using GIMP. You've learned:

◆ How to use layers to build up a composite image from SketchUp output

◆ How to create and edit layer masks to avoid erasing

◆ How to use filters to modify SketchUp output

◆ How to use the Dennis technique to produce fast, sketchy, watercolour art

◆ How to do eerily realistic pencil art

These methods will become the staple of your visual output, simply because they're quick and easy to achieve, yet the client can be seriously impressed with it. These styles are sketchy and loose, ideally suited to presenting early design concepts. In the next chapter, you can take your concept designs further into a photo-realistic reality.

8

Photo-Realistic Rendering

In this chapter, you will learn how to render photo-realistic architectural visuals with SketchUp and Kerkythea. You will already be familiar with the basic process from Chapter 1, Quick Start Tutorial. This chapter goes into a little more detail, giving you the why, as well as the how.

You will cover the following topics:

- ◆ How to do clay renders for lighting checks
- ◆ How to import and merge from SketchUp to Kerkythea
- ◆ Inserting photo-real 3D Studio Max entourage
- ◆ Setting up photo-realistic materials
- ◆ The best render settings for lamp-lit and sun-lit scenes
- ◆ Bump and clip maps
- ◆ Time-saving preview render settings

But best of all, by the end of this chapter you will be able to render your SketchUp models to look better than the real thing.

The learning feedback loop

Photo-realistic rendering is not learned overnight. That's mostly because the learning feedback loop is so long. The feedback loop is the time taken for you to see the results of an action, so that you can analyze it and feed back that knowledge into your next step. This is the way many people learn most effectively, but with rendering that's difficult because it can literally take a whole day to view rendered output!

A learning strategy despite long render times

In this chapter, I'm going to suggest a learning strategy that will largely combat this problem. We'll start with render settings that show you what you need to know, quickly, so that you can learn from what you see. These settings may not give you beautiful renders at once, but later you'll learn the settings used for the final render too. For those among us who love the quick fix, Chapter 1 is all about that, so don't forget to give that a go if you haven't already.

Photo or hyper, what's the difference anyway?

We need to define what we're trying to achieve at the outset, so we can tell when we've achieved it. There are a couple of categories of photo-real—real or hyper-real. Hyper-real is an image that is impossible to distinguish from reality; it's a fake photo with warts and all. Real is more like a staged photograph. For example, there might be a dream-like or a too-perfect feel about it. What we're aiming at in this book is photo-real as opposed to hyper-real, because with arch-viz you're trying to get a realistic, but pleasing image for marketing or sales.

Setting up for photo-real rendering

In Chapter 2, you found out about the software and plugins required for rendering with SketchUp and Kerkythea. You also found out where to get add-on packs for Kerkythea, such as the material libraries and global scenes. If you haven't looked at this yet, you might like to do so now. It's as easy as accessing a few websites, and it's all free! In particular, you need to make sure you have the SU2KT plugin installed, and a few materials and global libraries installed in Kerkythea. The tutorials in this chapter assume you have the Windows version of Kerkythea 2008.

The SketchUp - Kerkythea rendering process diagram

In this section there is a diagram that shows the SketchUp and Kerkythea rendering process. This is a good way of doing it because you achieve great results in little time. For example, why find out that a material hasn't mapped at the right scale only after an hour long render? Using the following process, you would find that out in 30 seconds with a low quality test render.

Step 1: Check integrity and the modify/testrender loop.

Step 2: Insert extra entourage.

Step 3: Define lighting.

Step 4: Refine materials.

Step 5: Test the production render.

Step 6: Production render.

Step 7: Post-production renders.

We're going to look at each of these in detail using a fairly large scene lit by the sun. Later in the chapter we'll go back into SketchUp, add some indoor lights, and do a night render. You can use any scene you've set up yourself in SketchUp, or you can use the scene used in this chapter, which you can find by searching for *Acme Gold* in the 3D Warehouse (`http://sketchup.google.com/3dwarehouse/`).

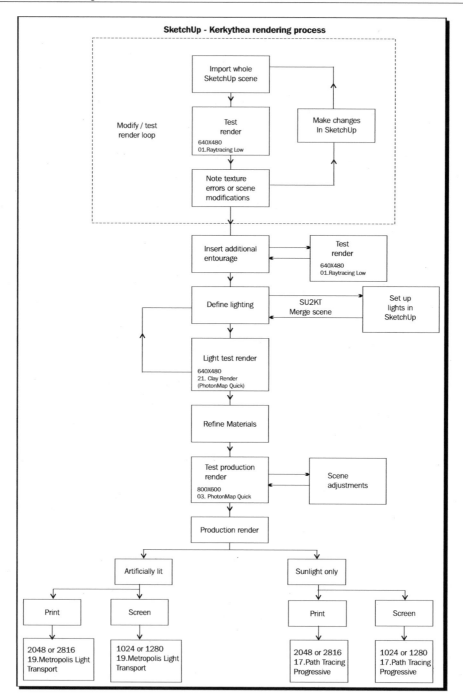

SketchUp - Kerkythea rendering process

Import whole SketchUp scene

Modify / test render loop

Test render
640X480
01.Raytracing Low

Make changes In SketchUp

Note texture errors or scene modifications

Insert additional entourage

Test render
640X480
01.Raytracing Low

Define lighting

SU2KT Merge scene

Set up lights in SketchUp

Light test render
640X480
21. Clay Render (PhotonMap Quick)

Refine Materials

Test production render
800X600
03. PhotonMap Quick

Scene adjustments

Production render

Artificially lit

Sunlight only

Print

Screen

Print

Screen

2048 or 2816
19.Metropolis Light Transport

1024 or 1280
19.Metropolis Light Transport

2048 or 2816
17.Path Tracing Progressive

1024 or 1280
17.Path Tracing Progressive

Step 1: Checking integrity and the modify/test-render loop

1. Open your SketchUp model.

2. Make sure the SketchUp window is maximized, and the button bars are as you're going to keep them throughout.

3. Click the **SU2KT** Export model to Kerkythea button.

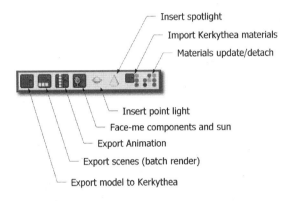

4. Select the options required in each box as shown in the following screenshot. Usually you will need Geometry and Lights unless you have used Photo-Match or stretched images over surfaces, in which case select Photomatched too.

5. Select the save location and input a file name. Click **Save**.

6. Click **Yes** to open the model in Kerkythea

7. If this is the first time you have done this, a message will come up asking you to find the `Kerkythea.exe` file.

If you haven't done this step before, you will be asked where the Kerkythea program file is located. Just navigate to where you installed Kerkythea, usually `C:/Program Files/Kerkythea Rendering System`. You'll find the program file in there (see the following screenshot). Click on it and click **Open**.

The Kerkythea program will open and you will see your view just as you had it in SketchUp. The blue dotted-line rectangle is the extent of the view in SketchUp. When you produce your rendered image, this is the area that will be outputted. If you don't like it for whatever reason, close Kerkythea and go back into SketchUp to repeat the export process.

Time for action – the modify / test loop

You're now going to do a test render to see whether the model has come in right. You'll then modify what you need to and re-import it until you get it right. Depending on how well you modeled your scene in SketchUp, this might take no time at all.

1. Import into Kerkythea (you've already done that bit).

2. Hit *V* to see the model in colored solid view.

3. Click the running man (**Start Render**).

4. Select **Camera:** (Whatever you called your scene tab in SketchUp).

5. Set **Resolution** to **640x480**.

6. Set **Settings** to **01. Ray Tracing Low**.

7. Hit **OK**.

Your scene will render and you should see the progress in the **Quick View** window.

8. Click the **Image** button.

9. If lighting isn't sufficient, select **Gamma Correction** in the **Tone Map** menu.

10. Move the sliders to increase **Exposure** or **Gamma**.

11. Check if all the textures are in correctly place. Make a note of what isn't.

12. Close the window.

13. **Zoom** (rotate middle mouse button), **Pan** (right mouse button), and **Orbit** (hold middle mouse button) to go in close to detail.

14. Repeat the render, choosing **Current View** as your **Camera**.

15. Note discrepancies as before.

16. Close Kerkythea. Go into SketchUp, make changes and go back to step 1.

What just happened?

You exported your scene from SketchUp and imported it in Kerkythea, a light simulation engine. The scene came in with the light and camera set up exactly as it was in SketchUp. You then performed a few test renders at a basic setting and small image size just to show up errors in texture import. This is the most common problem with 3D import and export with SketchUp. These settings ensured fast render times for a quick evaluation of what we need to see, and not what we don't. You will have noticed that the lighting's not great. That's because Raytracing doesn't compute light bounce as in a real life situation.

This is the export check loop which you may have to repeat a few times. The more you get used to SketchUp and Kerkythea, the less you will need to do this. But for now, there's a lot to learn by doing this exercise, so the time is well spent.

Common import bugs and how to rectify them

The most common import bugs will be seen here at this first stage. Textures do not always scale or map correctly, which is the case with many rendering applications, not just Kerkythea. Here are some common problems, likely causes, and how to deal with them:

Problem	Usually happens when...	Solution
Textures look skewed in a weird angle over lots of faces	You've used the Photo-Match feature in SketchUp	Re-export the model but tick **Export PhotoMatch** in the SU2KT settings
Textures appear skewed or incorrectly scaled in a few isolated places	You've stretched photos over a surface using the texture features in SketchUp	In SketchUp select the face, Right-Click and select Make Unique Texture
Kerkythea tells me there's no lights in the scene	You may not have exported the sun from SketchUp	In SketchUp, ensure the Shadows setting is on. Re-export and ensure you've selected **Yes** for **Export Lights**
The scene renders completely blank	There may be a face in the way of the camera which didn't show up in the SketchUp view	In SketchUp remove or move faces that could be in the way, or change the view and update the scene tab.

 When exporting plain color materials from SketchUp, texturing coordinates (UV) are not exported. So, when you come to map a new material onto this color, the texture will be all wrong. To solve this, apply a random texture material in SketchUp (any will do, as long as it uses a texture image rather than a simple color) and re-export.

Step 2: Inserting extra entourage

More and more 3D content is now being produced, or converted into, `.skp` format. So, you might already have downloaded and inserted all you need directly into SketchUp. But sometimes you'll want to insert it directly into your rendering application yourself. This can also be the best way to go simply because you won't slow down your SketchUp file with high polygon additions, and you will be able to make use of the large amounts of free `.3ds` files we discussed in Chapter 6, *Entourage the SketchUp Way*.

So, now it's time to get to grips with the Kerkythea interface. You may have been a "Have a go hero" in Chapter 6 and realized you needed some more guidance. Let's cover this now.

Time for action – test rendering models in Kerkythea

Here's how to check if models you've downloaded will render correctly in your scene. For insertion into Kerkythea, the best model file formats to go for are 3DS or OBJ.

1. Download and unzip your files into an easily found directory.

2. In Kerkythea, go to **File | Open** and find the model file.

3. Once the model is open in Kerkythea, hit *V* to go to solid view.

4. Here you can see if the model and textures have imported correctly.

5. Hit the **Start Render** button and use the settings shown in the following screenshot:

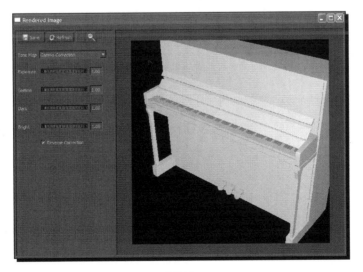

6. If there are no lights, click **Yes** to accept some default lighting.

7. A window will open with the rendered image. Here you can check more or less what the rendered model will look like in your scene.

What just happened?

You've done a quick render of the downloaded entourage just to check if it's fine to use. If the model doesn't have materials attached correctly, you might be able to fix it by assigning other materials to it in Kerkythea. This is covered later in the chapter. It's easiest for materials that don't use a texture image, such as metals, plastics, and other colored surfaces. Alternatively, you can try to find another better model instead.

Time for action – manipulating entourage in Kerkythea

Kerkythea has a slightly clunky interface, as do most rendering applications. That's why in Chapter 3, I suggested doing all design and composition of the scene in SketchUp. But once you learn the basics in Kerkythea it's perfectly possible to insert, move, and scale stuff in Kerkythea. Inserting entourage directly into Kerkythea has the advantage of keeping your SketchUp scene uncluttered, import the 3DS format better, and will also allow you to use the OBJ format not supported in SketchUp. You will use the entourage place markers you set up in Chapter 3 to guide where and at what scale to put it, then hide the place markers.

> **Selection in Kerkythea**
>
> Throughout this *Time for Action*, remember to revert to having the **Select** icon pressed in order for these steps to work (top of the main window). Editing or moving won't work if any of the view manipulation buttons are selected. See the diagram of the Kerkythea interface that follows.

1. Download a furniture model. Extract the ZIP file.

2. Click **File | Merge**.

3. Set the selections as seen previously, to leave your scene intact and just import the furniture.

4. You can see the Kerkythea interface in the following diagram:

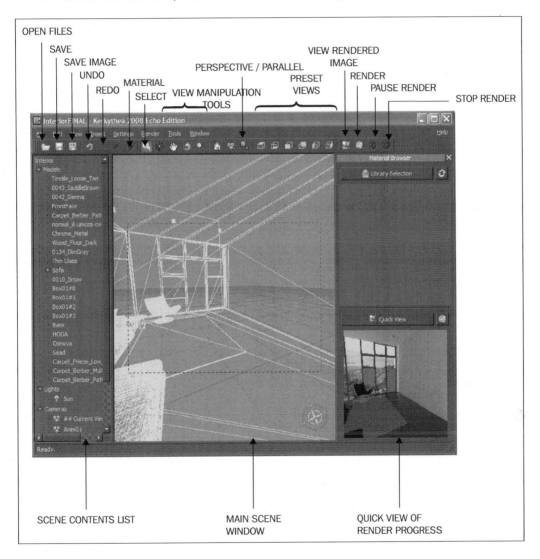

5. The model should have imported near the origin point, so click the **Top** preset view and use the scroll button and the right mouse button to scroll and pan to the origin.

6. My piano has come in far too large. First we need to select all the geometry making up the piano. Select them on the list (they should be the last few items on the **Models** list). When you select them, they'll go yellow, so you can see if you've got it right (see the following screenshot).

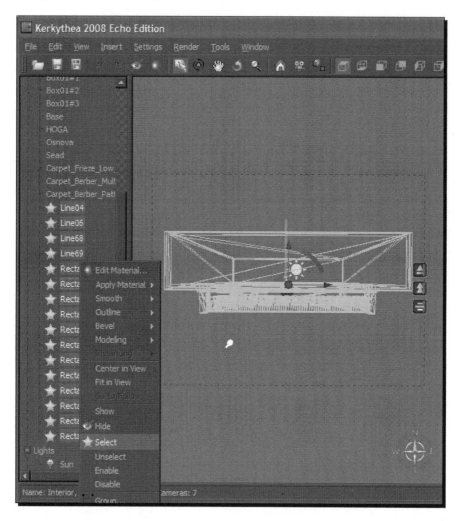

7. Right-click and select **Group**.

8. Name it *Piano* and hit **OK**.

9. Now you can select and modify the Piano in one go.

10. Select it, then go to **View | Gizmo | Scale**.

11. You can now scale the model up or down by clicking and dragging on the little box at the centre of the Gizmo.

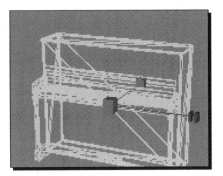

12. Go to **View | Gizmo | Translate/Rotate**.

13. Click and drag on any of the arrows to move in x, y, or z axes.

14. Click and drag the mouse on an arc segment to rotate.

15. Clicking **Parallel/Perspective** can help you line up and scale your model, as you can see in the following screenshot:

16. If you have set up place marker entourage in SketchUp, this will be really useful to help you orientate the new entourage.

17. You can now select and hide the place marker entourage (right-click on the list and select **Hide**).

What just happened?

You merged a model into your scene, and threw away all the settings (camera, lights, and so on) that you didn't want to import. You grouped geometry to make a selectable object. And you've learned how to scale, rotate, and move using the Gizmo tools. You also had a quick look at the Kerkythea interface. Most of the buttons there will become obvious once we come across them in the chapter.

Step 3: Defining the lighting

We need to check whether the light we have added to the scene (in this case the sun alone) is adequate and pleasing to the eye. We can do this with a simple light test. When applying extra lights at the end of this chapter we'll be spending much more time on this check because we will want to balance the strength of several light sources. The lighting test is conducted on a "clay model" of your scene. The reason for it is that we can focus on light alone without being sidelined by other issues. It will also speed up the render significantly by having only simple materials (clay) to render. Moreover, because all the model will have a light grey, matt surface, you'll be able to see exactly where light is falling and how strongly.

Time for action

1. In Kerkythea, go to **Insert | Globals** and select a sky (you will need to have installed some skies already from the Kerkythea library at `www.kerkythea.net`).

2. Select all windows in the scene. Right-click and select **Hide**.

3. Select the running man (**Start Render**).

4. Set **Camera**. (Whatever you called you scene tab in SketchUp).

5. Set **Resolution** to **640x480**.

6. Set **Settings** to **21. Clay Render (PhotonMap - Quick)**.

7. Click **OK**.

8. Now view the image to see if you like the lighting.

What just happened?

You chose the Clay Render preset, which converted all the materials to a basic matt grey. This is very render efficient because Kerkythea doesn't have to calculate reflection or highlights. If all materials change to clay, see-through materials like windows might now block light. So, you hid them temporarily to ensure light came through. This clay render allows you to see where the light is distributed.

You can now make changes to time and date back in SketchUp as required to alter the sun angle. Maybe the shadows aren't quite where you want them. If the amount of light needs adjustment you can also alter the exposure in the image view window.

> Some globals settings change your sun setup. If you notice this, you can reset the sun back to how you had it in SketchUp. Go to **File | Merge**, set everything as **Keep Current** and set the lights to **Replace With New - Throw Away Current**. Now select the file you exported from SketchUp and hit **OK**.

Have a go hero – adjusting lights in Kerkythea

There's also lots you can do to alter your lighting within Kerkythea. Try these two now to see what effect they have on your Clay Render.

To change the intensity/colour of the sky

1. Go to **Settings | Sun and Sky | Skip (sun already exists) | Intensity**.

2. Or, go to **Insert | Globals** and select another sky.

3. In the main window, select the sun and any other lights, right-click, and select **Disable**.

Now when you render you can see what effect the sky's ambient light is having on its own. Ambient light is always there even when the sun isn't visible. It's caused by the clouds and other particles in the air receiving sunlight and passing it on indirectly.

To change strength of the sun

1. Select **Sun** in the left selection pane.

2. Right-click and select **Edit Light**. Change the **Radiance** value or select a different color.

3. Change the **multiplier** to increase or decrease the light strength, as you can see in the following screenshot:

4. Make each of these changes and note the difference in render time and light quality.

 To obtain and compare render times, go to **Window | Console Log**. Scroll down and read the last line for the last render you did.

If you hid glass during this step, remember to unhide it before you carry on. Right-click on the material in the list and select **Show**.

Step 4: Refining materials

As you discovered in Chapter 1, *Quick Start Tutorial* tweaking the materials you already set up in SketchUp is really all you need to do to achieve a realistic render. So, in this step we'll stick with that method for most of the materials in your scene. In addition you will want to replace the materials that are:

◆ **Translucent**: Glass objects, windows, and liquids
◆ **Metallic**: Such as gold, silver, steel, and chrome
◆ **Plastic**: Shiny or glossy plastic objects render better using the library materials

Have a go hero – applying preset materials in Kerkythea

You've already set up your scene with the correct lighting and texturing. It is now time to make the best of Kerkythea's materials libraries in your scene. Let's have a go at this using a metallic material.

1. Select a material in the main window you want to make metallic.
2. In the list on the left of the screen, notice which item on the list has a yellow star next to it. This is the one you selected.

3. Right-click on this. Select **Apply Material**. Pick a material pack (you will have already installed some of these) and select a metallic material. Here's what that would look like with the Metals library:

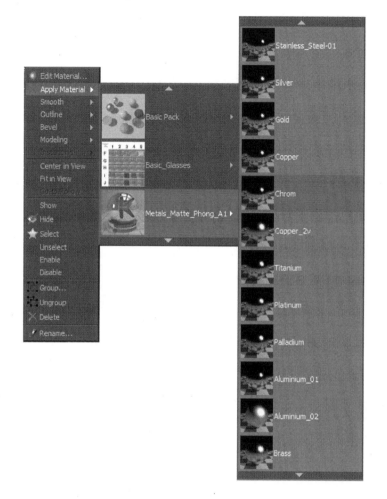

Go through other materials like this. Change only the materials you couldn't create in SketchUp, such as the ones previously listed. These will all render better using the Kerkythea preset materials you've installed from the Kerkythea website (see also Chapter 2 for how to install these). But bear in mind, every additional one of these you use will increase render time. To check how your scene is getting along, use the same render settings as in *Step 1*.

Modifying SketchUp materials for render

For most outdoor scenes, the only materials you will need to change are windows, water, and metals. The rest of the time the colors and textures you set up in SketchUp will render just fine as they are. That's because most outdoor materials are matt, not shiny or reflective. They have bumpy surfaces, but that's already shown in the SketchUp materials because they're derived from photos of real objects with real shadows and lighting. You're now going to add a little reflection and shininess to some of the materials already in your SketchUp scene. You already touched on this in Chapter 1.

Time for action – adding specularity and reflections

Go through the SketchUp materials in your scene and add specularity (highlights) and reflectivity where necessary like this:

1. In Kerkythea go to **Settings | Materials....**

2. Right-click a tile and select **Select All**.

3. Right-click and select **Rebuild Selected**.

4. Thumbnails will update showing previews of the materials, like in the following screenshot. The left-hand pane shows the materials in your scene, and the right-hand pane shows materials in a library if you have opened one.

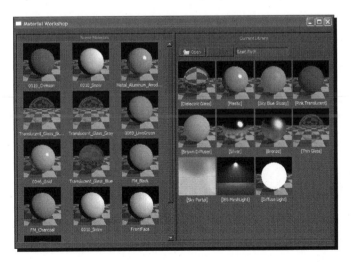

5. Double-click on a material in the left-hand pane that you think could do with some specular highlights.

6. Once in the material editor, right-click on **Specular** and select the first icon (**Add Colour**).

7. Drag the cursor along only the right-hand edge of the triangle. Here you are selecting a shade of grey, no color (see the following screenshot). Select a very light grey.

8. Click **Accept**.

9. Look at the thumbnail (top left).

10. Now click on the icon next to **Specular** and change the grey to nearly black. Can you see what changes in the thumbnail?

11. Click **Apply Changes** and **Close Editor**.

12. Do the same with the **Reflection** channel and note what happens to the thumbnail.

What just happened?

The quantity of reflection and specularity of a material can be controlled by assigning a shade of grey to the channel. Black for none, and white for lots. You can select color too if you want, but for most materials this would not be correct. Think of the grey level as just a way of visually assigning a value. Notice when you click **OK**, the value has changed to between 0% and 100%, corresponding to the level of grey you selected.

This is just about all you need to know to get great looking Architectural Visuals using SketchUp with Kerkythea. You will use Kerkythea simply to create more realistic light, shadows and reflections where SketchUp can't. So, congratulations are in order! If you've started at the beginning of the book and worked through, you've now learned 90% of what you need to create great photo-real renders. Stop, pause, and ponder for a minute on what you've just learned, and don't be fooled by how easy it was to achieve. Just remember this golden rule:

Most architectural materials can be rendered straight from SketchUp or by adding specular and reflection. It is only when you deviate from this that you have to spend ages learning and fine tuning Kerkythea.

Time for action – controlling reflections in glass

1. In Kerkythea select a window in your scene. The material name should highlight in the list.

2. Right-click on this material and select **Apply Material | Basic Pack | Thin Glass**.

3. You've now assigned the basic glass material to your windows.

    If you rendered now you would get glass that looked like this:

    So, let's alter the glass to reflect more of the sky as it's a sunny day.

4. Right-click again and **Edit Material**. You're taken to the **Material Editor**.

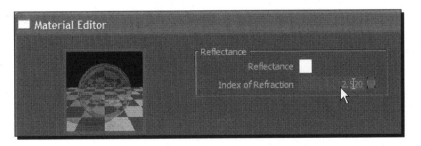

5. Here you're going to type over the value for an **Index of Refraction** to make the glass more reflective. Type in *2.5*. Notice the thumbnail preview image has changed.

6. You can also click on the square next to Reflectance and change the color value. Try a 50% grey.

7. Click **Apply Changes** then **Close Editor**.

Here's the same window with 50% grey and **Index of Refraction set** to **5** so you can see a pronounced effect. Notice the indoor light is only just visible?

What just happened?

You've assigned the basic glazing material to the windows on your building. If you're doing an external render looking at the outside of a building you usually don't need to look inside the rooms. You'll want to have more sky or scenery reflected in the windows. You accomplish this by simply changing the **Index of Refraction** value. The higher value you use, the less the window will allow you to see through it, and the more reflection you will see. However, when you do this the window will have a washed out white look to it. You can remedy this by selecting a grey color in the reflectance channel.

Step 5: Testing the production render

You're now ready to do a "dress rehearsal" of your final render, just to smooth out any other issues and make the final changes. This will be a copy of what you will produce with the final render, but at a lower resolution image and lower quality setting.

Time for action

1. Click **Start Render** and select your required camera/scene.

2. Set **Resolution** to **800x600.**

3. Select **PhotonMap Quick** and click **OK**

4. Allow it to render out to the end. This will produce a test render with the correct textures, lighting, shadows, and light bounce (combining both the test methods you used earlier).

5. Go make a cup of tea or coffee.

Here's my test render using PhotonMap Quick.

What just happened?

The PhotonMap group of settings uses Global Illumination to work out not only where light strikes a surface, but also how those surfaces will provide indirect light. It's like if you shone a spotlight at the ceiling, the whole room would be lit by the glow of light bounced from the ceiling. So, PhotonMap is an accurate light simulator that will give you an accurate idea of what your production render will look like. You chose "Quick" to force the light engine to take some shortcuts to speed things up, and you also set the image resolution to 800x600 to reduce the amount of detail the renderer had to cope with.

Can I simplify materials to reduce render time?

When you get back from making the tea, if the render is still less than half way through (the window title shows you a percentage complete), you might want to press the red stop button and simplify some materials in order to reduce render time. If you've used bump maps (see later in the chapter), metals, or lots of reflective surfaces, ask yourself if you really need them. You might be able to change those materials for a simpler plastic material or a texture. Bear in mind that however long the test render took, the production render will take many times longer than this. So, the primary focus of your test production render is to check your full render won't take days. For example, I have done test renders which were only 1% done after an hour. That's an alarm bell that something's wrong.

Forum assistance

If you have a render that's taking far too long, you've checked your materials and settings and still don't know why, try asking for help on the Kerkythea forum. The users there can often come up with the solution straight away.

You can now make other small changes too if you need to. Then when you're happy with the test image, and it's rendering quickly enough, go to Step 6 to give it the full works! Sometimes you may even think the image is already good enough for what you want to use it for. In this case, you may not need a production render. Just notch up the settings a little to **PhotonMap – Medium + AA 0.3,** and re-render. This is a great, rapid, render setting I use all the time. "AA" means **Anti-aliasing**, which is used to get rid of jagged edges for a smoother image.

Step 6: Production render

So, imagine you've spent all of your adult life, and most of your childhood, planning to take over the world. You've employed despicably able scientists and morally short-circuited engineers from all over the world to design and build you a secret under-water bunker complete with nuclear rockets. These are aimed at all the important centers of world government. As you unclip the steel cover from the big red button, you take a moment to breathe in..

And that's how you should be feeling now! The button's ready to be pressed. You've waited oh so long for this. So lets breathe in... and do it.

No, not the rockets! I meant the render!

Time for action – settings for a render using only sunlight

For the lighting setup you've been using so far in this chapter, which would apply for the majority of outdoor scenes, you've used only the sun and sky for light. This is brought over automatically from SketchUp. For this kind of scene, preset **17. Path Tracing Progressive** is a really good render setting. You will be able to get it going and stop it whenever you feel the quality is up to scratch.

1. Hit the **Start Render** button.

2. Select the camera.

3. Now choose a resolution: 2048 or 2816 widths are great for large prints, 1024 and 1280 widths will look good on screen. 1600 is a compromise if you need to reduce render times.

4. Select **17. Path Tracing Progressive**.

5. In **Threads**, select the highest number shown. This means your computer will be entirely busy with rendering so you may not be able to use it for anything else at the same time.

6. Select **Apply** then click **Yes** if a message comes up.

7. Click **Cancel** to exit this dialog box for now.

8. Select the Sun in the list on the left and right-click and select **Edit Light**.

9. Tick the **Soft Shadows** box and click **OK**.

10. Go back to **Start Render**.

11. Hit **OK** and go do something else for a while! Your render will turn out great because you already made sure it looked good in the test render stages.

Saving the final image

12. When you're happy, click the **Stop** button.

13. Click the **Image** button.

14. Use the **Gamma** sliders if necessary.

15. Hit **Save** and type in a filename.

16. Select either PNG or TIFF in the **File Filter** box.

What just happened?

After 40 or 50 passes the image should be done . You can leave it longer or stop it earlier, it's up to you. Don't worry about the slight "grainy" quality of the image, as you'll learn how to remove this in Chapter 9, *Important Compositing and After Effects in GIMP*. Here's my final daylight render:

Step 7: Post production renders

You might have thought you were finished, but not quite yet. There are a few highly specialized renders that you need to take if you really want your image to stand out. These special renders will allow you to do all sorts of post-processing wizardry in GIMP, which is the subject of the next chapter.

Time for action – the Depth Render

1. Using exactly the same settings as before, render at preset **24. Depth Render**.

2. In the **Rendered Image** window lower the **Gamma** setting until you can make out a difference in shade between the foreground and background.

3. Save the image as a PNG

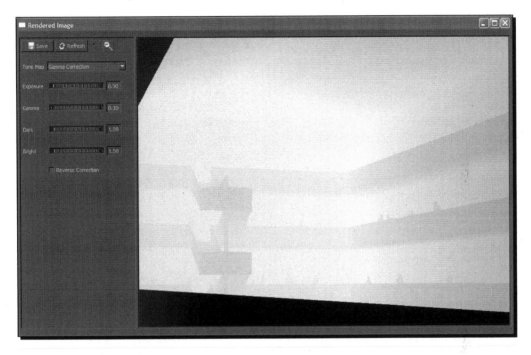

What just happened?

The depth render shows foreground in black, background in white, and objects in between as shades of grey. You'll use this to tell GIMP what to blur for out of focus parts of the image to simulate a real photograph. Focus is yet another way of drawing the eye into parts of the image you want to draw attention to.

Mask render

With a mask render you can select anything you individually want to have the outline to. The render will show whatever you selected as white, and the rest as black. This is especially useful when you need to replace the outdoor view through windows. You'll do this in Chapter 9.

Time for action

1. Using the mouse, highlight everything under **Models** in the tree view on the left.

2. Right-click and click **Select**.

3. Click on your window glazing, right-click and de-select.

4. Render using preset **25. Mask Render** and select the same image size as your final render.

5. Click the **Image** button.

6. Set **Tone Map** to **None.**

7. Save the image as a PNG.

Artificially lit indoor scenes

As you've seen, you can get a really nice, really quick render using SketchUp's sun and sky settings without changing much in Kerkythea. SketchUp passes on all the necessary environment information on to Kerkythea. But what about indoor scenes with artificial lighting? In this *Time for action* we're going to take the same scene and turn off the natural light, then add lights back in SketchUp to export to our Kerkythea scene. You can use any scene you used for the first half of the chapter.

Time for action – creating spot-lights in SketchUp

1. You will only be using SketchUp to set up and export lights. So you can hide all unnecessary geometry to help you place lights more easily. Your main scene is already open in Kerkythea.

2. Click the **Insert Spotlight** button on the **SU2KT** toolbar.

3. Click somewhere on the ceiling to place it.

4. Move the cursor down along the blue axis and click near the floor.

5. Click **OK** to accept the default settings.

6. **Export Model** to Kerkythea.

7. Select **Yes** on **Export Lights** only. Leave the rest set to **No**.

8. Name the file "spotlights only" and click **Save**.

9. When asked to open in Kerkythea, click **No** because we want to merge instead

10. Back in Kerkythea select **File | Merge**.

11. Set **Lights** to **Replace With New – Throw Away Current**.

12. Change all other settings to **Keep Current – Throw Away New**.

13. Click **OK**. Select the "spotlights only" file and click **OK**.

14. The new light imports into Kerkythea.

15. Perform a clay render as you did earlier in the chapter.

What just happened?

You set up a spotlight in SketchUp with default settings. You then moved the cursor down along the blue axis to show the spotlight where to point to. The further you move the cursor before you click, the greater the light power. Using the **Merge** function instead of Open allowed you to import only that single light into Kerkythea and leave everything else the same. You performed a clay render to check the lighting as before. Notice that the sun and sky still light the scene, and these still need to be switched off. Do this now as follows.

Time for action – switching off sun and sky lighting

1. Right-click on the Sun in the left-hand list. Click **Disable**.

2. Now go to **Settings | Sun and Sky | Next**, and set **Sky Type** to **Background colour**.

3. The Map/Color preview image will go black. Click **Finish**.

4. Zoom in closer to the area containing the light.

5. Do a clay render using **Current View** in the **Camera** list.

6. You should get an image like the one shown in the preceding screenshot.

What just happened?

You disabled the sun. But this is not the only light present in Kerkythea for a daylight render. The effect of the sky is present too. So, you switched this to black to turn it off. In reality a night scene is also lit by the moon and stars, and this can be simulated by turning the **Intensity** setting down instead. You did a clay render on a single light so you can check the power setting before you assign more lights in SketchUp. Check out the render now and note if the light needs to be brighter or less bright. To change this, do the same as you did with the sun earlier, changing **Light Power**. Re-render and note the power setting once you've got it right.

Changing light parameters in SketchUp

You can also change light settings in SketchUp before you export the lights to Kerkythea.

1. Back in SketchUp, click on the spotlight. Right-click and select **SU2KT:Edit Spotlight**.

2. Change the **Light Power** setting to the value you worked out in Kerkythea.

3. Copy this light wherever you need it.

4. You now have a basic idea of the light power you need. Alter the settings for individual lights in SketchUp higher or lower now if you need to.

5. Re load into Kerkythea and re-render. Below you can see the scene with the same spotlight copied multiple times, then adjusted as necessary.

Have a go hero

Omni lights are just the same to set up as spotlights, except they don't have direction, hotspot, and falloff settings. Try adding some more lights in SketchUp, both Spot and Omni, and altering the settings in SketchUp. Try altering falloff and hotspot settings too. Export the new lights and replace them in Kerkythea. Do a test render to see what effect these settings have. This is the best way to learn, remember, and get a feel for what light settings are required.

Adding light-emitting materials

To finish off the lighting in this scene we need some larger ceiling lights. In order to simulate this, you're going to create some simple rectangles in SketchUp and set up a light-emitting material in Kerkythea. It's similar to the one you did in Chapter 1, where you used a ready made diffused light material, but this time you'll create the material yourself.

Time for action – radiant materials

1. In SketchUp, draw a rectangle where you want a ceiling light.

2. Make sure the grey (front) face is facing down.

3. Assign a color material to it, a material you've not used elsewhere in this scene.

4. Make a component of the rectangle and copy it to several locations near the ceiling.

5. Select each instance of this component.

6. Export to Kerkythea selecting **Export Selection Only** and **Export Geometry** as you can see here:

7. In Kerkythea go to **File | Merge**, and set **Models** to **Merge - Add New to Current**.

8. Leave all other settings as **Keep Current – Throw Away New**.

9. In the list, right-click on the material you just assigned to the rectangle.

10. Select **Edit Material**.

11. Next to where it says **Diffuse**, right-click on the color and click the red cross (**Delete Texture**).

12. You've now removed that color from the light you set up in SketchUp. You've also removed the diffuse channel. This means the object won't attract diffused light from elsewhere, which would be pointless.

13. In **Radiance** select a pure white color and change **Power** to a higher number. In this large scene a high number—between 5 and 10—works well. You'll work out your own value when you do a clay render in a moments time.

14. Click **Apply Changes**.

15. Select all the spotlights. Right-click and select **Disable**.

16. Now do a Clay Render like this one. It should show only the ceiling lights.

What just happened?

You disabled all the spotlights so that you could check the level of lighting from the rectangular overhead lights by themselves. You changed the material so that the rectangles act as light-emitting materials, and deleted the diffuse color so that they would not absorb light themselves. You did a clay render to see the effect. Notice how uniformly the light is spread from a rectangular light source, just as you would have from normal strip lights. You can now enable all the other lights you disabled earlier and clay render again with all the lights on.

The final indoor render

You are now ready to render a preview image and final image of your artificially lit indoor scene. Because the scene is complex with many light sources and reflective materials, we're going to do a preview render with setting **01. Ray Tracing - Low**. This won't calculate light bounce (Global Illumination), but this doesn't matter when you've got a lot of lights in a scene as you can see in the following screenshot. Most areas will be lit directly. And what's most important, your render won't grind to a halt!

Go ahead and do a test render with preset **01. Ray Tracing – Low**.

The setting we're going to use for this indoor scene is preset **19. Metropolis Light Transport**. This setting works really quickly when there are lots of lights and lots of reflective surfaces. So, select your image resolution and hit **OK**. The final image is shown below after about 50 passes. It's now ready to go on to post-processing in GIMP; the subject of the next chapter.

Advanced materials techniques

Now that you've learned all you need to know for success the majority of the time, here's some other skills and techniques you can learn if you want to. You'll find them useful, but not essential. So, if you want to, you can just come back to this part when you need it. This is by no means a complete description of all the features you'll find in a rendering program. It's just some exercises showing you a couple of advanced functions which I think you'll find useful in your SketchUp workflow.

Time for action – applying Alpha transparency to face-me components

If you have photo-based 2D trees or people in your SketchUp scene, these might have Alpha maps. This means that parts of the image are made transparent. To view this correctly in Kerkythea you may have to save the material image from SketchUp and apply it as a map in Kerkythea, otherwise it'll render like the preceding image. Confused? No need to be, it's as simple as this:

1. Open a scene in SketchUp and place a 2D tree in it from the 3D Warehouse.

2. If it's been made by using Alpha transparency, it'll look slightly fuzzy at the edges in SketchUp, like this:

3. Now go to the materials pallet and click the **In Model** tab.

4. Select the thumbnail that corresponds to the 2D tree.

5. Right-click and select **Export Texture Image** and save it in the same place as your Kerkythea scene.

6. Now export your scene to Kerkythea as usual.

7. In Kerkythea, right-click the tree material and select **Edit Material**.

8. This opens the material editor (see the following screenshot).

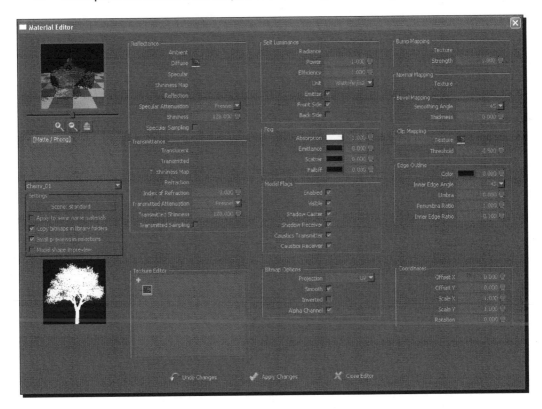

9. Click **Diffuse**.

10. Click the texture thumbnail under texture editor.

11. Under **Clip Mapping**, right-click **Texture**.

12. Select the second icon (**Add Bitmap**).

13. Select **Browse**, and find the image you saved from SketchUp.

14. Click on the thumbnail in texture editor again.

15. Then under **Bitmap Options,** tick **Alpha Channel.** (This option will only appear when you click the thumbnail).

16. The large thumbnail (bottom left) will now have changed to a black and white image showing the alpha channel (clip map).

17. Click **Apply Changes**.

18. Re-render.

19. You should now have fixed the problem as you can see here:

What just happened?

2D trees and people are often created as PNG files with transparency. The transparency information is saved in the form of a channel, called the Alpha channel. Normal images have just three channels, red, green, and blue. This is just an extra one. All you've done here is to tell Kerkythea where to find that Alpha channel, and that you want it to be used to clip the image. If you want to you can create clip maps manually in GIMP for your materials. For example, to create holes in a fence.

Have a go hero

Have a go at making a clip map. To do this just make a copy of the texture image and open it in GIMP. Then create a new black layer and paint white on it wherever you want a hole to be. Hide the original layer and save it as an image. Then just load the black and white image into the Clip Map slot in Kerkythea.

Creating bump map materials

Some materials need a bumpy surface to render accurately. You can do this with wood grain, leather upholstery, and even water. It's the same principle as clip maps, but this time the black and white image refers to how far the surface is raised. Try these steps to see it in action.

Time for action

1. In SketchUp draw a cube and apply a tile material to each face.

2. Set up shadows and rotate the view so that the shadows are facing towards you.

3. Go to **View | Animation | Add Scene**.

4. Export to Kerkythea.

5. In Kerkythea go to **Insert | Omnilight**. This places an omni-directional light at the location of the camera (like a headlamp) to light the scene head on.

6. Select the tile material and add a high amount specular in the material editor (say 65%) and set Shininess to 125.

7. Perform a render using **Raytracing Low**, and you'll get an image like this one:

Notice that whilst the two sides look fine, the top surface with sunlight reflecting off it looks wrong because the specular highlight is uniform (see top right of the box). This is why for outdoor scenes, where very few materials have specularity, plain flat photo textures look fine without bump. But when you have a shiny, bumpy floor indoors, we need some help!

8. In SketchUp go to the materials pallet and click **In Model**.

9. Right-click on the tile and select **Export Texture Image**.

10. Save it where you exported your Kerkythea scene.

11. In GIMP, open the image you just saved.

12. In the Layer pallet, select **New Layer** (bottom left).

13. Use the **Magic Wand** to select the tiles. Change the **Threshold** if you need to. Finding the right value for this is a matter of trial and error until you select the whole tile as you can see here:

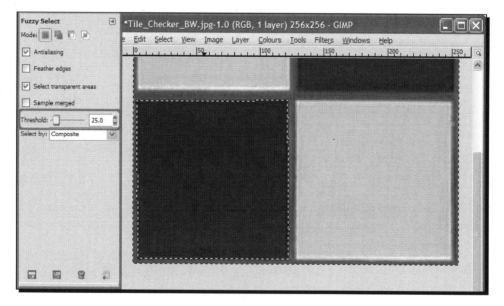

14. Hold down *Shift* and select the other tiles too.

15. Select the **Paintbucket** tool from the main tool pallet.

16. Click the double arrow under the pallet to change the foreground color to white.

17. Click on one of the tiles to fill the whole selection with white.

18. Now go to **Select | Invert**.

19. Click the double arrow again to select black foreground color and use the **Paintbucket** again in the selection.

20. Go to **Select | All** then **Filters | Blur | Gaussian Blur** to create a less sudden gradient from black to white (a less harsh bump effect in Kerkythea).

21. Set **Radius** to 2 then hit **OK**.

22. Save the image as a JPG or PNG file. You should have something like this:

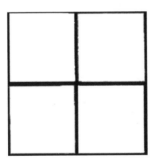

23. In Kerkythea add the image to the Bump channel of the floor tile material just like you did for the clip map.

24. Re-render using **02. Raytracing - High +AA** and see the difference!

What just happened?

You just added a black and white image to the bump channel of the floor tile material. This image tells Kerkythea that wherever there is black there should be depressions in the surface, and white should be raised. Notice how this effect is only noticeable on the surface where highlights exist. The omni light was used as a fill-in light for the sides of the box which were in shadow. When you insert an omnilight it appears at the position you're viewing from.

Pop Quiz

1. Which render setting is a good "one size fits all" setting for quick renders?

2. What does a depth render show?

3. Is it possible to import and update selected parts of a SketchUp model into a Kerkythea scene without changing the rest?

4. What's the best render preset for a sunlit scene?

5. What setting would you use if a scene has lots of lights and reflective surfaces?

Summary

In this chapter, you've learned how to take the scene you've set up in SketchUp and give it photo-realistic lighting. This is as easy as exporting the file and clicking **Start Render** in Kerkythea because SketchUp exports both Sky and Sun lighting information. You learned a time-saving method of using the right render presets in Kerkythea to preview and change materials and lighting. You then learned how to tweak SketchUp materials in Kerkythea to add a little Specular and Reflection here and there.

You also learned a few more advanced techniques which you can build on:

◆ How to replace or edit SketchUp materials within Kerkythea

◆ How to check and rectify common texturing import problems

◆ How to set up and modify lights in SketchUp and import to Kerkythea

◆ How to quickly check light levels in the scene with Clay Renders

◆ The most effective render presets for various lighting setups

◆ How to create bump materials in GIMP

◆ How to assign Alpha maps for clip mapping

Now's the time to go away and experiment with your own renders to put these techniques into practice. Why not make some great renders of your previous SketchUp projects so you can show them off and put them in a portfolio? Keep this book to hand and dip into it as and when you need it and don't forget the great help forums at www.kerkythea.net and www.cgarchitect.com, where you'll be lent a hand.

 If you want to look into other rendering software, I've listed the ones most commonly used with SketchUp in Appendix A, *Rendering Software*, along with their main features based on this book's suggested workflow. Many of these have offered discounts to readers; details can be found at www.provelo.co.uk/renderoffers/

In the next chapter, you'll learn how to further enhance your render by post-processing with GIMP.

9

Important Compositing and After Effects in GIMP

In Chapter 8, Photo-Realistic Rendering, you created a photo-real rendering of your interior or exterior architectural model in Kerkythea. That's a big achievement! But whatever you do, don't stop there! There are some important things you need to do to your image before it's truly worthy of your portfolio. Your grandma might think it's lovely as it is, but Santiago Calatrava is not going to employ you on the strength of unfinished work.

In this chapter, you're going to learn the tricks in GIMP which the pro 3D visualizers use. They probably have Photoshop with all the bells and whistles attached, but we can do it just as well in GIMP. You'll find out how GIMP can help you to:

- ◆ Modify **levels** to give ultra-realistic lighting
- ◆ Produce a **vignette** to draw the eye into your scene
- ◆ Add **bloom** to give glow to highlights
- ◆ Blur foreground or background to simulate camera **depth of field**
- ◆ Add lighting effects in GIMP
- ◆ Composite several images together to insert your model into real life scenes

It's a lot to cover, so let's get going. You can use some of the scenes you've already created in earlier chapters.

Part 1: Tweaks and lighting levels

Rendered output from Kerkythea is superb. There's no doubt about it. And that's because it's a physically accurate light simulator. When you click **Start Render** it fires light beams at the scene and recaptures them in the camera. So, it's really just a digital camera with simulated digital light. What that means to you and me, apart from the superb results, is that light levels (saturation, white balance, and so on) aren't always right, straight out of the box. And that's where GIMP comes in.

Here's the piano scene you saw in the last chapter, which went on to become the front cover image. Note the imperfections which detract from the realism:

♦ Light shades are dull and washed out

♦ No clear contrast between light and dark areas

♦ Daylight quality is somehow unrealistic

Often when you've done a render you will not be entirely pleased with the result, and won't know why. This is usually down to something called **Levels**. Let's have a go at adjusting levels in GIMP so you can see what they are, and what are their results.

Have a go hero – adjusting levels automatically

There are a lot of ways to fix the levels in a rendered image. Some of them are easy, and these are the ones you should try first. After that you'll look at the more involved way of doing it, which will usually yield better results.

1. Open your render in GIMP.

2. For a quick levels fix, first go to **Colours | Auto | Equalize**.

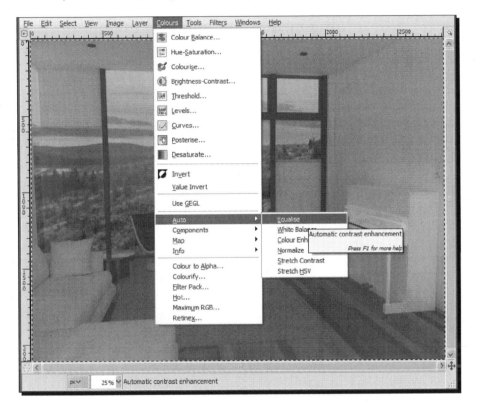

You can see five other **Auto** levels options on the menu. If **Equalize** doesn't do it for your image, hit **Edit | Undo** and try some of the others on the menu:

- ❑ **White Balance**: Corrects photos that have impure white or black colors

- ❑ **Color Enhance**: Colors should come out more vivid without changing brightness

- ❑ **Normalize**: Scans the image and stretches the brightness values across the full spectrum to make the darkest black, and the lightest white

- ❑ **Stretch Contrast**: Same as Normalize but does this for each color channel independently, so you may find that colors change
- ❑ **Stretch HSV**: Not usually used as the effects can be a bit random

3. Alternatively, if you have access to other image editing software that's designed for quick digital photo correction, try some of the auto-fix settings on those (for example, Photoshop Elements or Picasa). They tend to be very good and hassle free.

4. The last, and possibly best, way of automatically tweaking levels is to open the **Levels** dialogue and click the **Auto** button. Do this by going to **Colour | Levels**.

What just happened?

You found the color settings in GIMP and tried out a few automatic levels tools to see what they did to your image. A lot of these settings are to individual taste, but they're all there on the color menu for you to try out and see what you think. Often they won't work because the image has more than one problem. Remember to make use of the **Undo History** on the **Layers, Channels, Paths, Undo** pallet, which can be accessed in the **Windows** menu, as you experiment.

Adjusting levels manually

You're now going to learn one of the most powerful and versatile image editing techniques available. Once you get into this method you will not need any one-click presets and you'll be able to tweak light exactly how you want it. This is worth learning as it will give your images that extra edge.

Time for action – the levels dialogue

1. Once you have your image open in GIMP, go to **Colors | Levels**.

2. The levels dialogue box opens. You should see something like this:

The graph, called a histogram, shows the light values in the image (or layer) from lightest (to the left) to darkest (on the right). So, as you can see from this histogram, all the detail in the image is happening in the middle of the graph. The very light and very dark areas of the graph aren't being used at all. This makes for a very washed out, low contrast image as you can see from part of the image here:

3. Click on the black arrow on the left of the histogram and drag it to the right until you hit the base of what looks like a mountain range.

4. Do the same with the white arrow to the right. You can see where I've placed mine in the histogram shown.

5. Click **OK**. You will now have corrected the contrast in the image.

Can you see how much clearer this image is?

6. Go to the levels dialogue again and notice the change in the histogram. It might look a bit like this one:

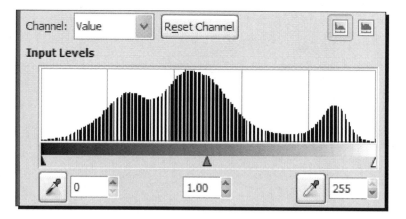

What just happened?

You took the lighting level information contained in the image and stretched the most used part to fit over the entire light range. Notice how the mountain range now fits the entire area? Each pixel in your image can now have a value of between 0 and 255, whereas before the image was confined to something like between 14 and 188 (see the first histogram). By dragging the white and black arrows you told GIMP to forget the flat areas before and after the mountain range, enhancing the contrast.

Time for action – adjusting light quantity

1. While you're still in the levels dialogue, click on the middle arrow and drag it to the left. The image preview becomes lighter.

2. Now drag it to the right. The preview image becomes darker.

3. Move it where you're happiest and click **OK**.

What just happened?

The middle arrow controls the Gamma value. This tells GIMP whether to favor the left (light) or right (dark) side of the histogram. This is the correct way to brighten the image because none of the actual image information is lost. If you close and open the levels dialogue again, you will see that the histogram has not changed in any way.

Correcting individual color channels

Now comes the really good bit; I hope you're up for a challenge. Did you know that most digital images are split up into red, green, and blue channels? Using levels you can edit each of these separately in exactly the same way as before. This will allow you to balance the light levels out perfectly and get rid of unrealistic color tints, or even introduce some for your own purposes:

- **Red**: Warmer lighting for interiors
- **Green**: Increase this for leafy outdoor scenes, but it makes interiors look ill
- **Blue**: Increase this for realistic natural light

Have a go hero

Notice above the histogram, is a box saying **Channel: Value**. This means the histogram is taking the combined value of all the red, green, and blue channels together. If you click in that box you can select any of the three color channels to edit separately. Do this now and edit the three arrows for each color separately. Once you've done all three colors, go over them again until you're happy with the result. Then before you finish, go back to **Value** and give the whole ensemble a final tweak.

Removing unwanted image noise

Now let's look at the final render from Chapter 8. If you look carefully, or zoom in to a small area of the image, you can see a speckled effect.

Grainy images like the one above are the hallmark of progressive render techniques such as **Metropolis Light Transport (MLT)** or **Path Tracing Progressive**, which you will have used for your final render in Chapter 8. It can add an appealing film grain effect a bit like the crackle on an old vinyl record. But too much crackle and we don't enjoy the performance. If you master the noise removal technique you will be shown here, you will save bags of render time, because you don't need to wait for so many render passes.

Time for action – find a way of removing noise

1. Take your final render and open it in GIMP.

2. Duplicate the layer by clicking on the button at the bottom of the **Layers** pallet.

3. Select this duplicate layer.

4. Use **Filter | Blur | Gaussian Blur**. Try a small radius of say 2-4 pixels.

5. Use the **Opacity** slider (shown in the previous screenshot) to adjust the effect of this layer on the original image beneath. It's a trade-off between less noise and more detail.

6. Here's the same area again with Gaussian Blur radius 3, and layer opacity set to 75%.

7. Create a layer mask if you want to block out areas you don't wish to apply the effect to (go ahead and check back to Chapter 7 if you can't remember how to do this, though it's not an essential step here).

8. When you're done, select the upper layer and go to **Layers | Merge Down**.

9. This makes the change permanent and puts everything back to one layer ready for you to carry out other image edits.

What just happened?

You created a slightly blurred copy of the image and overlaid it on the original. You then adjusted the opacity of the blurred layer so that the effect of the layer would reduce or increase. This way you can fine tune the effect. Getting rid of noise is never perfect. Either you will lose detail, or you will have a lot of detail but lots of noise. Of course, the alternative is to go back to Kerkythea and render for longer. Finally, you can also try the **Depth of Field** effect which you'll be covering in a few pages. An additional benefit of this is also to reduce image noise.

Do you notice it when you print?

When printing out your image, often the noise/grain doesn't show in the print. So, give it a test print and see, you may be worrying about nothing!

Have a go hero

A more involved alternative to the quick fix you've just learned is to try downloading and installing the **G'MIC** plugin for GIMP. You can find it at `http://gmic.sourceforge.net/gimp.shtml`. The dialog box within GIMP is shown here:

Here's the G'MIC version of our image after applying the **PhotoComiX** smoothing filter with the settings shown in the previous screenshot.

If you're up for it, download and install the plugin now using the instructions on the website. Open your image in GIMP and try some of the filters and settings until you get a great result.

 If you have some money to spend, **Neat Image** by ABSoft is hard to beat, with exceptional quality output, speed, and ease of use. You can get a free trail of this software at http://www.neatimage.com

Light bloom

On bright days the sun puts a halo of light round objects in direct sunlight. You can achieve this effect easily in GIMP. This is a good way to soften an image, making it more dreamlike.

Time for action

To add some soft glow to the edge of lights, take your final render and just follow these steps. Let's start with this small area of the final render:

1. Open it up and create a copy of the image layer in GIMP.

2. Use **Gaussian Blur** of radius 5-10 depending on how big the image is.

3. Now increase the brightness and contrast of this layer using **Colors | Brightness**. Contrast so you have something like this image:

4. Set the layer to **Hard Light** or **Lighten Only** and adjust the **Opacity** to get the effect you want.

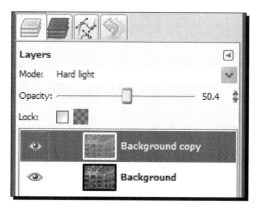

5. Go to **Layer | Merge Down** to fix the effect and allow further work on the image.

6. Here's the doctored image. You can see the light "blooms" out rather than having a sharp edge like before.

7. To see the effect more pronounced take a look at this image rendered in Modo (there are details of Modo and other renderers in the appendix). Rendering and texturing is by Ahmed Alireza and modding by Branko Jovanovic.

8. Now that you've spent some time learning that little trick, why not go back to your original image and try **Filters | Artistic | Softglow** and see which version you prefer?

What just happened?

You created a copy of the image over the top of the original one. You blurred and increased brightness to get a halo effect. Setting the upper layer to **Hard Light** meant it only changed the contrast of the layer below. After you've finished, use **Layer | Merge Down** to reduce it back to a single layer again. This allows us to do some of the other effects more easily. Then you found out the whole thing can be done automatically with the Softglow filter; such is life. But you now have two methods—a quick fix for the whole image, and a manual one so you can exactly control the effect in different parts of the image using masks.

Simulating depth of field

This is a technique you'll use all the time. It adds a photographic realism to your image like nothing else can. Depth of Field is an effect created by the aperture settings in your camera. If you have a digital "point and shoot" you probably won't even be aware of it. It basically means that what you're focused on is sharp, while the foreground and background are blurred. The reason you might want to see this effect in your renders is because that's the way we see things through our own eyes. Most things are blurred apart from what we're focusing on, therefore the focus is a way of drawing attention to a particular area or element. So, let's give it a go. The following three images illustrate this concept:

First the render itself. Notice all of it is in focus; you can see the brick pattern clearly on each box.

Here's the depth render. You learned how to produce this in the previous chapter.

And here's the final image after the effect was applied in GIMP. You can tell the focus is on the box in the foreground, because the other two boxes are progressively more blurred.

Time for action – depth of field using a depth render

You will have output a depth render from the previous chapter. It should look something like this one here. Shades of black are closer to the camera, and whiter shades furthest away.

1. Open your main image in GIMP.

2. Go to **File | Open as Layers....**

3. Select the depth render image and click **OK**. You should now have your render as the background layer, and the depth map on top.

4. Click on the Foreground square in the main tool pallet. You are taken to the **Change Foreground Color** dialog box.

5. Click on the eyedroper tool (circled in the following screenshot).

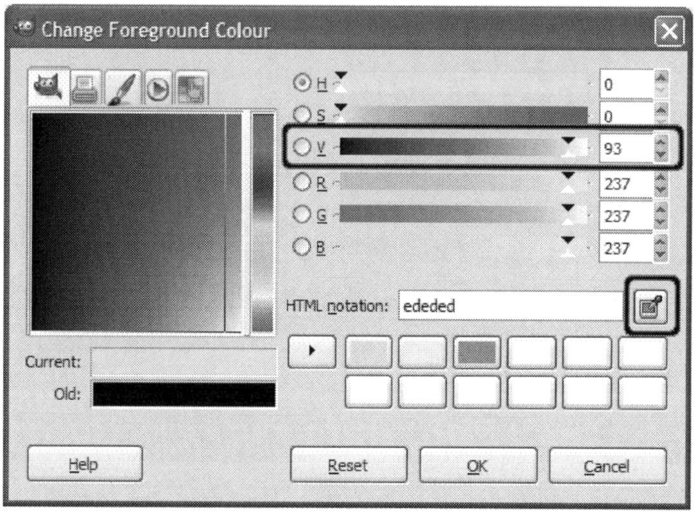

6. Make sure the depth render layer is selected, and now move the eye dropper tool over the image.

7. Hold down the left mouse button and watch the **V** value change (circled in the previous screenshot). It moves between **0** and **100** as you move it around over the depth map, depending on the grayscale value.

8. The values you are reading are a percentage of how far away something is from the camera. Note down the value you get when you pass over the area that you want to be in focus.

9. That's all you need from this dialogue. Click **Cancel**.

10. Download the **Focus Blur** plugin for GIMP from `www.registry.gimp.org` focus blur binaries the `focusblur.exe` file into the GIMP plugins folder (usually `Program Files\gimp-2.0\lib\gimp\2.0\plugins`).

11. Save your progress and restart GIMP and you will be able to access the new plugin.

12. Turn off the depth map layer (use the eye icon) so that you can see the main image.

13. Select the main image layer so that the following **Blur** filter works on that layer.

14. Access the plugin by going to **Filters | Blur | Focus Blur**.

15. Select **Gaussian**, change the **Radius** setting to control amount of blur required (according to your preference).

16. You can see the effect in the preview image. Move around with the sliders to see more of the image.

17. Select **Use Depth map** and select the depth render layer in the list box.

18. In the **Focal Depth** box, input the value you noted previously.

19. And that's it! Click **OK** to apply the effect.

20. You can do this for any percentage value (**1** to **100**) to blur different areas of the image.

21. You can see in my image that the balustrade has been blurred and the stair remains sharp.

 Apply some blur to the depth map image first. Sometimes this gives a better effect. The Kerkythea depth render isn't perfectly accurate at sharp corners and valleys, so applying a little blur can smooth this error out.

Lighting effects

What about some of the light effects you can add at the post processing stage? Let's not leave those out. Some exceptional artists can render a scene with just plain ambient light and then add all the other lighting using image editing software afterwards. So, while you probably don't need to do that, you might want to know how to do it as part of your toolbox. For example, you might wish to put some shining dots where the ceiling light bulbs would be. This technique is often applied with night scenes and street lighting.

Time for action – adding light effects in GIMP

Open your artificially lit render from Chapter 8.

1. Go to **Filters | Light and Shadow | Supernova**.

2. Click the zoom icon to zoom closer in the preview image.

3. Click where you want the centre of the light to be.

4. Adjust **Color**, **Radius**, and **Spokes** as necessary (refer to the following screenshot).

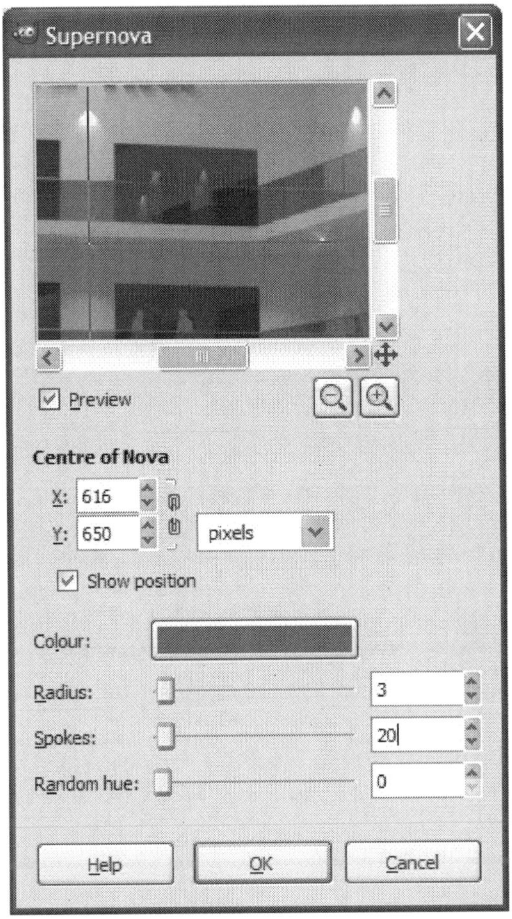

5. The values for **Radius** and **Spokes** I've used are 5 and 100 respectively, for the light you can see on the right of the preview image, but have reduced the values for the current light because it's at a shallower angle to the camera.

6. Repeat for each light bulb.

Here's the image with these Supernovas applied:

Have a go hero – discovering weird and wonderful lighting filters

GIMP has some great, some not so great, and some plain "far out" lighting effects that you've just got to sample for yourself to believe. They can be found under **Filters | Light and Shadow**. Try some of these out on your image and see what effects you can get. You might find some that are so good that you can leave out some lights in SketchUp or Kerkythea and add them in quicker GIMP on your next project.

Pop quiz

Now it's time for a quiz because I need to check whether you've really been listening; not daydreaming about the new chicken double mayo with mung-bean and sprout salad bap at Burger King. You'll have plenty of time to get your chops round that little beauty after your homework! But for now, clear your mind of temporal bliss and concentrate... Ready?

1. What are the options within GIMP for reducing noise in rendered images?

2. What color are the separate channels in an RGB image?

3. What do you do to the levels histogram to increase contrast?

4. Where do you get the figure between 1 and 100 to put into the depth of field box in the Focus Blur dialog?

Using a vignette layer to finish the image

When you're happy with your image, all that's left to do is further draw the viewer's eye into the image. This final process is the **Vignette**, which is a posh word for a dark border.

You've already learned all the skills you need for this in Chapter 7, *Non-Photo-Real with Sketchup*. It was slightly different in that case because you used a white border to let the image fade out at the edges. With photo-real images you'll darken the edges slightly instead.

Time for action – fade out the edges with a vignette

To draw the eye to the areas of the image you wish to focus on, parts of it need to be lit more than others. The edges especially should be darker. The following screenshot is an exaggerated image showing where the vignette could go on this particular image:

1. In GIMP, create a new layer. For **Layer Fill Type** select **Transparency**. This is your vignette layer.

2. Select the **Paintbrush** tool.

3. Click on **Foreground & background colors** (shown circled in the screenshot) to get colors back to black and white.

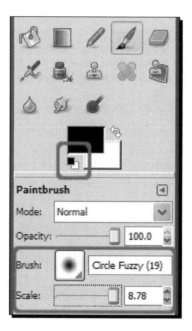

4. Select a fuzzy circle brush and increase the scale to get a bigger brush.

5. Start round the edges of the image and apply black paint all round.

6. Change the brush **Opacity** to **50** and gradually come in from the edge where you want slightly more light.

7. Repeat with the setting still at 50 to overlay your paintbrush strokes, as you can see from the exaggerated image.

8. You can use a 20 opacity brush for fine tuning if you need to.

9. Remember, work fast because you can change this at any time. Simply click the eraser and paint over the areas you need to alter. Set the Eraser Tool at **50** if you need a less definite effect.

10. As you've done this really roughly, do a **Gaussian Blur** on the vignette layer at a high radius value (**20** - **100** pixels) to smooth things out a little.

11. Now lower the **Layer Opacity** until you have just a subtle effect (I've used 30).

What just happened?

You added a final flourish to help draw the viewer's eye into the picture. This was achieved with a simple darkened overlay. Using this process you can emphasize or minimize certain areas of the composition. Here are the two images for comparison:

That's the end of this section of the chapter related to image enhancements. You have learned how to give your image that extra pizzazz that makes all the difference!

Part 2: Compositing multiple images

It's time in this second half of the chapter to go on to compositing multiple images. You will have learned a lot of the skills needed here already in Chapter 7, so, you're already half way there! The following few pages will equip you to stitch together finished images from different component parts.

Time for action – using the Kerkythea mask render for windows

You'll find this trick useful again and again in all sorts of ways as you progress with your post-processing skills. We're going to go through just one application of this, but there are all sorts of other uses you'll discover yourself. Remember in that Chapter 8, *Photo-Realistic Rendering*, you removed the windows in Kerkythea and executed a mask render. You'll put this to good use now.

1. Open your day-lit scene in GIMP.

2. Go to File | **Open as Layer...**, select the mask render and click **OK**.

3. Repeat with a sky image, or even a holiday snap with some sky showing.

4. Select the sky image layer and use **Move** to place it over the window area. You may need to resize it using **Layer | Scale Layer**.

5. Select the mask render in the layer pallet. Now go to **Select | All**.

6. Go to **Edit | Copy**.

7. Right-click on the sky layer and select **Add Layer Mask | Add** and click **Add**.

8. Now click on the layer mask that just appeared in the layer pallet.

9. Go to **Edit | Paste**.

10. Select the pasted item in the **Layer** Pallet. Then right click and **Anchor**.

11. You have now set the **Mask Render** to the layer mask associated with the sky layer. But it still looks wrong! That's because you need to invert the mask.

12. Select the mask, then go to **Colours | Invert**.

13. Now set the sky layer to **Multiply**.

Here's the image and layer stack you should end up with:

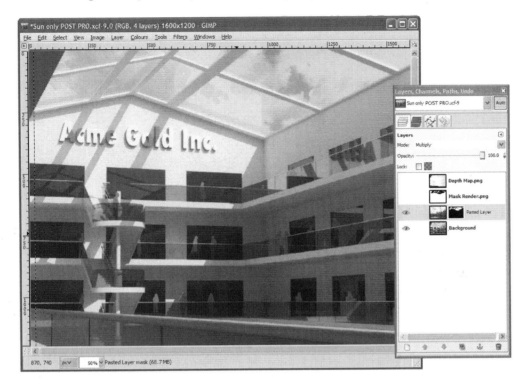

What just happened?

You produced a mask render in Kerkythea which had all the image in black apart from the outside showing through the windows, which was left white. You assigned this mask render to the mask channel of a sky image, so that only the sky portion showed through. This sky layer was set to **Multiply** so that both the sky and the reflections in the glass would show together.

This technique is great when you don't have a sky or background image in an indoor render. You just add it later in GIMP.

SketchUp window reflections without rendering

With this technique you can take your SketchUp image and instantly add sky reflections to your windows without rendering! Take a look at the following image. Apart from my badly applied brick texture, can you distinguish it from a render?

I din't think you would. So, follow this simple *Time for action* to learn the trick.

Time for action

1. Open a SketchUp scene and zoom in to a window looking from below, like the one shown here.

2. Output a colored view in your preferred style.

3. Use the same view and click the shaded view button.

4. In the **Styles** Pallet, turn off **Display Edges** and **Profiles**.

5. In the **Shadow Settings** pallet change **Light** to *0*, and **Dark** to *100*

6. You can see the results here:

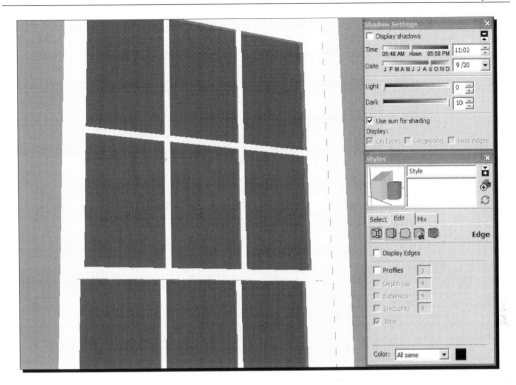

7. You will now have an image with flat colors like the one in the previous screenshot. Output this too, making sure you haven't changed the view from the one before.

8. In GIMP, open the images as layers, as you've done previously.

9. Click on the flat colors layer.

10. Select the **Select by Color Tool** from the main tool pallet.

11. Click somewhere on the window. This will select only the window glazing.

12. Insert a sky image as before and create a layer mask for this new layer.

13. Select **Selection** and click **Add.**

14. Adjust the opacity of the sky layer and mask out areas you don't need, like I've done with the lower sash window here:

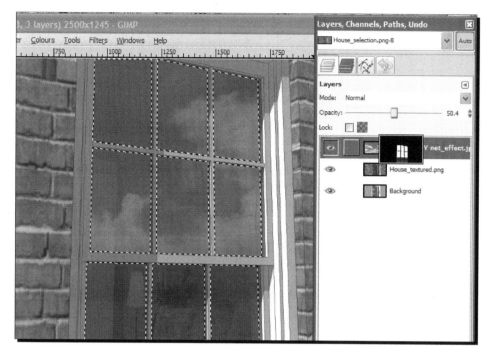

You can now use this technique to selectively replace, enhance, or blur any part of your SketchUp scene.

Have a go hero

Use the **Fuzzy Select Tool** (magic wand) or the **Select by Color Tool** in combination with a SketchUp flat colors layer to select areas of your image and blur, darken, lighten, sharpen, or delete areas of your main image. Now use the same technique as above to overlay other images or textures over parts of your scene. How many uses for this technique can you find to enhance your image? Enhancing doesn't just mean cleaning up, this can also be used to grunge up or add variation to textured surfaces.

Using Paths to mask photos

If you have set up your scene using Photo-Match (or by eye) to insert a building into an existing photograph, you're going to need to do some masking in GIMP to separate the foreground and background from the rendered image. You should be able to mask the outline of your building in Kerkythea using a mask render so that there's no problem inserting a background. The foreground may be more tricky as you'll see now.

I want to take this serene picture and insert a riverside hut. It's where I'm planning to retire once everyone knows how to use SketchUp!

Like all strapped for time architects, I'm simply going to download a design from the 3D-Warehouse and claim it as mine. Here it is rendered in Kerkythea on a plain background:

I've rotated the view by eye in SketchUp to vaguely match the photo, using *Alt + Tab* (*CMD + Tab* on the Mac) to switch between windows. I couldn't use Photo-Match because there are no right angles in the image. When you get it about right by trial and error you can try to match the sun/shade and export the image for rendering.

Time for action

So, you're in GIMP now with both the images opened as layers, just like you learned before.

1. Turn down the opacity on the hut layer and use the move tool to place it (see the following screenshot).

2. Select the **Scale Tool** to size it. Hold *Ctrl* (*CMD* on the Mac) to keep the aspect ratio correct.

3. Select the background with the **Select by Color Tool** and hit *Delete*.

4. You now need to copy the photo layer to sit over the top (for the foreground elements).

5. Select the photo layer, then click the **Duplicate Layer** button and move the new layer to the top of the list.

6. Right-click and select **Add Layer Mask | Selection | Add**.

7. Go to **Select | None**.

8. Click on the **Layer Mask.** Click the little **Double Arrow** in the main layer pallet to swap from black to white.

9. Click the paintbrush tool and select a rough brush. Make sure the opacity is set back to 100.

10. Paint in bits of grass or whatever you want in the foreground as you can see in the screenshot below:

11. Turn off the rendered image layer.

12. Select the **Paths Tool** from the main pallet as shown in the following screenshot.

13. Click around any foreground elements, such as this tree (using *Ctrl* + middle mouse button to zoom in).

14. When you've finished creating a closed boundary around the object, click the right mouse button then go to **Select | From Path**.

15. Click the **Layer Mask**.

16. Select the **Bucket Fill Tool** and fill the selection with white.

17. Turn on the hut layer so you can see the result.

18. Use the **Burn Tool** to darken the edges of your foreground objects if you need to.

19. Go to **Select | None.**

20. Adjust the **Brightness / Contrast** of the rendered image layer to match the image better.

21. Go to **Image | Flatten Image.** Here's the final result:

What just happened?

You created what's called a **Clipping Path** around the area of the tree trunk that overlaid the hut. You then turned this Path into a selection and filled the selection with white in the layer mask. This made this area of the Layer visible again. This is the basic method of clipping and masking any foreground or background elements in your scene. Paths are very versatile and it's well worth reading more about Paths in GIMP or Photoshop help websites

Summary

In this chapter you have learned how to extend your skills 200% as a rendering artist. You have learned how to take renders and native SketchUp images and add some seasoning. In particular, I think you will keep coming back to:

- ◆ Compositing photos and renders into one image
- ◆ Tweaking levels to give realistic lighting
- ◆ Creating the "straight out of the camera" depth of field effect
- ◆ Adding reflection to windows without even touching a render application!

These are some of the main skills a 3D artist needs to get to grips with, and along the way you picked up the skills to use these tools and methods in many other ways too. You have now graduated from SketchUp Architectural Visualization school and may go home...

...that is, unless you want to do some animation?

10
Walkthroughs and Flyovers

In this chapter, you're going to learn the basic skills you need to produce animated walkthroughs and flyovers. SketchUp can be the ideal software to produce these types of animations. In fact, the film industry uses SU as a previsualization tool. They work out the basic shots, camera angles, timing, and so on within SketchUp before they shoot it for real! And that's how we're going to use it too.

In this chapter, we will cover:

- ◆ What to include in your animation
- ◆ How to create a simple walkthrough in SketchUp
- ◆ Using paths for a smooth flythrough
- ◆ Stitching animated sequences together into a video
- ◆ Photo real animated renders
- ◆ Video compositing, file types, and compression settings

The same principles for stills and animation

Creating moving images, or movies for architectural visualization, takes a slightly different but related mindset to still images (stills). That's because an animated sequence shows off more of the scene than in a still. For example, you might see the back of a building which you wouldn't have bothered modeling for a still. Now you have to model it. But all the same principles apply that you have already learned about in Chapter 3, *Composing the Scene*.

Here's a recap:

- If you can't see it, it isn't there (don't model it)
- If it's in the background, make it low poly or a 2D cutout
- Use interesting and varied camera angles

But this time, all this has to be kept in mind for the duration of a 30-second, 5-minute, or even feature length presentation made up of many views of the model. This can quickly become an overwhelming premise. So, we need to do it like all good movie producers do it. And guess what? You already know what that is, and practice it just about every day, because we're simply talking about *breaking it down into bite sized chunks*.

Rome wasn't built in a day

Some architect didn't sit down one day and start sketching Rome, starting with the Coliseum and working outwards until he'd finished the whole city. It took ages (literally) and involved many different designers and designs. So, Rome was made up of component parts, and each component part was made up of individual bricks. Just like you do every day with other design projects, home DIY, life goals, or even a holiday itinerary, you're going to break down your animation scene by scene and shot by shot.

Making a start: Sketch it out

Even if you already have a fully detailed model that you can quite happily view from any angle, you need to start by planning what you want to see in your animation. Actually, that's a complete lie. Why would the client want to see what *you* want to see? You're interested in buildings for pity's sake! So, we must start by filling the boots of the client or "audience" and from now on only think in terms of their wishes. If there wes a switch to turn them on, what would it be?

Most of this principle has been covered also in Chapter 6, *Entourage the SketchUp Way*, because it's entourage (people, cars, and trees) that tell the audience "this could be you in this scene!" and "wouldn't you like to be in this environment?"

Time for action – write out your itinerary

If you were to visit the quaint English village of Bourton-on-the-Water, what would be the absolute "must sees" of your trip? If you have travelled for 17 days to get there, you knew you could never go back there again, and you were the last one to go with a film camera before it was leveled by hungry bulldozers? So, write out your itinerary. There's a method of doing this that's completely easy and foolproof. You can do it when you're on the train or eating your cornflakes:

1. Take an A3 sheet of paper.

2. Start at the centre of the page and write down a feature of the building you're "selling" to your audience.

3. Rotate the page randomly and write another somewhere in a blank space.

4. Do it again and again.

5. Go completely crazy and write down whatever pops into your head (such as "dishwasher", "great drainage", or "south facing").

6. When you've filled the page, collect them all up in a list.

7. Put three columns down the right-hand side, labeled Quality, Desirability, and a blank column

It doesn't matter if you spell desirability wrong. That's the point of the exercise, no wrong answers, don't worry about spelling or getting the best stuff down. Just get the flow going.

When you're done, in the Quality column give a rating 1 to 5 for how "nice" this part of this particular development is:

8. Now do a valley fold to hide the first column.

9. In the Desirability column, give a rating 1 to 5 for how desirable such a building feature is to your audience. You need to divorce this from your particular building completely. Rate it purely on how your audience would view this feature on *any* building. Does anti-vandal paint on a bin store make someone want to buy a property?

10. When you're done, multiply the first and second column and put the total in the third.

What just happened?

Without knowing it or finding it remotely difficult, you have written the itinerary for your animation. Easy wasn't it? You probably don't think you've achieved much, but you have. By using this method you were forced to be dispassionate about your design or model. You were also forced to separate out what you like (as a building feature lover) and what your audience wants (as the ones wanting to *be in it*!). What you have in the third column is a definitive rating of the impact of each feature on your audience. Go ahead and label it "impact" now.

Generating the story board

You are now ready to sketch out the storyboard, because you now know what to include in your animation and what to leave out. Take a pink marker and highlight everything with a score of 20-25. This is your prime real-estate. Take an orange marker and highlight scores of 12-16. And take a yellow marker to all the nines. Nines are just about tolerable. What you now have is a color coded scene allocation system. When deciding what to put into your animation, you should get all the pinks in as many times as you can. You should get the oranges in the rest of the time. And you should use the yellows to pad the content out where necessary and give an overall context to the presentation. And guess what? Anything you've not colored will actually detract from the presentation and stop people buying the property. Don't you dare even model them!

Dealing with detractions

As you've discovered, anything in your list that didn't get colored could easily detract so much from your presentation that someone who would normally be enamored with it is left cold instead. So, these areas should be minimized if possible, but what do you do if they're a central feature and have to be included for context (or honesty)? For example the electricity enclosure, the bin store, or the plant room? Here's a quick list of ways to overcome this problem:

◆ Leave non-critical areas blank and un-textured, giving the context but not the detail

◆ Cover or mask with entourage

◆ Leave unfocussed in the background (with moving images this only possible when using professional level compositing software)

◆ Use viewing angles that obscure these features

Probably as much of your effort should be spent in minimizing bad features as promoting good ones. You should aim at showing the development in its best light and greatest potential.

Time for action – the storyboard

Now that you've decided what needs to be included and what needs to be left out, you need to decide how long to allocate to each, and what the camera views should be. Do the following on paper with sketches.

1. Split up your list into scenes, including wide views and close-up views.

2. Decide how long the whole animation should last. Add a couple of seconds for cutting out later.

3. What about transitions? Are you going to travel from one scene to the next, or cut to it?

4. Work out how long to spend on each scene, each transition.

5. Create a rough sketch for the start of each scene.

6. Scan them into your computer.

 The following steps are shown specific to Windows Movie Maker, but are similar to all basic video editing software (Adobe Premiere Elements, Final Cut Express, iMovie, or similar)

7. In Windows Movie Maker or similar, import each picture.

8. In **Import Pictures** hold *Ctrl* to select more than one then click **Import**.

9. The pictures will open in the **Collections** area.

10. Drag them one by one into the **StoryBoard** in the sequence you want

11. Click **Show Timeline**. Drag the edge of each image out to the correct time-length.

12. Press play on the preview viewer.

13. Keep adding scene sketches and editing the timing until you're happy.

14. Add voice or music to the audio channel if you want to key the scene transitions to that as follows:

15. Click **Import Audio or Music**. Navigate to the file, then drag into the storyboard as before.

16. Remember to save the project.

What just happened?

You just storyboarded your whole animation so that you now know exactly where and what you need to go and model. You did this in Movie Maker or something similar, creating place markers so you can easily import your moving clips later. This saves an enormous amount of time in the long run because you will only model, texture, animate, and render what you're going to see, not what'll get left on the cutting room floor. If you already have your SketchUp scene completed, you could take screenshots from that instead of sketching it out. You can use this later, as a template to insert the actual animations into.

> When you're doing a complex project such as an animation, it's vital to get a second or third pair of eyes onto it early on. Use your rough and ready movie to talk it through with a colleague, tutor, or a "clued up" friend. It's important to do it at this early stage because you haven't invested lots of time and emotion into it yet.

You're now at the stage where you slot in to Chapter 3 and compose each scene.

Animating in SketchUp

Now comes the really fun bit! We're going to look at the main ways you can get animation out of SketchUp. And don't forget, whatever you animate in SketchUp can be turned into a render in Kerkythea. So, SketchUp is a pre-visualization tool for rendering as well as a visualization tool in itself.

Time for action – a simple walkthrough

1. Create the simple scene illustrated here in SketchUp. The tallest object is about 2 meters (6.5 feet) tall.

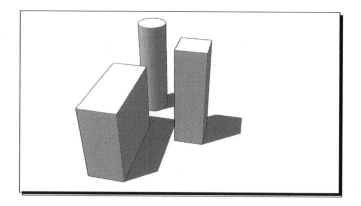

2. Texture all the faces differently so that you can recognize where you are at any time.

3. Now go to **View | Toolbars | Walkthrough**.

4. Select the **Walk** button.

5. Type in your **Eye Height** and hit *Enter* (see the following screenshot).

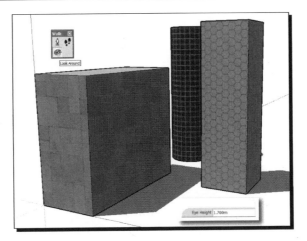

6. Click the **Look Around** button to move your eyes around.

7. This can be the start of your walkthrough. Go to **View | Animation | Add Scene**.

8. We're going to walk in between the boxes and look what's on one of the surfaces we can't see.

9. With the **Walk** button selected, click on the screen, hold the left mouse button, and move the mouse forward. You start to walk! Move the mouse from side to side to steer.

10. Walk in-between the boxes. Now add another scene.

11. Use the **Look Around** function to turn on the spot and look directly at the right hand box. Add another scene.

12. To see how you've done, go to **View | Animation | Play**.

What just happened?

You set up a simple scene and told SketchUp you wanted to view it from eye level. Using the **Walkthrough** tool bar you simulated a person walking through your SketchUp model. This in itself is a highly effective presentation tool. You used the **Look Around** tool to change your view without altering eye height or camera position. It's important to use these tools to change views rather than your usual **Pan** and **Orbit**, in order to maintain a level eye height. You then created scenes to act like key-frames for the animation.

When you viewed it, you will have noticed the animation paused, flew quickly in-between the boxes, paused again, and then rotated the camera to the right. The settings that control the speed of a scene transition's length of pause are in the **View | Animation | Settings** dialog box. Go there now for a look.

> **Use your laptop for real time walkthroughs**
>
> The walkthrough tools you've seen right here are really useful for helping people visualise a design. There's nothing better than interacting with an environment and viewing it as you would see it in real life. Why not take your laptop to meetings and allow people to see your models first hand?

Animation settings

The animation settings dialog box looks like this:

You'll notice there are very few settings here and it's not possible to control individual scene timings. That's a pity in one way, but it does help keep everything simple. You'll look at how to control individual scene timing using a plugin a little later in the chapter. Here's what each setting does.

Function	What it does	Uses
Scene Transitions	Controls the time it takes to travel from one scene to the next	Enter a number (seconds)
Enable Scene Transitions	Allows travel from one Scene to the next	Un-tick to operate as a slideshow
Scene Delay	Sets the amount of time to dwell at each scene	Set it to zero to go directly from one transition to the next without pausing

For now, you're going to add some intermediate steps to your walkthrough to smooth out the movement, and also slow things down a little.

Time for action – getting the timing right

1. Still in the settings dialog, change the scene transitions to *2* seconds.

2. Change **Scene Delay** to *0*.

3. Close the dialog box.

4. Click on **Scene 1**.

5. Walk half-way between **Scene 1** and **Scene 2**.

6. Right-click on **Scene 1** and select **Add Scene**. **Scene 4** appears between 1 and 2.

7. Play the animation again and note the difference.

8. Click to go back to **Scene 4** and now move your position or eye view, then update **Scene 4** (right-click and select **update**).

9. Play the animation again and repeat until you get a smooth timing between scenes.

10. Now create further scenes as you walk around the back of the cylinder and back through to where you started.

11. Click on each scene tab to view, edit, and update as necessary.

What just happened?

You just learned how to adjust animation properties and create a regularly paced animated walkthrough. You set up the scenes and were able to go back and tweak each one to get the desired effect. You will have noticed that the animation can still be a little jerky, and we still want to alter individual transition timings. Thankfully, there's a plugin for that and we're going to look at it now.

Time for action – adding individual timing to scenes

1. Get `scenes_transition_times.rb` from `http://morisdov.googlepages.com`.

2. Drop the plugin into your plugins folder and restart SketchUp.

3. Go to **Plugins | Scenes Transition Times**.

4. Type values (in seconds) into the boxes (**-1.0** leaves it as default).

Scenes Transition Times	
Scene 1	2.0
Scene 4	3.0
Scene 2	4.0
Scene 3	-1.0
Scene 5	-1.0
Scene 6	-1.0
Scene 7	-1.0
Scene 8	-1.0
Scene 9	-1.0

OK   Cancel

5. Play the animation again to see the difference.

6. Now find the scene in which you're turning your head to look at the box. Type *4* here.

7. Play the animation again to see the difference.

What just happened?

You installed a plugin that allows scene transitions to be adjusted individually. You then increased the scene transition time to four seconds when you turn to look at the box beside you. You may have worked out that the value goes in the box relating to the scene after the one you need to edit.

Note that the animation is still jerky. This may be good enough for your current project, especially if you stitch together different scenes into a collage of moving views in your video editing software. You just cut out the dodgy transitions. But for an altogether smoother animation there are some further techniques that you can work on now.

Creating flythroughs from paths

The usual way of creating flyover presentations in rendering software, such as 3D Max, is to create a travel path. The camera is then attached to this path and told how fast to travel along it, where to point, and when. This is exactly what you can do in SketchUp too. This method is usually preferable to the walkthrough you've already looked at because:

- Travel is smooth, and not "jerky"
- The speed of travel is constant
- There's greater control over where you go and where you look
- Scenes are created automatically

To prepare for this *Time for action*, first you need to download and install the following plugins:

- `Flightpath.rb` from `http://www.smustard.com/script/flightpath`
- `Bezierspline.rb` from `http://www.crai.archi.fr/RubyLibraryDepot`

Time for action – smooth transitions

You're going to simulate an aircraft flying through some tall buildings. This will teach all the slightly more advanced skills you need for your architectural video, although you might be working on a smaller scale with a single building or site. You're going to use a 3D Warehouse city rather than your own project so you can practice all you like and not worry about getting it just right.

1. Click on the **Get Models** button to enter the 3D Warehouse.

2. Type in *3d cities exhibition* and select **Collections.**

3. Grab a city you want to fly through. I'm going for Rocane 2020.

4. First delete or hide all the polygon intensive trees and stuff as follows:

  ❑ In **Outliner**, click **Details | Expand All**

  ❑ Type in "Tre" into the **Outliner** text box (in case tree is spelt wrong, as it is in this case)

5. Go through it and select, right-click and **Hide/Delete** what you can. This will really speed things up (refer to the following screenshot).

6. Start by going to the **Plan View** and switch to the monochrome view style. Also turn off shadows. This will speed up manipulating and viewing the model and animation.

7. From your new **Bezier Spline** toolbar (**View | Toolbars | BZ_Toolbar**), select **Cubic Bezier Curve** and draw the path you want on the plan view, as shown in the following screenshot:

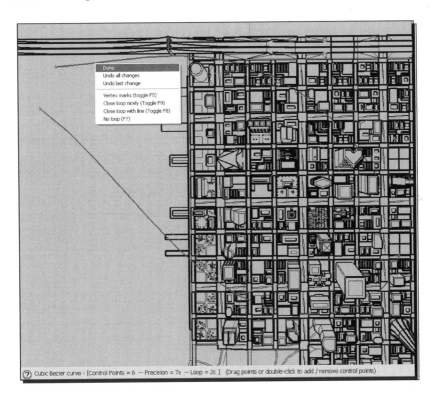

8. Right-click and select **Done**.

9. Orbit your view as you can see below, then move the path up off the ground in the blue axis.

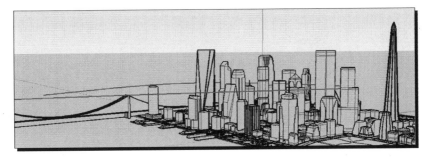

6. Now set the view style and shadows exactly as you want them.

7. Unhide anything you want to see in the animation.

8. Save the model. This is important because you can't undo the flight path easily.

9. Select the path you just created.

10. Right-click and select **Flightpath**.

11. Enter the speed you require. 88 meters per second is 60 mph (car speed). I'm going for 500.

12. Now go to **View | Animation | Settings** and reduce **Scene Delay** to *0*.

13. Go to **File | Export | Animation**.

14. Reduce the size to 320x240 and set **Frame rate** to 10. This is a test render size.

15. If after you view the animation you need to make path adjustments, re-open your saved SketchUp file and edit from there.

What just happened?

You created a 3D curved path for the camera to follow. The flightpath plugin creates scenes for each step in the path and sets the transition speed between scenes to keep the flight speed constant. You entered a speed in meters per second to control this. You now have a camera path converted to scenes which you can edit individually. This is really great because as you'll see in a minute, you can fine tune what the camera does every step of the way!

But best of all, did you notice how smooth it was?

Fine tuning with camera controls

Now it's your turn to add some real panache to finish off your flythrough! Install the `CameraControls.rb` camera plugin from `http://www.smustard.com/script/CameraControls`

This plugin's a little more difficult to install because you need to create a new folder in your `Plugins` folder. Details are in the `readme.txt` file you get when you download it. This plugin gives you fine control over camera pan, roll and tilt, and allows you to see values for these at each step of the animation.

 Currently the `CameraControls.rb` plugin only works for the PC, not MAC. If you're a MAC user you can still achieve these camera effects manually though. The plugin is just there to give tighter control over the values.

Have a go hero – camera pan, roll, and acceleration

Add camera effects to each scene along your path using the camera controls plugin. Here are some examples of what you can do with pan, tilt, and roll. Remember to update each scene after your changes.

	Example of effect	Method
Pan	Focus on a building as you go past it to simulate a passenger looking out of the window	Use the Pan slider to keep the camera trained on a building through several scenes
Tilt	When you want to simulate lift as the car or motorcycle sets off or brakes	Increase or decrease the Tilt value on one scene.
Roll	When you want to bank to the side like an aircraft when turning	Add progressively higher values of roll to adjacent scenes, then do the opposite to come out of a roll.

Let's put it together

Now that you've got the skills together for creating moving scenes in SketchUp, it's time to put it all together. Using the skills you've learned, render out a couple more simple moving camera shots. Go to Chapter 3, *Composing the Scene* to get some more ideas on viewpoints and camera focal settings. I'm trying the following with our city scene:

- Travel along the bridge approaching the city:

- Top down flyover emphasizing the height of buildings:

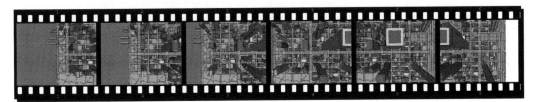

◆ Slow travel along a road looking up at sky:

◆ Some close-up shots:

◆ Moving shadows or night shots:

◆ Free-fall spinning camera:

◆   Different SketchUp styles (Monochrome, Sketchy, Blueprint, and so on):

All this will then be mixed in with the main flythrough sequence. The beauty of this is that the audience is getting a constantly fresh, changing perspective, rather than a monotonous flyover. These scenes are interspersed to create this variety. They're also used to mask over the bits of your flythrough you don't particularly want to see.

Have a go hero – interesting details and viewpoints

So, it's your turn now to grab the mouse, zoom into the SketchUp model, and capture some really interesting viewpoints, camera angles, and perspectives. Make each of these no more than a couple of scenes long, and keep them to a few seconds each. The whole idea here is variety. Start with a saved copy of the model from before you added the flythrough scenes. Save each mini animation as a separate .skp file for easy access later, so when you need to you can export each animation as production size 768 x 576 JPEG frames, as you can see in the following screenshot, or render it in Kerkythea.

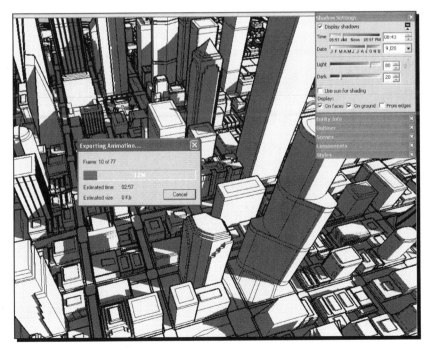

Authoring video sequences

So, you've got a bunch of clips. These may or may not relate to the storyboard you set up at the start, but it doesn't matter. You're just practicing. What you need to do now is put your SketchUp animations together.

1. Open Windows Movie Maker (or similar software).

2. Go to **File | Import Into Collections.**

3. Drag the main flythrough clip onto the timeline.

4. You're now going to insert the short clips into the main flythrough.

5. Move the slider (see the following screenshot) to where you want to cut.

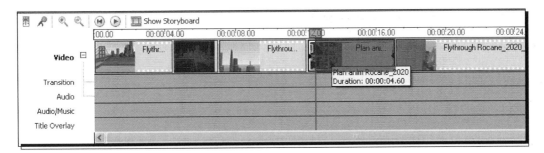

6. Click the **cut** button (circled in the following screenshot).

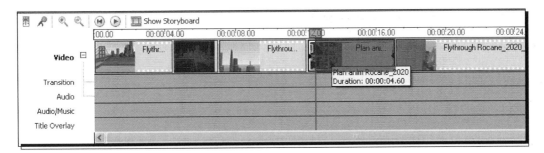

7. Cut again further on if you want to remove a section, or leave it if you want to come back to where you left it.

8. Select the section and hit *Delete*.

9. Import one of your smaller clips and drag it into the space you created.

10. Adjust the start and end by clicking and dragging the ends of the clip in the timeline.

Windows Movie Maker isn't there anymore with the newest version of Windows (Windows 7). Apparently an earlier version of WMM does work, however, and can be downloaded at www.microsoft.com; type *Windows Movie Maker 2.6* into the search box.

Now that you've produced your low resolution quick mock up, and tweaked it to perfection, you're ready to render the final footage at a higher resolution in SketchUp, or photo real in Kerkythea. Kerkythea imports the scene, sun, and camera movements exactly as you have them in SketchUp, so you have done all the hard work already.

High resolution animation from SketchUp

If you're aiming for a SketchUp sketchy movie, you'll now need to output the full resolution animation frames, ready to be stitched together later. To do this go back to SketchUp, make any edits you need, and save. Then go to **File | Export | Animation** and use the following settings:

1. Select a save location (create a folder especially for this).

2. Select .jpg file format from the drop-down list (this will save on hard disk space).

3. Click **Options** and set the following parameters:

Time for action – animating with Kerkythea

1. Try this first for one of the short clips you set up earlier.

2. In SketchUp click **Export Model to Kerkythea** in the SU2KT toolbar. This will export the scene to the Kerkythea format.

3. Select appropriate settings and allow the scene to open in Kerkythea.

4. Make any adjustments as necessary (See Chapter 9, *Photo Realistic Rendering*) and do a few test renders until you're happy, using the sequence you followed in that chapter.

5. Now do a production render using preset **06. PhotonMap - Medium +AA 0.3**, resolution 768 x 576.

6. Note how long it takes by checking the last line in **Windows | Console Log**.

7. If the quality isn't good enough, try **07. PhotonMap - High +AA 0.3** or even **08. PhotonMap - Fine +AA 0.3**.

> **How long will my animation will take to render?**
>
> The render time of a single frame x 25 x number of seconds in animation.
>
> For example, 2 minutes x 25 x 5 seconds = 250 minutes. It is not unusual to allow the computer a day or two to render a short animation.

8. Alter **Exposure** and **Gamma** in the **Rendered Image** window if necessary, then close that window.

9. Go to **Start Render** and click **Apply**. Click **Yes** to the **Are you sure?** prompt, then click **Cancel**.

10. Save the scene using the same name as when it was exported. This is an important step.

11. You're now ready to export the animation details from SketchUp.

12. In SketchUp, click the **Export Animation to Kerkythea** button.

Animation export options	
Frames per second	25
Loop to first camera	No
Animated Lights and Sun?	No
Face-Me Components?	No
Full model per frame?	No
Resolution	768x576
Render Settings	06. PhotonMap - Medium + AA 0.3
OK	Cancel

13. Choose the above settings and click **OK**.

14. Choose **OK** in export settings. You've already set these up.

15. Type in a filename and click **Save**.

16. When asked to open in Kerkythea, click **No**.

 This is the most robust method of using this exporter and will work well with all versions of SketchUp and the SU2KT plugin. You might be able to get it to work automatically, but please note, that method is not always problem free.

17. Close SketchUp and switch back to Kerkythea.

18. When you're happy to start rendering, make sure other software is closed on your computer so as not to waste computing power.

19. Go to **File | Run Script**.

20. Select the animation path you saved from SketchUp. Click **OK**.

21. Kerkythea will save all frames in a new folder named the same as the scene filename.

22. The clock counts down the frames. After a couple of frames have rendered, check in this save folder to see if the animation frames are saving correctly.

What just happened?

You set Kerkythea to automatically render the animation frames generated by SketchUp. Kerkythea uses the scene you saved and reads info from the script to change camera details and sun position. These frames are saved as JPG files in the folder you specified when you exported in SketchUp. The Image resolution of 768 x 576 ensures that your work is future proofed and can be used in both TV, DVD, and on the Web. With this resolution you will be able to create crisp animations for all video formats. Of course, if you particularly need to go **High Definition (HD)** you will need to raise this to 1280 or 1920 pixels wide. Think carefully before you do this because it greatly increases render times. You will need to change export settings to **16:9** in the drop-down box.

Why save individual frames for animations?

This is a good question. Why save individual frames when Kerkythea / SketchUp could make an AVI video file directly? The answer is that this is a much more robust and flexible method. If the render you've left going overnight bombs out half way through, or there's a power cut, you can still retrieve all the frames rendered up until then. With a single AVI animation you would have lost everything. You can also check the progress of the animation immediately by opening the animation save folder and taking a look at the frames as they're produced. No more having to wait till the end of a four hour render to discover the lighting was wrong! And just as importantly, using your frames with the following workflow you can achieve far greater compression and video quality. You're now ready to stitch all this together into your final video.

Compositing in VirtualDUB

Virtualdub was introduced in Chapter 2, *How to Collect an Arsenal Rambo Would Be Proud of*. If you haven't obtained it yet, check out Chapter 2 for details. VirtualDub basically creates animations from still images, and has loads of other image filters too. In just a couple of steps you're going to take the individual frames saved from Kerkythea and turn them into an uncompressed AVI video.

Time for action

1. Find the `VirtualDub.exe` file or shortcut and double-click it.

2. In VirtualDub go to **File | Open Video File**.

3. Navigate to where Kerkythea saved the renders and click on the first image. Click **Open**.

4. You can also just drag the image into VirtualDub.

5. Click the **Play** button on the left.

6. In **Video | Framerate** change the frame rate to *25* if necessary.

7. You should now have a 768 x 576 video at 25 frames per second. This will give you the most flexibility in what you want to use the video clip for.

8. If you're going to further edit the video, or output to the Web, leave these settings as they are and skip to the step for editing levels.

> If you want to output for NTSC file format (US), you need a framerate of 29.97 and a size of 720 x 480. PAL (the UK format) has 25 frames per second, and size of 768 x 576, which must be squashed to 720 x5 76 in the next step.

9. To resize the video go to **Video | Filters | Add | Resize**.

10. You can now resize for any standard you wish. 720 x 480 is the NTSC standard so click **Letterbox/crop to size** and enter **720** and **480** (see the following screenshot). This will crop away a little from each edge of the frame.

11. Alternatively, if you prefer not to crop your movie, tick the **Disabled** button in **Aspect Ratio,** then enter these dimensions in the top boxes instead. VirtualDub will do a resize without cropping.

12. If the end use for this is a PAL TV screen (for example a DVD in the UK), leave settings as they are (768 x 576) and do the resize in the next step (MPEG Streamclip).

13. Click **OK**.

14. Now to edit the levels just like you did with your still image in Chapter 9, Click **Add** in the **Filters** dialog box.

15. Select Levels from the menu and click **OK**.

16. Click **Show preview**.

17. Click **Sample frame**. The histogram appears. Move the little arrows as you did in Chapter 9, *Important Compositing and After Effects in GIMP,* until you're happy with the preview image (see the following screenshot).

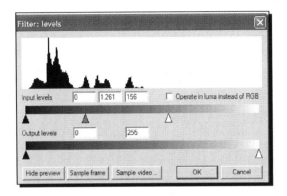

18. Click **OK**.

19. Now go to **File | Save as AVI**. VirtualDub will take the JPG frames, apply your filters, and export them as an AVI animation (see the following screenshot).

What just happened?

VirtualDub has taken the individual frames and stitched them together into an AVI file. This can be played using a standard viewer on your computer, or edited as part of your video sequence in Windows Movie Maker or something similar. When you save the AVI animation the file is not compressed, allowing you to use it in video editing software without losing further quality. If you'd saved it straight from SketchUp as an AVI, it would have already been compressed, and you would lose quality by further editing it.

Notice the AVI you've exported is a huge filesize! So what now? First of all, let's assume you want to use the animation as it is, and you'll prepare it for web use by compressing it massively. Then you'll go back and use the original AVI files in Windows Movie Maker.

Compressing and preparing for web use

The subject of video use on the web is a thorny one. Put on some gardening gloves before grasping this one! But as promised in Chapter 2, I've done most of the hard work for you, and it wasn't easy. The problem lies in the fact that there is no standard video format, standard compression format, or standard viewer. Those three combined make for a big headache. The solution is to make your video compatible with Flash, which most people already have on their computers. This will allow people to view your video on the web or straight from a CD/DVD without installing anything else, and the format happens to be highly compressed for easy downloading too. The following steps will allow you to post to YouTube and most other sharing sites, and will be viewable in all commonly used Internet browsers. The frame rate and video size you set earlier will also convert easily to TV and DVD and is even viewable on iPod, iPhones, and can be uploaded to iTunes.

Time for action – preparing an MP4 video with MPEG Streamclip

1. Open **Mpeg Streamclip**.

2. Go to **File | Open Files**.

3. Open the AVI file you just saved from VirtualDub.

4. Check it plays correctly in the viewer window.

5. Now go to **File | Export to MPEG-4**.

6. Here you have lots of options, but the suggested ones are usually the best way to go, you can see the settings I've used here for a web video:

7. Change **Sound** to **No Sound**.

8. Click **Make MP4**.

9. This file is now ready for upload to a web host such as YouTube, Screencast.com, or iTunes which will give you the option to show the MP4 video in a Flash player on your website.

10. For example, in YouTube, after you have uploaded your video, select the options you require, then go to embed, and copy and paste the code into your website or blog as you can see here:

What just happened?

You just compressed your video to MPEG-4 format with the `H.264` compression codec. This is immensely good news for three reasons:

◆ `H.264` allowed you to compress the video with little reduction in quality

◆ The AVI file is now something like 100 times smaller in size

◆ The video can be viewed online by anyone with a Flash viewer installed, and that includes most people

Creating the final video composition

You now have photo real clips from Kerkythea and/or non photo real clips from SketchUp that need to be put together into your final presentation. You will have already created a Windows Movie Maker project (or similar) with low resolution Sketchup clips or scanned in images. You now need to convert this to the final production. This is now just a matter of replacing the sketches or low resolution animations with your high resolution clips, then exporting in the correct format. Just follow the steps outlined here. Remember to use only uncompressed AVI files from VirtualDub for this, not any MP4 files.

1. Open your project in your favorite video editing software.

2. Hover over a clip in the timeline or storyboard. Read the clip length.

3. Insert your new production resolution clip next to it and adjust it to match the start/finish of the adjacent clip (if you trimmed it).

4. Click on the **Low Res Clip** and hit *Delete*.

5. When you've done all the clips like this, you will now have a high res version of your video presentation.

6. If you like, add scene transitions by dragging them into the slots in your storyboard view.

7. Save the project as a different filename. In Windows Movie Maker the process is as follows:

    ❑ Go to **File | Save Movie File**

    ❑ Select **My computer** and click **Next**

    ❑ Name it. Browse for a place to save it then click **Next**

    ❑ Click **Other settings | High Quality Video (PAL)**

    ❑ Check you've got enough hard drive space

    ❑ Click **Next**. The movie will be saved on your hard disk

Due to the way Windows Movie Maker saves or encodes files, you now need to go through the same process as before to open this in VirtualDub: save as an AVI, open in MPEG Streamclip and save as an MP4. You'll be amazed at how much this compresses files, I've just compressed a 3-second clip from 53 mega bytes to half a megabyte, that's 100 times smaller!

Pop quiz

1. How can you deal with parts of your design that will put off your viewers?

2. What plugin can you use to individually change scene transition times?

3. True or false: I can't edit lighting levels once I've created an animation.

4. Why should I export individual JPG frames rather than AVI video?

Summary

In this chapter you learned how to create flyovers and walkthroughs. You found out how to set up the camera to follow a path, and tweak individual views along the path. You then discovered how to put clips together into an over-all presentation. Some particular skills you picked up in this chapter were:

♦ Planning your animations the easy way

♦ How to render photo-real frames in Kerkythea

♦ How to best prepare files for viewing on the Internet

♦ Compression settings to achieve a 100 times (or more) reduction in file size

♦ Plugins you need to achieve smooth animations

All that knowledge will set you on the path to happily produce SketchUp animations for Architectural Visualization. As you have seen, it's not hard to generate great results with SketchUp and a few other free programs. Of course, if you find you're doing animations regularly you can take these skills and apply them to industry standard video compositing applications such as After Effects or Nuke.

11

Presenting Visuals in LayOut

This last chapter is all about presentation. Think about the types of visuals you've created so far—the many different media, styles, viewpoints, and angles on your building. Do these individual images speak for themselves? Do they individually have both context and focus? Usually the answer to this will be "no" because it takes several images to create an overall impression, in other words to communicate your design intent. You may already be skilled at displaying visuals as posters on websites or in presentations, but you may not yet have looked into LayOut. LayOut is Google's attempt to make easy work of communicating design intent with SketchUp, and this chapter is a brief introduction to it.

In this chapter, you will discover how to:

- ◆ Display plans and elevations
- ◆ Import SketchUp models and rendered images
- ◆ Add dimensions and text
- ◆ Set up a CAD style border
- ◆ Create PowerPoint style presentations
- ◆ Print to scale and control line-weights

LayOut comes part and parcel with SketchUp Pro, or you can try it free for 480 minutes when you install a try-out version. The free trial should easily be long enough to try out the *Time for action* and *Have a go hero* sections found in this chapter.

Getting started with LayOut

You will find that many things in LayOut remind you of SketchUp, so you'll feel at home with it as soon as you load it for the first time. It's designed completely from scratch for SketchUp. This is good because there's nothing redundant about it. And we can look forward to Google continuing to develop LayOut in years to come as their de-facto presentation tool. Some areas of LayOut in particular, such as dimensioning, are an exciting development as they extend SketchUp's reach into the domain where CAD programs reside.

First of all, let's start by taking one of the pre-installed page borders and customizing it into a familiar Architectural page border. It will be there for you to use whenever you need it.

Time for action – customizing a page border

1. Open LayOut. You'll be presented with this **Getting Started** screen:

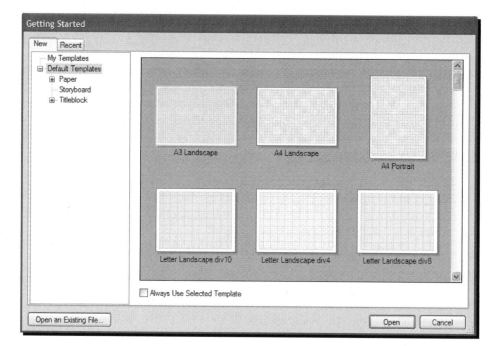

2. Here you can select any standard page size to start your project with. Click on the **+** sign next to **Titleblock** and select **Simple,** and then **A3 Landscape** as shown here:

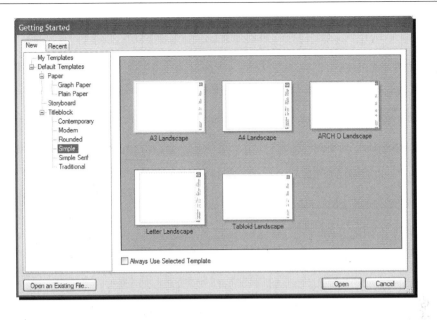

3. Click **Open**. The main **LayOut** window opens with the A3 page along with a simple border in the main window.

4. On the right are the pallets arranged one above another as you can see in the following screenshot. Click the title bar named **Pages** to expand the **Pages** pallet.

5. The **Pages** pallet opens up. Click on **Cover Page** or **Inside Page** to view each of these in the main window. The template you selected earlier came with both these pages already set up.

> Unlike in SketchUp, where the pallets are often moved around in the window or switched off, the LayOut pallets are best left where they are. Each pallet can be expanded or collapsed simply by clicking their title bar.

4. Use the middle mouse button to pan and zoom in and out of the main window.

5. Press the select arrow (top left of the screen) and double-click the title text. Why doesn't LayOut allow you to edit it?

6. Open the **Layers** pallet. Notice you have a lock symbol next to three of the layers? This means that items on that layer cannot be edited. It's a safety feature to stop you accidentally editing what you want to keep as it is.

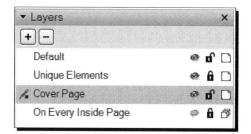

7. Click on **Cover Page** in the **Pages** pallet and click the lock for the **Cover Page** layer. The padlock symbol opens (refer to the previous screenshot).

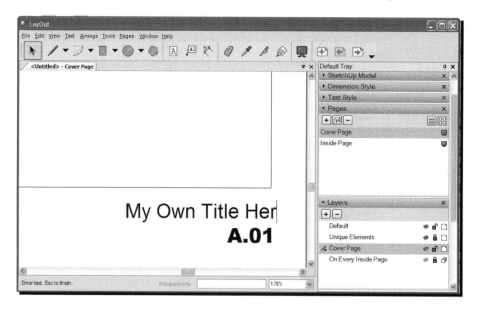

8. You can now edit the title and any other elements that are on the **Cover Page** layer. Add your own title now.

9. Click the lock again to stop your border elements being edited.

What just happened?

You selected a pre-made template to start your project with. This has been ready made by Google and includes a front page and inside page. That's two pages with different page borders. They've also set up elements of those pages - text and lines - on different layers. This allows you to keep them locked so as not to edit them accidentally. As you have seen, you can edit any of the text you want to, once the layer they're on is unlocked.

Have a go hero

Now it's a simple matter of changing the text you find in this template to reflect your project. Also add lines and rectangles to the title block or border to customize it. Make sure you're on the correct layer for the page you're on by clicking on it in the **Layer** pallet. The current layer you're drawing with shows a pencil next to it.

Have a go at this now, and when you're finished set the bottom three layers to locked again. Then click **File | Save As Template** and enter the name of the project. You can now grab this template whenever you start a new page.

Displaying SketchUp models in LayOut

Any view or scene in SketchUp can be viewed within LayOut. You don't need to export any images or files to do this. LayOut links to your SketchUp file directly, so whatever change you make to your model in SketchUp will be changed in LayOut too. This is great, because similar to animation storyboarding in the last chapter, you can set up dummy views in LayOut to flesh out later. Once set up you know exactly what views you have to work on in SketchUp, and you can check your progress through LayOut. It's just like having a page with windows in to your model.

Time for action – displaying a SketchUp 3D view

1. For the purpose of this tutorial, you might like to download an architectural model from 3D Warehouse, or use your own scene. I'm going for *Model of a Mixed Use Building* by Google.

2. In LayOut select the **Cover Page** in the pages pallet.

3. Go to **File** | **Insert** then navigate to your SketchUp model and click **Open**.

4. A window appears on your page with the SketchUp model shown in it. Click a corner of the window and stretch it to fill the page, like I've done here:

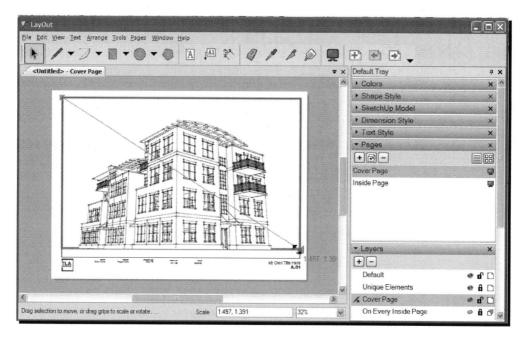

5. The view will resize to fill the window. Note you can snap to the corners or edges of the border, as you can see in the previous screenshot.

6. Double-click in the window you just inserted. This activates the window for editing. You can now move, zoom, and orbit the view how you want it.

7. Click the header bar of the **SketchUp Model** pallet. Then select the **Styles** tab and select the style you want to see. These are the same as the SketchUp styles. Click the little house icon to access the full list of styles:

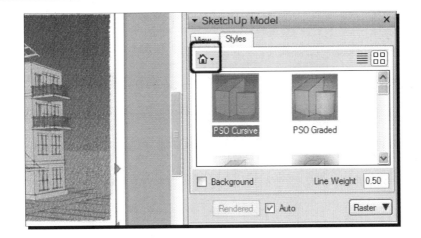

8. Double-click in the area outside the view when you want to stop editing it.

What just happened?

You inserted your own SketchUp model, or one which you previously saved from the 3D Warehouse. You edited the view and style just as you would in SketchUp, but now you can see exactly what it will look like on the page when it is printed out. This way of working is fundamentally different to other layout applications such as CorelDraw, Inkscape, or Pagemaker, because in LayOut the 2D images on display remain fully editable 3D entities. When they are changed in SketchUp, the page in LayOut will update too.

Multiple views of the same model

You're now ready to set up the internal pages of your presentation. Here you're basically going to show off as many views of the model as you can, now that you've done the hard work downloading it! This is just to practice with LayOut. For a live project you would want to think more carefully about what (and what not) to show. You already gained all the skills for planning your scenes at the start of Chapter 3, *Composing the Scene*, and in Chapter 10, *Walkthroughs and Flyovers* you learned an easy method to plan what to show in multiple scenes.

Time for action – orthographic views in LayOut

1. Click on the SketchUp view you inserted.

2. Then go to **Edit | Copy**.

3. Select the **Inside Page** and go to **Edit | Paste**. A copy of the view appears on the page.

4. Resize it using the corner grips. A little less than a quarter of the page should do it.

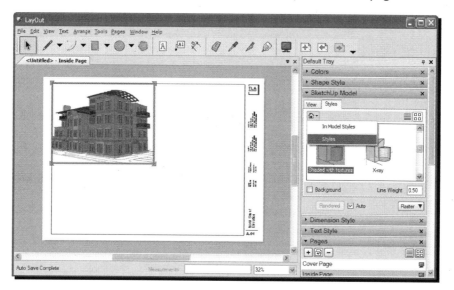

5. Go to the **Styles** tab and select the **Shaded with Textures** style. You should have something like the preceding screenshot (click the house icon and **Styles** as shown if you need to).

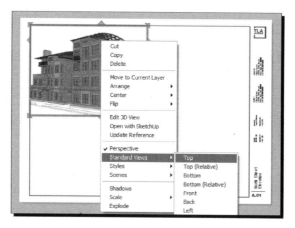

6. In the main window, right-click on the SketchUp view and select **Standard Views |
    Top** as shown in the preceding screenshot. Notice the view isn't in the right
    orientation (see the following screenshot), and also if you pan you can see it's
    still showing the view in perspective.

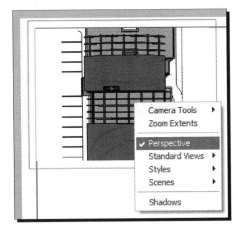

7. Right-click again and deselect **Perspective**. Your model shows in correct
    orthographic representation as you would with a 2D plan. Now to rotate it.

8. Select **Standard Views | Left**, then **Standard Views | Top (Relative)**. This will
    now orientate the plan relative to the left view you just had, as in the
    following screenshot:

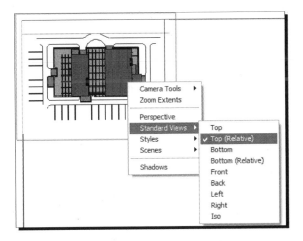

9. Double-click in the window and zoom and pan to get the view to fit the window.

10. Go ahead now and copy this view several times to create the elevations.

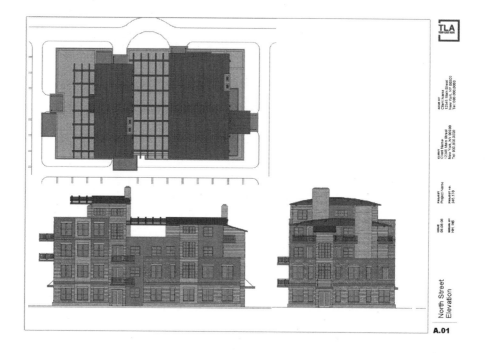

11. Go to **File** | **Save As** to save your progress.

What just happened?

First, selecting the standard view that relates your front elevation (in this case, **Left**) before doing the **Top (relative)** view told LayOut that you wanted to view the plan relative to the left-hand side. You then copied this window several times, which meant that the same scale was retained in each window.

Setting scale

You can set the scale of an inserted SketchUp model in LayOut by selecting **Scale** in the right-click menu and selecting from the list.

Orientating a view using SketchUp Scenes

But what if your SketchUp model isn't set up to the standard left, right, front, and back? Take the following model, for example, a plan view of a hotel downloaded from the 3D Warehouse:

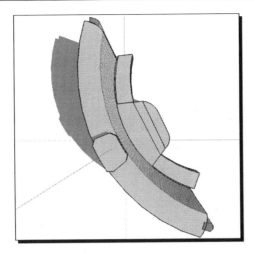

As you can see here, the model is both curved and rotated in plan. So, when you insert it into LayOut the standard views will not help. Try the following to regain control.

Time for action – align the view using a face

1. In SketchUp, double-click on the front face of the model until you can select the face itself.

2. With the face selected, right-click and select **Align View**.

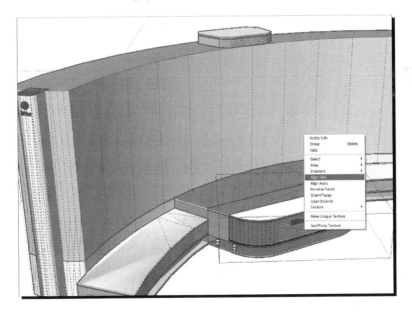

3. If the face you wanted to select is curved (like the one in the previous screenshot), first go to **View | Hidden Geometry**. You'll now be able to select a facet of the curved face and perform the **Align View** command.

4. Go to **Camera | Parallel Projection** and then set up a scene (**View | Animation | Add Scene**).

5. Save the model, and back in LayOut right click the window. Select **Update Reference**.

6. Your window will update with the last view you had in SketchUp. You can now select the scene by going to **Scenes** in the right-click menu.

What just happened?

You aligned the view in SketchUp to be in the same plane as the face you selected. You then set up a scene so that this view could be readily accessed in LayOut. Did you notice how LayOut read any changes you made to your SketchUp model and updated it?

Have a go hero – layout dimensions

Adding dimensions is pretty much self-explanatory. Just click on the dimensions button and snap to parts of the building. Some features can be adjusted in the **Dimension Style** box shown in the following screenshot:

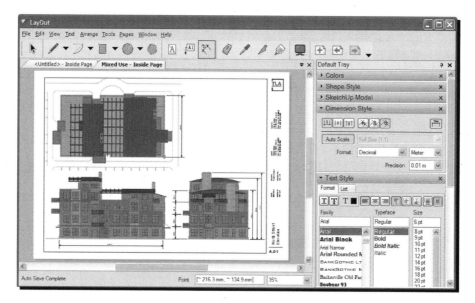

Use the dimension, text, and label tools now on your drawing. They work just like the dimension tools in SketchUp or any CAD program. Have a go at all the different buttons in the **Dimensions** and **Text Style** pallets.

Displaying SketchUp sections

There is currently no function to create building sections in LayOut, so you need to create sections in SketchUp first. Once you add them in a SketchUp model, the LayOut version will contain them too.

Time for Action – creating sections

1. Right-click on a SketchUp window in LayOut and select **Open with SketchUp**.

2. Click on the **Section Plane** button and click on a surface. The section plane will be created in plane with that surface.

3. Use the **Move** tool to move the section plane where you want it and then manipulate your view to how you want it to appear in LayOut.

4. Create a **Scene** tab. Right-click on the tab and go to **Scene Manager**.

5. Make sure **Active Section Planes** is ticked.

6. Type in *Section A-A* into the **Name** box.

7. Save the model. Now in LayOut right-click and select **Update Reference**.

8. The view in LayOut will automatically update showing the section. But the problem is, all the other views will now include the section cut too!

9. Go back to your SketchUp model and set up another scene tab.

10. Right-click on the section and un-tick **Active Cut**.

11. Right-click again and select **Hide**.

12. Now right click on the **Scene** tab you just created and select **Update**. You now have one scene with, and one scene without the section cut showing.
Leave the view on the scene without, and **Save**.

13. In LayOut your views now revert to their original state without the section cut.

14. For the window in which you intend to display the section, right-click, and select the *Section A-A* scene you set up earlier. It's now the only window showing the section cut.

Aargh! My LayOut views keep changing!

If you want to avoid your LayOut views changing every time you change something in SketchUp you could consider saving different versions of a SketchUp model. Also, setting up dedicated scenes in SketchUp will let you control what you see in each window in LayOut.

Slideshows and presentations

LayOut is a cross between CAD, desk-top publishing and PowerPoint. If you set up multiple pages in LayOut, they can be viewed as a slideshow just like PowerPoint (but without the scene animations you get in SketchUp) or printed as a portfolio of pictures. Here's how to do it.

Time for action – creating a presentation

1. Start a new file in LayOut; **File | New**.

2. Select a plain paper page in landscape.

3. Insert a SketchUp model as before.

4. In the **Pages** pallet, click the **Duplicate Selected Page** button.

5. Modify the view, style, and add text or other elements.

6. Do this for however many views you want.

7. In **Pages** click the **Thumbnail View** button (circled in the following screenshot) to get an overview of your pages so far:

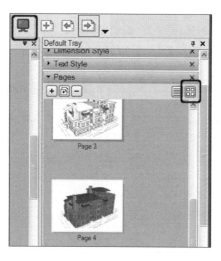

8. Hit the Start Presentation button (see previous screenshot) to view an onscreen slide-show.

Adding further elements to enhance LayOut pages

By inserting background images, adding shapes and controlling the view order of each element, you can build up interesting page layouts.

1. Start on a page with a SketchUp model shown large, as you can see in the following screenshot.

2. Click the arrow next to the **Rectangles** tool and select **Rounded**.

3. Draw the rectangle over your page and then use the **Shape Style** pallet to change the fill color and line attributes.

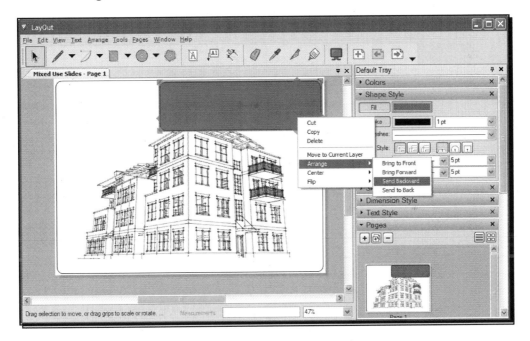

4. Right-click on the rectangle and **Arrange | Send Backward**. This will put the rectangle behind your building.

5. Go to **File | Insert** and navigate to a suitable background image.

6. Click on the image and drag the corners to scale it. It doesn't matter if it goes off the sides of the page because that part won't be viewed anyway.

7. For some SketchUp styles LayOut automatically clips the background (see the following screenshot). You also need to have **Background** unticked in the **SketchUp Model | Styles** pallet.

8. Below you can see how shapes can be used to mask areas. I didn't want to see the base of this image so I inserted a colored rectangle. Use the various **Arrange** options to make sure elements are stacked in the right order.

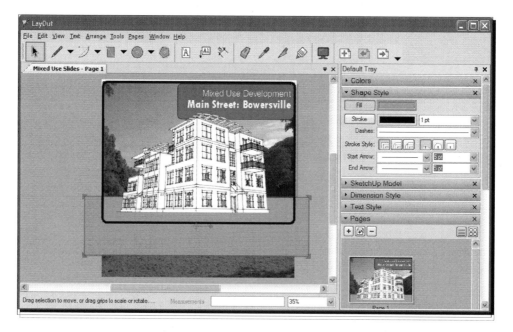

9. You can also import the rendered scenes or non photo real images you've created. Click the **Add** button to create a new page. Go to **File | Insert** and navigate to your rendered scenes.

10. Insert the images and stretch them using the corner grips.

11. You can combine any of the elements you've looked at with your output images.

What just happened?

You used LayOut to arrange several views of your SketchUp model, along with photos and previous renders or non photo real output. Each page can now be shown as a slide, or output as a PDF or individual images.

Exporting and printing

You can now export your whole slide-show, or individual pages as JPG or PNG images. Remember that PNG is lossless (it doesn't deteriorate every time you modify and save it) and JPG has a smaller file size but is lossy.

Time for action – exporting images from LayOut

1. Go to **File | Export | Images**.

2. Type in a filename, select PNG and click **Save**.

3. Select which slides you require and the image size you need.

4. You can see the export dialog box here:

5. Start by entering the **Resolution** at **300 pixels/inch**.

6. If you've already set up your page to the correct size for your print, the **Width** and **Height** will change to the values required.

7. Otherwise, think about the width of your printed image. If it's say 12 inches wide, do the math, 12 x 300 = 3600.

8. Type *3600* into the **Width** box. The **Height** and **Resolution** change automatically.

Image resolution values

Resolution is usually 72 or 96 for screen viewing, while 150 is fine for your home printer, 300 is standard for commercial printing, and up to 600 is used where you need really crisp text or line art. You can work out the number of pixels you need by:

Image Dimension (Inches) x Resolution = Pixels.

What just happened?

You've saved your page or pages as PNG or JPG images. These can be edited or printed from GIMP, displayed on the web, or stuck on a memory stick and printed at a digital photo machine.

You learned a little about image resolution so that your images will look right for the application you want them for, and file sizes won't be too big.

Exporting a PDF document from LayOut

If you choose the PDF option you get the following dialog box. **Output Quality** will affect the file size, so choose **Low** or **Medium** if you're placing it on the web; **High** if you mean to print it.

Output for print

Now it's time to print out your creations directly from LayOut.

1. Go to **File | Page Setup**.

2. Click **Printer** to select the printer you're going to use.

3. Go to **File | Document Setup**. Go to the **Paper** tab.

4. Set **Output Quality** to **High**.

5. Click **Close**. Go to **File | Print** and click **Print**.

Controlling the line-weight

For orthographic and other detailed views you will need to control the line thickness (line-weight). This can be done for each individual view.

1. Click the window you wish to change. Go to the **SketchUp Model** pallet.

2. Select the **Styles** tab and change **Lineweight** to a value between 0.1 and 0.25.

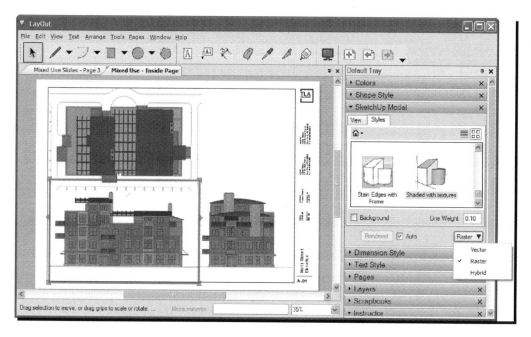

3. You can also change the view method from **Raster** to **Vector** or **Hybrid**. Raster renders the view exactly as in SketchUp, using pixels. Vector uses lines and color fills, so it will be better for line or solid color based images, but won't retain the sketchy quality. It's more like CAD output. Hybrid is a bit of both, so it can give the best image quality but takes longest to process.

4. Just to be sure, go to **File | Print Preview** and use the zoom and arrangement icons to view your pages as they will be printed.

Summary

In this final chapter you have briefly experienced the capabilities of the LayOut tool which comes with SketchUp Pro. This tool is coming on in leaps and bounds, and looks set to become a force to be reckoned with in the future, if it isn't already. You've learned how to:

◆ Create custom slide shows for output on a projector

◆ Carefully control print output including line weights

◆ Display a mix of SketchUp views, renders and other images

◆ Add text, dimensions, shapes, and borders

◆ Print and view SketchUp models to scale and with dimensions

I hope this chapter has given you a feel for LayOut and that you'll continue using it for your future projects. With the advent of dimensioning tools in LayOut 2.1 it is all the more worth purchasing a license of Pro, which is fast becoming the new standard for CAD, design, and visualization.

Choosing Rendering Software

At some stage you may wish to upgrade your rendering software and spend some money. What criteria should you use to decide on a "pay for" renderer? There are so many out there! But which of these integrate particularly well with your SketchUp workflow?

The following tables are a reference guide for you and will answer some of your questions. They're not exhaustive (for one thing, new renderers come out every day!) but you might find them a good starting point.

Am I outgrowing Kerkythea?

In general, my advice is to stick with Kerkythea until you're showing signs of outgrowing it. Some of the things you might like to have at your fingertips which Kerkythea currently doesn't enable are:

- ◆ Physics and particle animations
- ◆ Poser integration (3D people)
- ◆ Animating objects, not just cameras
- ◆ More access to quality entourage (for example automatic foliage creation in Vue)
- ◆ Simplified or enhanced interface
- ◆ Render directly within SketchUp

What should I look for in a renderer?

The tables have been created to show which renderers fulfil three basic categories or criteria. In general, for a photo-realistic architectural image the three basic criteria I've gone for are:

◆ Interoperability with SketchUp

◆ Global Illumination rendering quality

◆ Accessibility of training, support, help forums, and user generated content

I've chosen these three areas because I feel they make the most difference day by day in creating a realistic render quickly and consistently. In short, you need these things if you decide to go pro.

Interoperability with SketchUp

Contrary to popular opinion, this doesn't mean the renderer needs to work within SketchUp. Often this can be as much of a drawback as a benefit, because you can't carry on modeling when your SketchUp's locked in a rendering cycle for four hours! Also an external renderer usually handles imports of other file formats better. So, what you may like to look for is a few buttons within SketchUp that will help you export (just like SU2KT), or a renderer that supports the SketchUp native format really well. Next, does the export/import process retain lights, cameras, sun settings, animations, and component hierarchy? Does it allow you to merge in parts of a scene or do you have to start all over again whenever you change something in SketchUp?

Also be aware, some renderers require you to own a SketchUp Pro license, others will work with SketchUp for free. Tables 1 and 2 have been split up to make the difference obvious.

Global Illumination rendering quality

You might think Global Illumination is a strange choice, but I'm totally amazed by how many renderers there are out there that don't have this most basic of photo-realistic rendering capabilities' yet market themselves as photo-real renderers. **Global Illumination (GI)** (or indirect lighting) saves you having to add extra lights all over your scene to simulate indirect light bounce. It's the single most important aspect of getting a realistic render, yet many renderers out there don't tell you that they're just Raytracing (direct light) engines. Global Illumination rendering is slower than Raytracing, but this isn't important nowadays considering the awesome computing power of the most basic desktop PC. Furthermore, most GI renderers have a Raytrace setting too, so you can still use it if you wish (for example, to speed up rendering for an animation).

The tables below have been split into GI and Non-GI renderers so you can be sure all the renderers in the first two tables (1 & 2) simulate GI, and rendering quality will be more or less "accurate".

Training, support, help forums, and user-generated content

Once you start rendering regularly you will become more and more aware that rendering is more about time than quality. Once you have the quality sorted out (and you will), what matters is the amount of content (entourage, template scenes, help, and training material) that's available so that you can produce renders quickly and efficiently to schedule. The kind of thing to look for here is large forums, books on Amazon, good phone or email support, and external sites offering entourage and other content. You don't have to access it, just know it's there when you need it. What also matters here is that the major file formats are supported so that you can import stuff you find on the Internet, such as 3DS, Max, OBJ, and DAE.

Rendering software tables

The following tables have been compiled from questionnaires sent out to rendering software companies. As far as possible, the criteria are measurable and not too subjective. By seeing the software compared side-by-side you should be able to cut through the marketing hype and choose a few to investigate further. Several companies have offered to provide discounts of up to 25% off their rendering soft ware to readers of this book. Discounts are shown at the bottom of the tables, and up to date details of how to claim can be found at `www.provelo.co.uk/renderoffers/`. The tables are slightly abbreviated to fit in he book, and the full versions can be downloaded from the Packt website.

Table 1: Rendering Software for SketchUp Free/Pro

Name	Modo	Indigo Renderer	V-Ray for SketchUp	Twilight Render
Platforms	Win, Mac	Win, Mac, Linux	Win, Mac	Win
Internal to SketchUp?	Ext	Ext	Int	Int
Interoperability				
SketchUp import method	Collada (.DAE)	Exporter in SketchUp	Internal	Internal
Retain components	Yes	Yes	Yes	Yes
Import cameras/scenes	Yes	Yes	Yes	Yes
Import lighting	Yes	Yes	Yes	Yes
Merge scene capability	No	No	Yes	Yes
3D Import	DAE, OBJ, FBX	All that are supported by SketchUp	All that are supported by SketchUp	All that are supported by SketchUp
3D Export	DAE, OBJ, FBX, numerous others			Kerkythea XML
Render capabilities				
Render methods	GI, Raytracing, Physically-based, OpenGL *	Physically correct, unbiased	GI, Raytracing, HDRI *	Photon Mapping with GI, Path Tracing, Bidirectional Path Tracing, MLT, Clay, Depth, and more
Indirect Illumination (GI)	Yes	Yes	Yes	Yes
Clip from Alpha	Yes *	No		Yes
Training / Support				
Support options #	P W	E P	P W E	E
Training Available ##	B V S D	M S	M B V S D	M
Training Location	China, Japan	Italy	USA, UK, NL, AU, NZ	none
No. Licenses Worldwide	data not supplied	100	5000	500
Forum members	125000	3600	38300	400
Bundled entourage				
Materials	100+	190	75+	7 libraries
Vegetation	<100	3	None	None
Skies / environments	<100 *			
Additional Functions				
Animation: Camera	Yes	Yes *	Yes	Yes
Animation: Object	Yes	Yes	No	With Plugin
Physics engine	No	No	No	With Plugin
Poser/DAZ import	No	No	No	No
Buying Information				
Company	Luxology	Glare Technologies Ltd	ASGVIS, LLC	Twilight Render LLC
Version	401	2.2	1.5	1.1
Retail price (USD)	995	441	799	99
Discount with this book	None	None	15% discount	None
Website	luxology.com	indigorenderer.com	tinyurl.com/y8dr7rp	twilightrender.com

SU Podium	IRender nXt	3ds Max Design	Vue Infinite	Vue Esprit
Win, Mac	Win	Win	Win, Mac	Win, Mac
Int	Both	Ext	Ext	Ext
Exporter in SketchUp	Internal	SKP	SKP	SKP
Yes	Yes	Yes	Yes	Yes
Yes	Yes	Yes	No	No
No	Yes	Yes	No	No
Yes	Yes	Yes	Yes	Yes
All that are supported by SketchUp	All that are supported by SketchUp	3DS, AI, DEM, XML, DDF, DWG, DXF, FBX, DAE, IGES, IPT, IAM, OBJ, STL, VRML, OpenFlight, SAT, SKP, WIRE	3DS, 3DMF, COB, DAE, DEM, DXF, LWO, OBJ, PZ3, PZZ, RAW, SHD, SKP, VRML.	3DS, 3DMF, COB, DAE, DEM, DXF, LWO, OBJ, PZ3, PZZ, RAW, SHD, SKP, VRML.
		3ds, AI, DWG, DXF, FBX, IGES, DAE, OBJ, STL, VRML, M3G, DWF, W3D, OpenFlight, SAT	3DS, C4D, COB, DXF, LWO, OBJ, SHD.	3DS, C4D, COB, DXF, LWO, OBJ, SHD.
Raytracing, GI	Raytracing, GI *	All	OpenGL, GI, Global Ambience, Global Radiosity, HDRI, Ambient Occlusion, IBL	OpenGL, GI, Global Ambience, Global Radiosity, HDRI, Ambient Occlusion, IBL
Yes	Yes	Yes	Yes	Yes
Yes	Yes	Yes	Yes	Yes
W E	W E	W	W E P	W
V	V	M B V S D	M B V D	M B V D
US, UK, JP		Worldwide	Worldwide	Worldwide
12,000	N/A	100000 +	Not disclosed	Not disclosed
210	N/A	100000 +	Not disclosed	Not disclosed
200+	5000+	1200	550+	550+
200+	500+	500	170+ species (unlimited)	70+ species
	12+ HDRi skies	50	160+	160+
with SU Animate	Yes	Yes	Yes	Yes
No	No	Yes	Yes	Yes
No	No	Yes	No	No
No	No	No	Yes	Yes
Cadalog, Inc.	**Render Plus Systems**	**Autodesk**	**E-on software**	**E-on software**
1.7.2	3	2010	8	8
179	399	3,495	895	199
None	None	None	None	None
suplugins.com	renderplus.com	autodesk.com	e-onsoftware.com	e-onsoftware.com

Table 2: Rendering Software for SketchUp Pro

Name	Maxwell Render	Artlantis Render	Realsoft 3D	Carrara Pro	Cheetah3D
Platforms	Win, Mac, Linux	Win, Mac	Win, Mac, Linux	Win, Mac	Mac
Internal to SketchUp?	Both	Ext	Ext	Ext	Ext
Interoperability					
SketchUp import method	Exporter in SketchUp	Exporter in SketchUp	3DS	OBJ	FBX
Retain components	Yes	Yes	Yes		Yes
Import cameras/scenes	Yes	Yes	Yes	No	No
Import lighting	Yes	Sun only	Yes	No	Yes
Merge scene capability	Yes	Yes	No	No	Yes
3D Import	OBJ, STL, 3DS, LWO, PLY, XC2 DXF, FBX, DAE, MXS	DWG,DXF,DWF,FBX, OBJ,3DS,SKP	DXF, IGES, 3DS, OBJ, FBX, AI, VRML, DEM,PS, REALFLOW, BOUJOU, ICARUS	DAZ, PZ3, CR2, OBJ, DAE, FBX	FBX, 3DS, OBJ
3D Export	OBJ, MXS	FBX, OBJ, SKP, DWF, U3D	DXF, IGES, 3DS, OBJ, FBX, VRML, PS	DirectX, FBX, RPF, After Effects Camera Export, Match Mover Tracking	FBX, 3DS, OBJ
Render capabilities					
Render methods	Physically correct, unbiased	Radiosity, Raytracing	GI, Raytracing, OpenGL	OpenGL, Raytracing, GI, IBL, HDRI, etc	Raytracing
Indirect Illumination (GI)	Yes	Yes	Yes	Yes	Yes
Clip from Alpha	Yes	Yes	Yes	No	Yes
Training / Support					
Support #	E	W	W		E
Training Available ##	V S		M	M V	V
Training Location	Europe	Worldwide	Finland		none
No. Licenses Worldwide	12000	85000	10000	100000 +	
Forum members	65000	unknown	1000	Not disclosed	1800
Bundled entourage					
Materials	4000	165 + additional CDs	100		procedurals editor
Vegetation	None	7 + additional CDs	20		None
Skies / environments	20		10		
Additional Functions					
Animation: Camera	Yes	Studio version	Yes	Yes	Yes
Animation: Object	Yes	Studio version	Yes	Yes	Yes
Physics engine	No	No	Yes	Yes	No
Poser/DAZ import	No	No	No	Yes	No
Buying Information					
Company	Next Limit Technologies	Abvent	Realsoft	DAZ Productions, Inc.	MW3D Solutions
Version	2.01	3	7	7	5.2
Retail price (USD)	995	677	900	549	149
Discount with this book	10% discount	None	None	25% discount *	.None
Website	maxwellrender.com	artlantis.com	realsoft.com	daz3d.com	cheetah3d.com

Table 3: Non GI software - Raytrace / OpenGL / Other

Name	Piranesi	SPIRIT	nXtRender	Live Interior 3D Pro
Platforms	Win, Mac	Win, Mac	Win	Mac
Internal to SketchUp?	Ext	Ext	Int	Ext
Interoperability				
SketchUp import method	Exporter	SKP	Internal	SKP
Retain components	no	No	Yes	
Import cameras/scenes	Yes	No	Yes	No
Import lighting	yes	No	Yes	No
Merge scene capability	No	Yes	Yes	No
3D Import	DXF, MAN, 3DS, SKP, FBX	DWG,DXF,SKP,O2C,ACO,IFC	All that are supported by SketchUp	SKP,3DS,Ogre XML
2D/3D Export	JPG, PNG, TGA, BMP, TIFF, PSD	DWG/DXF, DWF, O2C, IFC, DAE, VRML, JPG, BMP, TIF, TGA, LWI, PS, QuickTime	JPG, PNG, HDRi, EXR	JPEG, PNG, GIF, BMP, QuickTime Panorama, (MPEG-4, H.264), Google SketchUp
Render capabilities				
Render methods	n/a	Raytracing, OpenGL *	Raytrace - Multi pass for processing of soft shadows .	OpenGL
Indirect Illumination (GI)	No	No	No	No
Clip from Alpha	yes	Yes	Yes	Yes
Training / Support				
Support options #	E	W E	W E	W E P
Training Available ##	S V	V	V	V M
Training Location	Worldwide	CA, DE		
No. Licenses Worldwide	not provided	25000	N/A	5 000
Forum members	unknown		N/A	
Bundled entourage				
Materials	1800	100+	none	1300+
Vegetation	200	None	None	20
Skies / environments	60	20	12+ HDRi skies	1
Additional Functions				
Animation: Camera	no	No	No *	Yes
Animation: Object	no	No	No	No
Physics engine	no	No	No	No
Poser/DAZ import	no	No	no	No
Buying Information				
Company	Informatix Software International Ltd	STI International, Inc.	Render Plus Systems	BeLight Software Ltd.
Version	2010	2009.05	2.1	2.3
Retail price (USD)	695	1995	79	130
Discount with this book	15% discount	None	None	15% discount
Website	piranesi.co.uk	softtech.com	renderplus.com	belightsoft.com

B

Suggested Basic Toolbar Layout

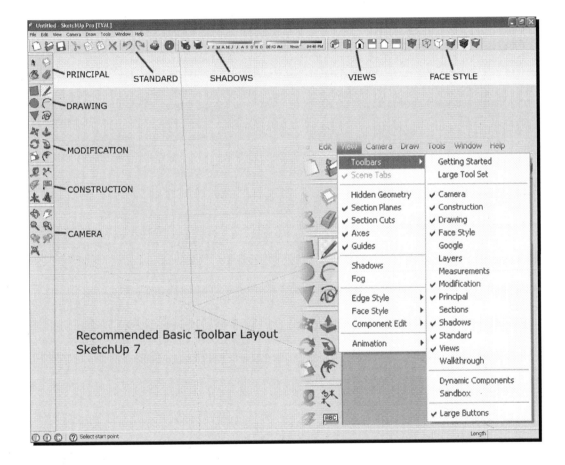

C

Pop Quiz Answers

Chapter 2

How to Collect an Arsenal Rambo Would Be Proud of

1)	b.
2)	http://www.crai.archi.fr/RubyLibraryDepot.
3)	False.

Chapter 4

Modeling for Visualization

1)	Will I see it? Can I replace it with 2D? Can I reduce the number of segments in an arc or circle?
2)	A component remains linked to all its copies (instances). So if you change one component it changes them all.
3)	Use Entity Info to input a smaller number of segments.
4)	False. Detail is best introduced by means of textures, or modeled later if you find you need it.

Chapter 5

Applying Textures and Materials for Photo-Real Rendering

1)	It locks (or unlocks) the aspect ratio between x and y dimensions for a texture.
2)	Select a face. Right-Click and select **Texture	Position**.
3)	True.
4)	Within the **Position** command (answer 2), right-click and untick **Fixed Pins**.

Chapter 7

Non Photo Real with SketchUp

1)	So if you make changes in SketchUp, you can re-export the same view again and replace the layer in GIMP.
2)	Controls where the focus is in the image, and takes away distractions at the edge of the image.
3)	Quick
4)	Click the **Update** thumbnail in the **Styles** pallet.

Chapter 8

Photo-Realistic Rendering

1)	**PhotonMap – Medium + AA 0.3**.
2)	Distance away from the camera.
3)	Yes, using **File	Merge**.
4)	Preset **17. Path Tracing Progressive**.
5)	Preset **19. Metropolis Light Transport**.

Chapter 9

Important Compositing and After Effects in GIMP

1)	◆ Gaussian Blur on a duplicate layer
	◆ Plugin filters such as the G'Mic plugin
	◆ External software such as NeatImage
	◆ The Focus Blur filter
	◆ Rendering for a longer period
2)	Red, Green, Blue (RGB).
3)	Crop away the flat areas around the "mountain" area of the graph.
4)	Use the **Eye Dropper Tool** and read off the grayscale value.

Chapter 10

Walkthroughs and Flyovers

1)	Leave them out of the animation, hide with entourage, or leave undetailed to show context only.
2)	`scenes_transition_times.rb`
3)	False. You can alter levels in VirtualDub.
4)	If the render fails you will still have all the frames rendered so far. You can also view your progress and can achieve greater video compression.

Image credits

Chapter	Page	Credit
2	49	Shane L. Fletcher: Partner, `TwilightRender.com`, Architect
3	62-66 (all images)	Photo texture: Draco2008, Flickr
3	60 and 61	David Cauldwell Architects
4	126	Photo texture: samualpedrete, Flickr
5	140	Photo texture: Google street view
5	144	REAL_ESTAGING, Flickr
5	149-150 (first image only)	`FreeDigitalPhotos.net`
6	186-191	Photo texture: pugetsoundphotowalks, Flickr
6	179	Image: REVI21ON visualization, Architect: Burns Morrissey Architecture + Design
6	183	Image: REVI21ON visualization, Design: Balongue Design, Owner: Overbrook Golf Club
6	195	Photo texture: Michael "Mike" L. Baird, Flickr, `bairdphotos.com`
7	198	Dennis Nikolaev, `ArchModeling.com`
7	203 (first image)	Dennis Nikolaev, `ArchModeling.com`
7	221	rjdesign, `rjdesign@optusnet.com.au`
9	289	Render: Ahmed Alireza, aalireza@3moon.com, Modding: Branko Jovanovi
9	305 (first image)	Unknown

Index

N

Neat Image **286**
ngPlant **194**
non photo real (NPR) visualization
      techniques 202
notice hierarchy **178, 179**

O

orthographic **77**
orthographic views, in LayOut **349, 350**
outliner
    about 110
    using 110, 111

P

parallel projection **77**
Path Tracing Progressive **283**
pencil sketch technique
    about 221
    Dirty Hands layer, importing in GIMP 227
    pencil shading, creating in GIMP 226, 227
    setting up 222-224
pencil sketch technique settings
    Dirty Hands layer 224
    Heavy Construction Lines layer 222
    Light Construction Lines layer 222
    Outline layer 223
    Pencil Shading layer 224
people cutouts, entourage
    2D people components, creating 187
    about 185-187
    face-me component, creating 191, 192
    halo, checking 190
    innards, drawing 191
    outline, tracing 188, 189
    person, scaling 188
    photo texture, applying 189
perspective tool **156**
perspective tricks, SketchUp
    orthographic 77
    parallel projection 77
    two point perspective 78

photo images
    about 21
    digital art, hanging 23-25
    scenery backdrop, setting up 22, 23
Photo-Match
    requisites 60
    scene, setting up with 62, 63
    setting up 60
Photo-Match textures **136, 137**
photo-realistic architectural image
    basic criteria 364
photo-realistic scene, modeling
    corner detail, adding 128, 129
    RoundCorner plugin, used 130
    sharp edges, issues with 127
photo-real rendering
    about 232
    setting up 232
    SketchUp - Kerkythea rendering process
        diagram 233
photos
    masking, Paths used 304-308
photo textures
    basic tileable textures, using 137
physical location, site
    north location, checking 67
    setting up 66
    time and date, setting up 67
plan
    sketching 71
Podium **47**
Portable Document Format **38**
post production renders
    about 256
    mask render 257

R

radiant materials **262**
random textures, tileable textures
    creating 156, 158
rendering, Kerkythea **30, 31**
rendering software
    about 47
    high end rendering software 47

Thank you for buying

SketchUp 7.1 for Architectural Visualization: Beginner's Guide

Packt Open Source Project Royalties

When we sell a book written on an Open Source project, we pay a royalty directly to that project. Therefore by purchasing SketchUp 7.1 for Architectural Visualization: Beginner's Guide, Packt will have given some of the money received to the Kerkythea project.

In the long term, we see ourselves and you—customers and readers of our books—as part of the Open Source ecosystem, providing sustainable revenue for the projects we publish on. Our aim at Packt is to establish publishing royalties as an essential part of the service and support a business model that sustains Open Source.

If you're working with an Open Source project that you would like us to publish on, and subsequently pay royalties to, please get in touch with us.

Writing for Packt

We welcome all inquiries from people who are interested in authoring. Book proposals should be sent to author@packtpub.com. If your book idea is still at an early stage and you would like to discuss it first before writing a formal book proposal, contact us; one of our commissioning editors will get in touch with you.

We're not just looking for published authors; if you have strong technical skills but no writing experience, our experienced editors can help you develop a writing career, or simply get some additional reward for your expertise.

About Packt Publishing

Packt, pronounced 'packed', published its first book "Mastering phpMyAdmin for Effective MySQL Management" in April 2004 and subsequently continued to specialize in publishing highly focused books on specific technologies and solutions.

Our books and publications share the experiences of your fellow IT professionals in adapting and customizing today's systems, applications, and frameworks. Our solution-based books give you the knowledge and power to customize the software and technologies you're using to get the job done. Packt books are more specific and less general than the IT books you have seen in the past. Our unique business model allows us to bring you more focused information, giving you more of what you need to know, and less of what you don't.

Packt is a modern, yet unique publishing company, which focuses on producing quality, cutting-edge books for communities of developers, administrators, and newbies alike. For more information, please visit our website: www.PacktPub.com.

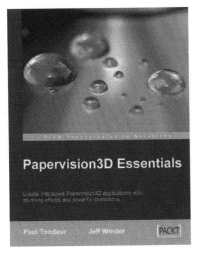